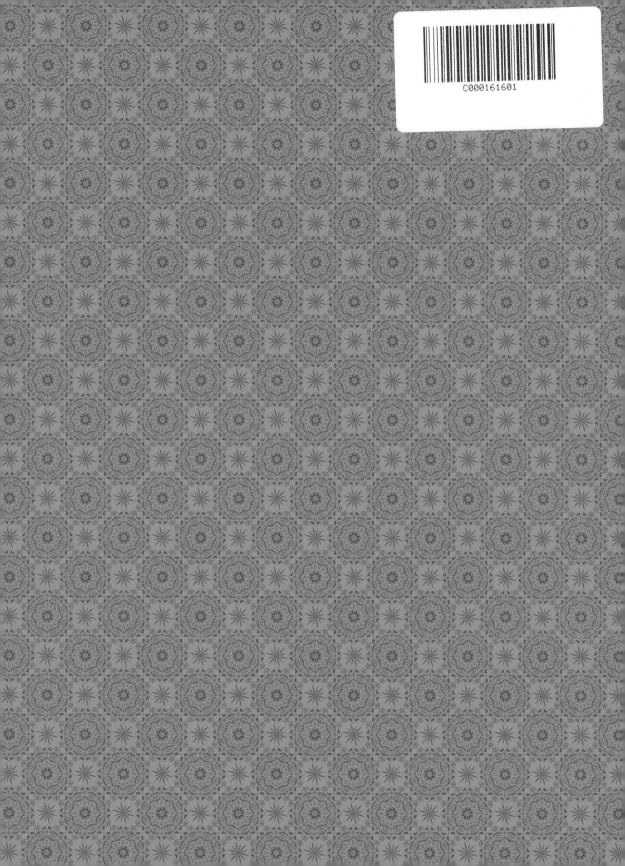

THE COOKERY COLLECTION

ORIGINAL AND DETAILED

500
RECIPES

Baking

Delicious everyday recipes from cakes
and breads to pastries and more

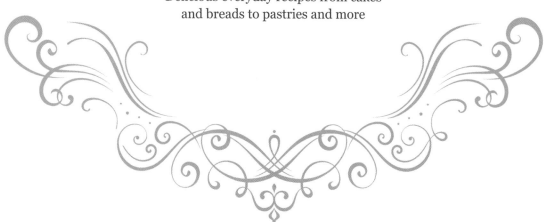

igloobooks

igloobooks

Published in 2018
by Igloo Books Ltd
Cottage Farm
Sywell
NN6 0BJ
www.igloobooks.com

LEO002 0218
2 4 6 8 10 9 7 5 3 1
ISBN 978-1-78810-194-3

All imagery: © iStock / Getty Images

Designed by Nicholas Gage
Edited by Richard Davis

Printed and manufactured in China

Contents

Sweet bakes 4

· · · · · · · · · · ·

Breads and other loaves 166

· · · · · · · · · · ·

Savoury bakes 218

Sweet bakes

Apple upside-down cake

PREPARATION TIME: 15 minutes
COOKING TIME: 35 minutes
SERVES: 8

300 g / 10 ½ oz / 2 cups self-raising flour
2 tsp baking powder
250 g / 9 oz / 1 ¼ cups caster (superfine) sugar
250 g / 9 oz / 1 ¼ cups butter, softened
5 large eggs
4 tbsp golden syrup
3 cooking apples, thinly sliced
50 g / 1 ¾ oz / ⅓ cup walnuts, chopped

- Preheat the oven to 170°C (150°C fan) / 340F / gas 3, then grease a 23 cm (9 in) round cake tin.
- Sieve the flour and baking powder into a mixing bowl, then add the sugar, butter and eggs. Beat the mixture until smooth and well-whipped.
- Spread the golden syrup over the base of the cake tin and arrange the apple slices on top.
- Spoon over the cake mixture and bake for 35 minutes. Test with a wooden toothpick; if it comes out clean, the cake is done.
- Transfer to a wire rack to cool, then sprinkle with chopped walnuts to finish.

Clementine upside-down cake
Replace the apple slices with 4 peeled and sliced clementines, and remove the walnuts to give this cake a zesty flavour.

Orange polenta cake

PREPARATION TIME: 10 minutes
COOKING TIME: 45-50 minutes
SERVES: 12

100 g / 3 ½ oz / ⅔ cup polenta
100 g / 3 ½ oz / ⅔ cup ground almonds
150 g / 5 ½ oz / ⅔ cup caster (superfine) sugar
150 g / 5 ½ oz / ⅔ cup butter
3 large eggs
2 tsp baking powder
1 orange, juice and zest finely grated
icing (confectioners') sugar to dust

- Preheat the oven to 180°C (160°C fan) / 350F / gas 4, then grease and line a 23cm (9in) round cake tin with greaseproof paper.
- Put all the cake ingredients in a large mixing bowl and whisk them together until pale and well-whipped.
- Scrape the mixture into the tin and level the top with a spatula.
- Bake for 45-50 minutes. Test the cake with a wooden toothpick; if it comes out clean, the cake is done.
- Transfer the cake to a wire rack to cool completely. Dust with icing sugar to finish.

Cherry and almond cookies

PREPARATION TIME: **10 minutes**
COOKING TIME: **10-12 minutes**
MAKES: **24**

100 g / 3 ½ oz / ½ cup butter, softened
100 g / 3 ½ oz / ½ cup caster (superfine) sugar
1 large egg, beaten
1 tsp vanilla extract
225 g / 8 oz / 1 ½ cups self-raising flour
24 glacé cherries
75 g / 2 ¾ oz / ⅔ cup blanched almonds,
finely chopped

- Preheat the oven to 180°C (160°C fan) / 350F / gas 4, then line two baking trays with greaseproof paper.
- In a large mixing bowl, cream together the butter and sugar.
- Stir in the egg and vanilla extract, then sieve the flour into the mixture and stir until combined.
- Dollop teaspoons of the mixture onto the prepared baking trays, then stud each one with a cherry. Sprinkle over the chopped almonds.
- Bake for 10–12 minutes or until cooked through.
- Transfer the cookies to a wire rack to cool before serving.

Cherry and hazelnut cookies
Replace the blanched almonds with the same quantity of finely chopped hazelnuts (cobnuts) for a different nutty flavour.

Walnut and chocolate squares

PREPARATION TIME: **10 minutes**
COOKING TIME: **30-35 minutes**
MAKES: **12**

150 g / 6 oz / 1 cup self-raising flour
2 tbsp unsweetened cocoa powder
2 tsp baking powder
175 g / 6 oz / ¾ cup caster (superfine) sugar
175 g / 6 oz / ¾ cup butter
3 eggs
100 g / 3 ½ oz / ⅓ cup walnuts, chopped

- Preheat the oven to 180°C (160°C fan) / 350F / gas 4, then grease and line a 20cm (8in) square cake tin.
- In a large mixing bowl, whisk together the flour, cocoa powder, baking powder, sugar, butter and eggs until pale and well-whipped.
- Fold in the chopped walnuts until evenly distributed.
- Scrape the mixture into the tin and level the top with a spatula, then bake for 30–35 minutes.
- Test the brownie with a toothpick; if it comes out clean, the brownie is done.
- Transfer the cake to a wire rack to cool completely before cutting into 12 squares.

Chocolate and peanut squares
Replace the walnuts with the same quantity of chopped, roasted peanuts to give these brownies a different nutty flavour.

Summer berry pudding

PREPARATION TIME: **10 minutes**
COOKING TIME: **35-45 minutes**
SERVES: **6**

75 g / 2 ½ oz / ⅓ cup butter
75 g / 2 ½ oz / ⅓ cup caster (superfine) sugar
300 ml / 10 ½ fl. oz / 1 ¼ cups whole milk
2 large eggs
50 g / 1 ¾ oz / ⅓ cup plain (all-purpose) flour
a pinch of salt
300 g / 10 ½ oz / 2 cups mixed berries
icing (confectioners') sugar to dust

- Preheat the oven to 190°C (170°C fan) / 375F / gas 5.
- Melt the butter in a saucepan over a low heat until it starts to smell nutty.
- Brush a little of the butter around the inside of a 20 cm (8 in) cake tin, then add a spoonful of caster sugar and shake to coat.
- In a mixing bowl, whisk together the milk and eggs with the rest of the melted butter.
- Sieve the flour into a mixing bowl with a pinch of salt, then stir in the rest of the sugar.
- Make a well in the middle of the dry ingredients and gradually whisk in the liquid, incorporating all the flour from round the outside until you have a lump-free batter.
- Arrange 200 g of the mixed berries in the prepared baking dish, pour over the batter and transfer to the oven.
- Bake for 35–45 minutes. Test with a toothpick; if it comes out clean, the pudding is done. Leave to cool.
- Arrange the remaining berries on top of the pudding and dust with icing sugar to finish.

Pound cake

PREPARATION TIME: 5 minutes
COOKING TIME: 45-55 minutes
MAKES: 1 loaf

450 g / 1 lb / 2 cups butter, softened
450 g / 1 lb / 2 cups caster (superfine) sugar
8 large eggs, beaten
450 g / 1 lb / 3 cups self-raising flour
icing (confectioners') sugar to dust

- Preheat the oven to 180°C (160°C fan) / 350F
  / gas 4, then grease and line a large loaf tin
  with greaseproof paper.
- In a large mixing bowl, cream the butter and
  sugar until well-whipped, then gradually
  whisk in the eggs, beating well each time.
- Fold in the flour, then scrape the mixture into
  the prepared loaf tin.
- Bake the cake for 45–55 minutes. Test with
  a wooden toothpick; if it comes out clean, the
  cake is done.
- Transfer the cake to a wire rack to cool, then
  dust with icing sugar to finish.

Apple and cinnamon cake

PREPARATION TIME: **15 minutes**
COOKING TIME: **55 minutes**
SERVES: **8**

225 g / 8 oz / 1 ½ cups self-raising flour
2 tsp ground cinnamon
100 g / 3 ½ oz / ½ cup butter, cubed
100 g / 3 ½ oz / ½ cup caster (superfine) sugar
1 large egg
75 ml / 2 ½ fl. oz / ⅓ cup whole milk
2 apples, peeled and grated (reserve some slices for decoration)

- Preheat the oven to 180°C (160°C fan) / 350F / gas 4, then grease and line a 23 cm (9 in) round cake tin.
- Sieve the flour and cinnamon into a large mixing bowl. Rub in the butter with your fingertips until it resembles fine breadcrumbs, then stir in the sugar.
- In a separate bowl, lightly beat the egg with the milk and grated apple, then add this into the dry ingredients until just combined.
- Transfer the mixture to the prepared cake tin, then top with the apple slices and bake for 55 minutes. Test with a toothpick; if it comes out clean, the cake is done. Transfer to a wire rack and leave to cool completely.

Apple and raisin cake
Stir 100 g / 3 ½ oz / ⅔ cup raisins into the cake mixture before transferring to the cake tin, then bake as normal.

Zesty orange cupcakes

PREPARATION TIME: **25 minutes**
COOKING TIME: **15-20 minutes**
MAKES: **12**

100 g / 3 ½ oz / ⅔ cup self-raising flour, sifted
100 g / 3 ½ oz / ½ cup caster (superfine) sugar
100 g / 3 ½ oz / cup butter, softened
3 large eggs
1 orange, zest finely grated

- Preheat the oven to 190°C (170°C fan) / 375F / gas 5, then line a 12-hole cupcake tray with paper cupcake cases.
- In a large mixing bowl, combine the flour, sugar, butter and eggs, then whisk together for 2 minutes or until smooth. Fold in most of the orange zest, reserving some for the garnish.
- Divide the mixture between the cupcake cases, then transfer the tin to the oven and bake for 15–20 minutes.
- Test with a wooden toothpick; if it comes out clean, the cakes are done.
- Transfer the cakes to a wire rack and leave to cool completely. Sprinkle with the remaining orange zest before serving.

Orange and sesame seed cupcakes
Add 2 tbsp black sesame seeds to the mixture along with the orange zest, stirring until evenly distributed. Bake as normal.

THE
COOKERY
COLLECTION

Egg custard tarts

PREPARATION TIME: 45 minutes
COOKING TIME: 15-20 minutes
MAKES: 12

FOR THE PASTRY
100 g / 3 ½ oz / ½ cup butter, cubed
200 g / 7 oz / 1 ⅓ cups plain (all-purpose) flour

FOR THE CUSTARD
2 large egg yolks
55 g / 2 oz / ¼ cup caster (superfine) sugar
1 tsp vanilla extract
2 tsp cornflour (cornstarch)
225 ml / 8 fl. oz / ¾ cup double (heavy) cream
icing (confectioners') sugar to dust

- Preheat the oven to 200°C (180°C fan) / 400F / gas 6.
- Make the pastry first. Using your fingertips, rub the butter into the flour and add just enough cold water to bind.
- Chill for 30 minutes, then roll out on a lightly floured surface. Cut out 12 circles with a pastry cutter, rerolling the trimmings as necessary, and use them to line a 12-hole cupcake tin.
- Whisk the custard ingredients together in a jug and spoon into the pastry cases, until they're about three-quarters full.
- Bake the tarts for 15–20 minutes, or until the custard has set and the pastry is crisp.
- Transfer to a wire rack to cool, or serve warm, sprinkled with icing sugar.

Nutmeg egg custard tarts
Grate a little nutmeg into the custard ingredients, then bake as normal. Sprinkle the finished egg tarts with ground nutmeg to serve.

Wholemeal glazed chocolate cake

PREPARATION TIME: 30 minutes
COOKING TIME: 35-40 minutes
SERVES: 10-12

150 g / 6 oz / 1 cup stoneground wholemeal flour
1 tsp baking powder
2 tbsp unsweetened cocoa powder
2 tsp baking powder
175 g / 6 oz / ¾ cup dark brown sugar
175 g / 6 oz / ¾ cup butter
3 large eggs

FOR THE GANACHE
200 ml / 7 fl. oz / ¾ cup double (heavy) cream
200 g / 7 oz milk chocolate, chopped
50 g / 1 ¾ oz / ¼ cup butter
2 tbsp runny honey

- Preheat the oven to 180°C (160°C fan) / 350F / gas 4, then grease and line two 23cm (9in) round cake tins.
- In a large mixing bowl, whisk together all the cake ingredients until well whipped.
- Divide the mixture between the tins and bake for 35–40 minutes. Test the cakes with a wooden toothpick; if it comes out clean, the cakes are done. Transfer to a wire rack to cool.
- Bring the cream to a simmer in a small saucepan set over a low heat, then pour it over the chopped chocolate and stir. Beat in the butter and honey until smooth.
- When the ganache has cooled to a spreadable consistency, use a third of it to sandwich the cakes together. Spread the rest over the top and sides of the cake with a palette knife.

Caramel and chocolate chip cookies

PREPARATION TIME: **10 minutes**
COOKING TIME: **12-15 minutes**
MAKES: **36**

225 g / 8 oz / ⅓ cup light brown sugar
100 g / 3 ½ oz z / 1 ⅓ p caster (superfine) sugar
175 g / 6 oz / ¾ c up butter, melted
2 tsp vanilla extract
1 egg, plus 1 egg yolk
250 g / 9 oz / 1 ⅔ cups self-raising flour
100 g / 3 ½ oz /⅔ cup caramel pieces
100 g / 3 ½ oz / ½ cup chocolate chips

- Preheat the oven to 170°C (150°C fan) / 340F / gas 3, then line two baking trays with greaseproof paper.
- In a large mixing bowl, cream together the two sugars, butter and vanilla extract until pale and well-whipped. Beat in the egg and yolk, then stir in the flour, caramel pieces and chocolate chips until the mixture is fully combined.
- Dollop tablespoons of the mixture onto the prepared baking trays, leaving room for spreading. Bake in batches for 12–15 minutes or until the edges start to brown, but the centres are still chewy. Transfer to a wire rack to cool.

Caramel fudge cookies
Replace the chocolate chips with pieces of chopped vanilla fudge for a more intense vanilla flavour, and an even chewier centre.

Chocolate and hazelnut loaf cake

PREPARATION TIME: **15 minutes**
COOKING TIME: **45 minutes**
MAKES: **1 loaf**

225 g / 8 oz / 1 cup butter, softened
225 g / 8 oz / 1 cup soft light brown sugar
4 large eggs, beaten
225 g / 8 oz / 1 ½ cups self-raising flour
2 tbsp unsweetened cocoa powder
100 g / 3 ½ oz / ⅔ cup milk chocolate, chopped
100 g / 3 ½ oz / ⅔ cup hazelnuts (cobnuts), chopped

- Preheat the oven to 180°C (160°C fan) / 350F / gas 4, then grease and line a large loaf tin with greaseproof paper.
- In a large mixing bowl, cream together the butter and sugar until well-whipped, then gradually whisk in the eggs, beating after each addition.
- Sieve over the flour and cocoa powder, then fold in the chopped chocolate and hazelnuts.
- Scrape the mixture into the tin and bake for 45 minutes. Test with a wooden toothpick; if it comes out clean, the cake is done. Turn the loaf out onto a wire rack and leave to cool.

Chocolate, raisin and hazelnut loaf cake
Add 100 g / 3 ½ oz / ⅔ cup raisins to the mixture along with the chocolate and hazelnuts to give this loaf a fruit and nut flavour.

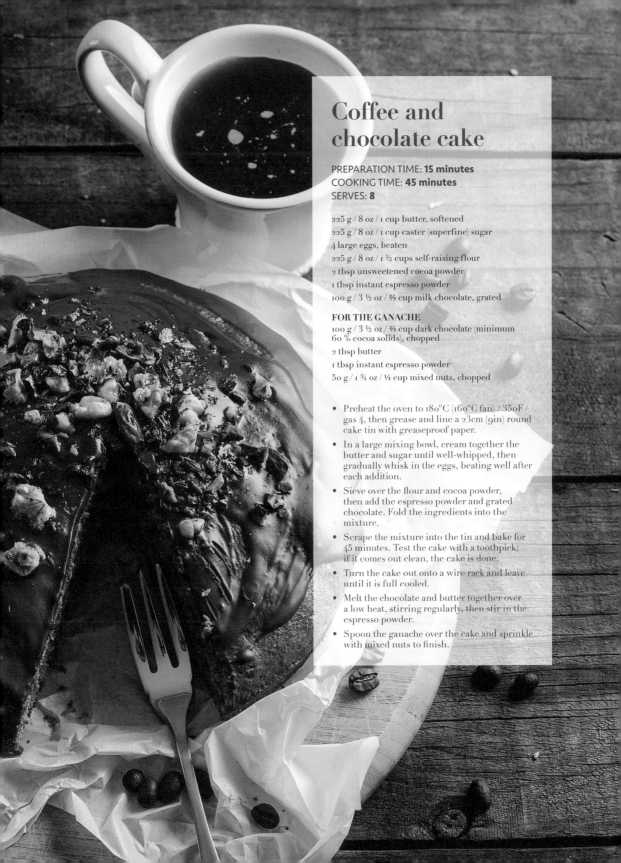

Coffee and chocolate cake

PREPARATION TIME: 15 minutes
COOKING TIME: 45 minutes
SERVES: 8

225 g / 8 oz / 1 cup butter, softened

225 g / 8 oz / 1 cup caster (superfine) sugar

4 large eggs, beaten

225 g / 8 oz / 1 ½ cups self-raising flour

2 tbsp unsweetened cocoa powder

1 tbsp instant espresso powder

100 g / 3 ½ oz / ⅔ cup milk chocolate, grated

FOR THE GANACHE

100 g / 3 ½ oz / ⅔ cup dark chocolate (minimum 60 % cocoa solids), chopped

2 tbsp butter

1 tbsp instant espresso powder

50 g / 1 ¾ oz / ⅓ cup mixed nuts, chopped

- Preheat the oven to 180°C (160°C fan) / 350F / gas 4, then grease and line a 23cm (9in) round cake tin with greaseproof paper.

- In a large mixing bowl, cream together the butter and sugar until well-whipped, then gradually whisk in the eggs, beating well after each addition.

- Sieve over the flour and cocoa powder, then add the espresso powder and grated chocolate. Fold the ingredients into the mixture.

- Scrape the mixture into the tin and bake for 45 minutes. Test the cake with a toothpick; if it comes out clean, the cake is done.

- Turn the cake out onto a wire rack and leave until it is full cooled.

- Melt the chocolate and butter together over a low heat, stirring regularly, then stir in the espresso powder.

- Spoon the ganache over the cake and sprinkle with mixed nuts to finish.

Pecan and cranberry oat cookies

PREPARATION TIME: 10 minutes
COOKING TIME: 12-15 minutes
MAKES: 36

75 g / 2 ½ oz / ⅓ cup butter, softened
100 g / 3 ½ oz / ⅓ cup honey
225 g / 8 oz / 1 ½ cups self-raising flour
100 g / 3 ½ oz / ½ cup caster (superfine) sugar
75 g / 2 ½ oz / ⅔ cup dried cranberries
75 g / 1 ½ oz / ⅔ cup oats
1 large egg, beaten
75 g / 2 ½ oz / ⅔ cup pecan nuts, chopped and whole

- Preheat the oven to 180°C (160°C fan) / 350F / gas 4, then line two baking trays with greaseproof paper.
- Melt the butter and honey together in a saucepan over a low heat.
- In a large mixing bowl, mix together the flour, sugar, cranberries and oats, then stir in the melted butter mixture and the beaten egg.
- Use a teaspoon to dollop the mixture onto the prepared baking trays, leaving room for the biscuits to spread. Press the pecan nuts onto the top of the cookies.
- Bake in batches for 12–15 minutes or until golden brown.
- Transfer the biscuits to a wire rack and leave to cool and harden.

Wholemeal banana and apricot loaf

PREPARATION TIME: **10 minutes**
COOKING TIME: **55 minutes**
MAKES: **1 loaf**

3 very ripe bananas
110 g / 4 oz / ½ cup soft light brown sugar
2 large eggs
120 ml / 4 fl. oz / ½ cup sunflower oil
125 g / 4 ½ oz / ¾ cup stoneground wholemeal flour
2 tsp baking powder
100 g / 3 ½ oz / 1 cup dried apricots, chopped

- Preheat the oven to 170°C (150°C fan) 340F / gas 3. Line a large loaf tin with greaseproof paper.
- In a large mixing bowl, mash the bananas roughly with a fork, then whisk in the sugar, eggs and oil.
- Sieve the flour and baking powder into the bowl, then add dried apricots. Stir just enough to evenly mix all the ingredients together.
- Scrape the mixture into the loaf tin and bake for 55 minutes. Test the cake with a toothpick: if it comes out clean, the cake is done. Transfer the cake to a wire rack and leave to cool completely.

Banana and apricot loaf
Replace the stoneground wholemeal flour with the same quantity of plain (all-purpose) flour.

Peach cake

PREPARATION TIME: **15 minutes**
COOKING TIME: **55 minutes**
SERVES: **8**

225 g / 8 oz / 1 ½ cups self-raising flour
100 g / 3 ½ oz / ½ cup butter, cubed
100 g / 3 ½ oz / ½ cup caster (superfine) sugar
1 large egg
75 ml / 2 ½ fl. oz / ⅓ cup whole milk
4 peaches, halved and stoned
icing (confectioners') sugar to dust

- Preheat the oven to 180°C (160°C fan) / 350F / gas 4, then grease a 23cm (9in) round baking dish.
- Sieve the flour into a large mixing bowl and rub in the butter with your fingers until it resembles fine breadcrumbs, then stir in the sugar.
- In a jug, lightly beat the egg with the milk, then stir it into the dry ingredients until just combined. Scrape the mixture into the baking dish and level the top with a palette knife.
- Press the peach halves into the mixture, cut side up. Bake for 55 minutes. Test with a wooden toothpick; if it comes out clean, the cake is done.
- Transfer the cake to a wire rack and leave to cool slightly, then dust with icing sugar to finish.

Nectarine cake
Try using nectarines instead of peaches, then bake as normal and dust with icing sugar to finish.

Raspberry cheesecake brownies

PREPARATION TIME: 10 minutes
COOKING TIME: 30-35 minutes
MAKES: 9

FOR THE BROWNIE BATTER
150 g / 6 oz / 1 cup self-raising flour
2 tbsp unsweetened cocoa powder
2 tsp baking powder
175 g / 6 oz / ¾ cup caster (superfine) sugar
175 g / 6 oz / ¾ cup butter
3 eggs
100 g / 3 ½ oz / ⅔ cup fresh raspberries

FOR THE CHEESECAKE BATTER
225 g / 8 oz / 2 ¼ cup cream cheese
50 g / 1 ¾ oz / ¼ cup caster (superfine) sugar
1 egg
½ tsp vanilla extract

- Preheat the oven to 180°C (160°C fan) / 350F / gas 4, then grease and line a 20cm (8in) square cake tin.
- Make the brownie batter first. In a large mixing bowl, whisk together the flour, cocoa powder, baking powder, sugar, butter and eggs until pale and well-whipped.
- In a separate bowl, soften the cream cheese with a spatula. Fold in the sugar, egg and vanilla extract until completely smooth.
- Scrape half of the brownie mixture into the prepared tin, then scrape in the cream cheese mixture. Swirl the mixture slightly using a spatula to give it a marble effect.
- Scrape the rest of the brownie mixture over the top and level with a spatula.
- Press the raspberries into the mixture, then bake for 30–35 minutes.
- Test the brownie with a toothpick; if it comes out clean, the brownie is done.
- Transfer the cake to a wire rack to cool completely before cutting into squares.

Black cherry cheesecake brownies
Replace the fresh raspberries with the same quantity of halved black cherries to give these brownies an indulgent flavour.

Blueberry and orange muffins

PREPARATION TIME: **25 minutes**
COOKING TIME: **20-25 minutes**
MAKES: **12**

1 large egg
120 ml / 4 fl. oz / ½ cup sunflower oil
120 ml / 4 fl. oz / ½ cup milk
375 g / 12 ½ oz / 2 ½ cups self-raising flour, sifted
1 tsp baking powder
200 g / 7 oz / ¾ cup caster (superfine) sugar
1 orange, zest finely grated
100 g / 3 ½ oz / ⅔ cup blueberries

- Preheat the oven to 180°C (160°C fan) / 350F / gas 4 and line a 12-hole muffin tin with paper cases.
- Beat the egg in a jug with the oil and milk until mixed.
- In a large mixing bowl, mix together the flour, baking powder, sugar and orange zest.
- Pour in the egg mixture and stir just enough to combine, then fold in the blueberries until evenly distributed.
- Divide the mixture between the paper cases and bake for 20–25 minutes.
- Test the cake with a wooden toothpick; if it comes out clean, the cakes are done.
- Transfer the muffins to a wire rack and leave to cool completely.

Fig and orange muffins
Replace the blueberries with 4 chopped figs and add 1 tbsp honey to the mixture to give these muffins a fig infusion.

Rhubarb loaf cake

PREPARATION TIME: **10 minutes**
COOKING TIME: **55 minutes**
SERVES: **8**

300 g / 10 ½ oz / 2 cups self-raising flour
2 tsp baking powder
250 g / 9 oz / 1 ½ cups light brown sugar
250 g / 9 oz / 1 ¼ cups butter, softened
5 large eggs
2 sticks rhubarb, chopped

- Preheat the oven to 170°C (150°C fan) / 340F / gas 3, then line a large loaf tin with greaseproof paper.
- Sieve the flour and baking powder into a mixing bowl and add the sugar, butter and eggs.
- Beat the mixture until smooth and well-whipped, then fold in the rhubarb.
- Scrape the mixture into the prepared loaf tin and bake for 55 minutes. Test with a wooden toothpick; if it comes out clean, the cake is done.
- Transfer the cake to a wire rack and leave to cool.

Rhubarb and apple loaf cake
Add 2 peeled, cored and chopped eating apples to the mixture, along with the rhubarb, to give this loaf cake an extra fruity flavour.

Chocolate cream cherry cupcakes

PREPARATION TIME: **25 minutes**
COOKING TIME: **15-20 minutes**
MAKES: **12**

100 g / 3 ½ oz / ⅔ cup self-raising flour, sifted
2 tbsp unsweetened cocoa powder, sifted
100 g / 3 ½ oz / ½ cup caster (superfine) sugar
100 g / 3 ½ oz / ½ cup butter, softened
3 large eggs
75 g / 2 ½ oz / ⅓ cup glacé cherries, chopped
TO DECORATE
225 ml / 8 fl. oz / 1 cup double (heavy) cream
2 tbsp icing (confectioners') sugar
½ tsp vanilla extract
12 fresh cherries
chocolate shavings

- Preheat the oven to 190°C (170°C fan) / 375F / gas 5, then line a 12-hole cupcake tin with paper cases. In a large mixing bowl, combine the flour, cocoa powder, sugar, butter and eggs and whisk together for 2 minutes or until smooth, then fold in the chopped cherries.
- Divide between the paper cases, then transfer to the oven and bake for 15-20 minutes. Test with a wooden toothpick; if it comes out clean, the cakes are done.
- Transfer to a wire rack to cool. In a clean bowl, whip the cream with the icing sugar and vanilla until thick, then spoon it into a piping bag fitted with a round nozzle. Pipe the cream on top of each cake, then top each one with a fresh cherry and a sprinkle of chocolate shavings.

Chocolate cream and raspberry cupcakes
Replace the glacé cherries with the same quantity of fresh raspberries, then top each cupcake with a few raspberries and white chocolate shavings.

THE COOKERY COLLECTION

Almond crescent biscuits

PREPARATION TIME: 55 minutes
COOKING TIME: 15 minutes
MAKES: 24

300 g / 10 ½ oz / 3 cups ground almonds

100 g / 3 ½ oz / 1 cup icing (confectioners') sugar, plus extra to dust

1 tbsp orange flower water

almond extract

1 large egg white, beaten

2 tbsp butter, melted

50 g / 1 ¾ oz / ½ cup blanched almonds, chopped

FOR THE PASTRY
1 egg yolk

2 tbsp orange flower water

2 tbsp butter, melted

300 g / 10 ½ oz / 2 cups plain (all-purpose) flour

- Make the pastry first. In a large mixing bowl, beat the egg with the orange flower water, butter and 125 ml of cold water.

- Stir in the flour and bring the mixture together into a pliable dough. Knead for 5 minutes, then chill for 30 minutes.

- Preheat the oven to 180°C (160°C fan) / 350F / gas 4, then grease and line a large baking tray.

- In a separate mixing bowl, mix together the ground almonds with the icing sugar, orange flower water and almond extract.

- Stir in the egg white, followed by the melted butter until a stiff paste forms.

- Roll out the pastry on a lightly floured surface and cut into 24 rectangles.

- Shape a tablespoon of the almond paste into a log and lay it along one long edge of a pastry rectangle. Roll it up and pinch the ends to seal then curl it into a crescent.

- Repeat with the rest of the mixture and bake for 15 minutes, then dust liberally with icing sugar to finish.

Lemon-ginger apple cake

PREPARATION TIME: 15 minutes
COOKING TIME: 45 minutes
SERVES: 8

300 g / 10 ½ oz / 2 cups self-raising flour
2 tsp baking powder
250 g / 9 oz / 1 ½ cups dark brown sugar
250 g / 9 oz / 1 ¼ cups butter, softened
5 large eggs
juice and zest of 1 lemon
1 tsp ground ginger
3 eating apples, cored and chopped
100 g / 3 ½ oz / ⅔ cup dates, pitted and chopped

- Preheat the oven to 170°C (150°C fan) / 340F / gas 3, then grease a 23cm (9in) round cake tin.
- Sieve the flour and baking powder into a large mixing bowl, then add the sugar, butter, eggs, lemon juice and zest, and ground ginger.
- Beat the mixture with a whisk until smooth and well-whipped.
- Stir in the apples and dates until evenly distributed.
- Spoon the mixture into the cake tin and bake for 45 minutes. Test the cake with a toothpick; if it comes out clean, the cake is done.
- Transfer to a wire rack to cool completely before serving.

Lemon-ginger cake
Omit the apple for a different take on this recipe

Quinoa and cranberry cookies

PREPARATION TIME: 40 minutes
COOKING TIME: 20-25 minutes
MAKES: 36

150 g / 5 ½ oz / 1 ½ cup quinoa flakes
50 g / 1 3/4 oz / ½ cup porridge oats
125 g / 4 ½ oz / ¾ cup stoneground wholemeal flour
1 tsp baking powder
175 g / 6 oz / ¾ cup butter
150 g / 5 ½ oz / ¾ cup soft brown sugar
100 g / 3 ½ oz / ⅔ cup dried cranberries

- In a large mixing bowl, mix together the quinoa flakes, oats, flour and baking powder.
- In a separate bowl, cream together the butter and sugar, then beat into the dry ingredients. Stir in the dried cranberries until evenly distributed. Chill the dough for 30 minutes.
- Preheat the oven to 180°C (160°C fan) / 350F / gas 4 and line two baking trays with greaseproof paper. Use a teaspoon to dollop the mixture onto the prepared baking trays, leaving room for the cookies to spread.
- Transfer the biscuits to the prepared trays and bake for 20–25 minutes or until cooked through and golden brown. Cool on a wire rack.

Quinoa, raisin and chocolate cupcakes
Replace the cranberries with the same quantity of raisins and chocolate chips, stirring until evenly distributed.

Coffee and chocolate chip cookies

PREPARATION TIME: 10 minutes
COOKING TIME: 12-15 minutes
MAKES: 36

225 g / 8 oz / 1 ⅓ cup dark brown sugar
100 g / 3 ½ oz / ½ cup caster (superfine) sugar
175 g / 6 oz / ¾ cup butter, melted
2 tsp instant espresso powder
1 egg, plus 1 egg yolk
250 g / 9 oz / 1 ⅔ cup self-raising flour
175 g / 6 oz dark chocolate, grated
100 g / 3 ½ oz / ½ cup chocolate chips

- Preheat the oven to 170°C (150°C fan) / 340F / gas 3, then line two baking trays with greaseproof paper.
- In a large mixing bowl, cream together the two sugars, butter and espresso powder until pale and well-whipped. Beat in the egg and yolk, then add the flour and grated chocolate.
- Dollop tablespoons of the mixture onto the prepared baking trays, leaving plenty of room to spread. Sprinkle chocolate chips on top.
- Bake the cookies in batches for 12–15 minutes or until the edges are starting to brown, but the centres are still chewy. Cool on a wire rack.

Double chocolate coffee cookies
Melt 100 g of milk chocolate in a bowl set over a saucepan of simmering water, then dip one side of the baked cookies into the melted chocolate. Leave to cool and harden on a wire rack.

Dutch caramel waffles

PREPARATION TIME: 20 minutes
COOKING TIME: 1 minute (per waffle)
MAKES: 18

400 g / 14 oz / 3 cups self-raising flour
150 g / 5 ½ oz / ⅔ cup caster (superfine) sugar
110 g / 4 oz / ½ cup butter, softened
3 large eggs, beaten
2 tsp baking powder
3 tbsp warm milk

FOR THE FILLING
350 g / 12 oz / 1 cup treacle
200 g / 7 oz / ¾ cup soft brown sugar
50 g / 1 ¾ oz / ¼ cup butter
1 tsp ground cinnamon

- Combine the waffle ingredients in a large mixing bowl.
- Knead on a lightly floured surface for 10 minutes, or until you have a smooth, elastic dough, then leave to rest for 45 minutes.
- To make the filling, heat the ingredients in a small saucepan set over a medium heat. Mix well, then set aside until the waffles are ready.
- Preheat a pizzelle iron until very hot, then place a heaped teaspoon of batter in each indent and close the two halves together.
- Cook the waffles for 30 seconds to 1 minute, or until cooked through.
- Remove the waffles with a spatula or palette knife, then repeat with the rest of the mixture.
- Carefully split the waffles into two rounds while they are still warm; do not wait until they are cool, as they will break.
- Spread a little of the filling onto one of the halves, then sandwich with the other half of the waffle to finish.

Coffee sponge fingers

PREPARATION TIME: **20 minutes**
COOKING TIME: **10-15 minutes**
MAKES: **40**

4 large eggs
125 g / 4 ½ oz / ½ cup caster (superfine) sugar, plus extra for dusting
1 tsp instant espresso powder
a pinch of cream of tartar
115 g / 4 oz / ⅔ cup plain (all-purpose) flour

- Preheat the oven to 190°C (170°C fan) / 375°F / gas 5, then grease and line two baking trays with greaseproof paper.
- Separate the eggs, then transfer the yolks to a bowl with half the sugar and the espresso powder. Whisk until very thick and pale.
- In a separate bowl, whisk the egg whites with the cream of tartar until the mixture reaches the soft peak stage.
- Gradually whisk in the remaining sugar.
- Sieve the flour over the egg yolk mixture and fold in the egg whites, keeping as much air in the mixture as possible.
- Spoon the mixture into a piping bag, then pipe 10 cm (4 in) fingers onto the baking trays, leaving room for the sponges to spread.
- Bake the biscuits for 10–15 minutes.
- Transfer to a wire rack and leave to cool completely, then dust with sugar to finish.

Chocolate sponge fingers
Replace the instant espresso powder with 1 tsp cocoa powder, and fold in 50 g / 1 ¾ oz / ⅓ cup chocolate chips just before baking. Sprinkle with cocoa powder instead of sugar to finish.

Frosted apple loaf

PREPARATION TIME: **10 minutes**
COOKING TIME: **55 minutes**
SERVES: **8**

300 g / 10 ½ oz / 2 cups self-raising flour
2 tsp baking powder
250 g / 9 oz / 1 ½ cups brown sugar
250 g / 9 oz / 1 ¼ cups butter, softened
5 large eggs
2 eating apples, cored and chopped
100 g / 3 ½ oz / ½ cup icing (confectioners') sugar
juice of 1 lemon

- Preheat the oven to 170°C (150°C fan) / 340F / gas 3, then line a large loaf tin with greaseproof paper.
- Sieve the flour and baking powder into a mixing bowl, then add the sugar, butter and eggs. Beat the mixture with a whisk for 4 minutes or until smooth and well-whipped. Fold in the apple, then scrape the mixture into the loaf tin.
- Bake for 55 minutes or until a skewer inserted comes out clean. Transfer to a wire rack and leave to cool completely.
- To make the drizzle, mix the icing sugar with lemon juice to form a thick icing. Use a spoon to drizzle the icing over the cooled cake to finish.

Frosted pear loaf
Replace the eating apples with 2 peeled, cored and chopped pears, folding into the cake mixture before baking.

Chocolate-dipped hazelnut shortbread

PREPARATION TIME: **20 minutes**
COOKING TIME: **15-20 minutes**
MAKES: **16**

225 g / 8 oz / 1 ½ cup plain (all-purpose) flour
2 tbsp ground hazelnuts (cobnuts)
75 g / 2 ½ oz / ⅓ cup caster (superfine) sugar
150 g / 5 oz / ⅔ cup butter, cubed
100 g / 3 ½ oz / ⅔ cup milk chocolate

- Preheat the oven to 180°C (160° fan) / 350F / gas 4, then line a baking tray with greaseproof paper.
- In a large mixing bowl, mix together the flour, hazelnuts and sugar, then use your fingertips to rub in the butter.
- Knead gently until the mixture forms a smooth dough, then roll out to a 1 cm (½ in) thickness.
- Transfer the shortbread to the prepared baking tray and bake for 15–20 minutes, turning the tray round halfway through.
- Transfer the biscuits to a wire rack and leave to cool.
- Meanwhile, melt the chocolate in a bowl set over a saucepan of simmering water.
- When the shortbread has cooled, dip the ends into the melted chocolate, then leave to leave to cool and harden on a wire rack before serving.

White chocolate hazelnut shortbread
Melt 100 g / 3 ½ oz / ⅔ cup white chocolate for dipping, instead of milk chocolate, to give these shortbread biscuits an indulgent finish.

Pumpkin spice loaf cake

PREPARATION TIME: 15 minutes
COOKING TIME: 55 minutes
MAKES: 1 loaf

225 g / 8 oz / 1 cup pumpkin purée
2 eggs
120 ml / 4 fl. oz / ½ cup sunflower oil
75 ml / 2 fl. oz / ¼ cup water
300 g / 10 ½ oz / 1 ⅓ cup caster (superfine) sugar
300 g / 10 ½ oz / 2 cup self-raising flour
2 tsp baking powder
1 tsp ground cinnamon
1 tsp ground nutmeg
100 g / 3 ½ oz / ⅔ cup pumpkin, grated
icing (confectioners') sugar to dust

- Preheat the oven to 190°C (170°C fan) / 375F / gas 5, then grease a large loaf tin .
- In a mixing bowl, mix together the pumpkin purée, eggs, oil, water and sugar until mixed.
- Sieve the flour into a separate bowl, then stir in the baking powder, cinnamon, nutmeg and grated pumpkin. Add to the pumpkin purée mixture and stir until just combined.
- Scrape the mixture into the prepared loaf tin and bake for 55 minutes.
- Test the cake with a wooden toothpick; if it comes out clean, the cake is done.
- Transfer to a wire rack to cool, then dust with icing sugar to finish.

Orange and cinnamon rolls

PREPARATION TIME: 2 hours, 30 minutes
COOKING TIME: 10-12 minutes
MAKES: 12

400 g / 14 oz / 2 ⅔ cups strong white bread flour
½ tsp easy-blend dried yeast
4 tbsp caster (superfine) sugar
1 tsp fine sea salt
1 tbsp olive oil
75 g / 2 ½ oz / ½ cup dark brown sugar
2 tbsp butter, softened
1 orange, zest finely grated
1 tsp ground cinnamon
1 egg, beaten
3 tbsp sugar nibs

- In a large mixing bowl, mix together the flour, yeast, caster sugar and salt.
- In a jug, stir the oil into 280 ml of warm water, then stir the liquid into the dry ingredients.
- Knead the mixture on a lightly oiled surface for 10 minutes or until the dough is smooth and elastic.
- Cover the dough with oiled cling film, then leave to rest for 1–2 hours or until doubled in size. Roll out the dough into a large rectangle.
- In a clean bowl, cream together the brown sugar and butter, then stir in the orange zest and cinnamon.
- Spread the mixture over the surface of the dough, then roll it up tightly.
- Cut the roll into 12 slices and spread them out on a greased baking tray. Cover with oiled cling film and leave to prove for 1 hour or until doubled in size.
- Preheat the oven to 220°C (200°C fan) / 425F / gas 7. Brush the rolls with beaten egg and sprinkle with sugar nibs.
- Bake the rolls for 10–12 minutes or until they are cooked through and golden brown.

Treacle and oat cookies

PREPARATION TIME: **10 minutes**
COOKING TIME: **12-15 minutes**
MAKES: **36**

300 g / 10 ½ oz / 1 ¾ cups caster (superfine) sugar
175 g / 6 oz / ¾ cup butter, melted
2 tbsp treacle
1 egg, plus 1 egg yolk
250 g / 9 oz / 1 ⅔ cups self-raising flour
100 g / 3 ½ oz / 1 cup porridge oats

- Preheat the oven to 170°C (150°C fan) / 340F / gas 3, then line two baking trays with greaseproof paper.
- In a large mixing bowl, cream together the sugar, butter and treacle until pale and well-whipped.
- Beat in the egg and the yolk, then beat in the flour and oats.
- Dollop tablespoons of the mixture onto the prepared baking trays, leaving room for the cookies to spread.
- Bake the cookies in batches for 12–15 minutes or until the edges start to brown, but the centres are still chewy.
- Transfer to a wire rack and leave to cool.

Sticky oat and banana cookies
Mash 2 bananas, then cream together with 200 g / 7 oz / ¾ cup sugar, the butter and treacle, to give these cookies a chewy, fruity texture.

Almond and raspberry loaf cake

PREPARATION TIME: **10 minutes**
COOKING TIME: **45 minutes**
SERVES: **8**

225 g / 8 oz / 1 cup butter, softened
225 g / 8 oz / 1 cup caster (superfine) sugar
4 large eggs, beaten
125 g / 4 ½ oz / ¾ cup self-raising flour
100 g / 3 ½ oz / 1 cup ground almonds
100 g / 3 ½ oz / 1 cup fresh raspberries
2 tbsp flaked (slivered) almonds

- Preheat the oven to 180°C (160°C fan) / 350F / gas 4, then grease and line a large loaf tin with greaseproof paper.
- In a large mixing bowl, cream the butter and sugar together until well-whipped, then gradually whisk in the eggs, beating well after each addition.
- Fold in the flour and ground almonds, then scrape two-thirds of the mixture into the prepared loaf tin.
- Sprinkle over the raspberries in an even layer, then top with the remaining cake mixture. Sprinkle over the flaked almonds.
- Bake the cake for 45 minutes. Test the cake with a toothpick; if it comes out clean, the cake is done. Cool the loaf on a wire rack.

Almond, raspberry and white chocolate loaf
Add 100 g / 3 ½ oz / ⅔ cup chopped white chocolate to the mixture along with the ground almonds, then bake as normal to give this cake an extra sweet flavour.

Iced cinnamon hearts

PREPARATION TIME: 1 hour, 15 minutes
COOKING TIME: 25-30 minutes
MAKES: 36

100 g / 3 ½ oz / ½ cup caster (superfine) sugar
100 g / 3 ½ oz / ½ cup butter, softened
1 tsp vanilla extract
1 tsp ground cinnamon
1 large egg, beaten
300 g / 10 ½ oz / 2 cups plain (all-purpose) flour

TO DECORATE
150 g / 5 ½ oz royal icing powder
red food dye

Iced rose water hearts
Replace the ground cinnamon with 1 tbsp
rose water for the biscuits, then stir 1 tsp
rose water into the royal icing powder to give
these hearts a floral flavour.

- In a large mixing bowl, cream together the sugar, butter, vanilla extract and cinnamon until pale and well-whipped. Beat in the egg, then beat in the flour.
- Shape the mixture together into a ball, then wrap with cling film and chill for 45 minutes.
- Preheat the oven to 190°C (170°C fan) / 375F / gas 5, then line two baking trays with greaseproof paper.
- Roll out the dough on a lightly floured surface to 5mm thick, then use a heart-shaped cutter to cut 36 biscuits.
- Transfer the biscuits to the prepared baking trays and bake in batches for 8–10 minutes.
- Transfer the biscuits to a wire rack and leave to cool.
- Whisk the royal icing powder with a few drops of red food dye and 25 ml water until it forms a thick icing. You can use different food dyes to create different coloured icing.
- Spoon the icing into a piping bag and pipe over the surface of the cookies.

Wholemeal chocolate loaf

PREPARATION TIME: 2 hours, 30 minutes
COOKING TIME: 35-40 minutes
MAKES: 1 loaf

200 g / 7 oz / 1 ⅓ cup stoneground wholemeal flour
200 g / 7 oz / 1 ⅓ cup strong white bread flour
½ tsp easy-blend dried yeast
4 tbsp brown sugar
2 tbsp unsweetened cocoa powder
1 tsp fine sea salt
1 tbsp olive oil
100 g / 3 ½ oz dark chocolate (minimum 60 % cocoa solids), grated

Chocolate and walnut loaf
Add 100 g / 3 ½ oz / ⅔ cup chopped walnuts to the mixture along with the grated chocolate, kneading to make sure the ingredients are evenly distributed. Bake as normal.

- In a large mixing bowl, mix together the flours, yeast, sugar, cocoa and salt.
- Stir the oil and grated chocolate into 280 ml warm water, then stir it into the dry ingredients.
- Knead the mixture on a lightly oiled surface for 10 minutes or until the dough is smooth and elastic.
- Transfer the dough to a lightly oiled bowl, cover with oiled cling film and leave to rest for 1–2 hours, or until doubled in size.
- Knock the air out of the dough, then knead again for 2 minutes.
- Flatten the dough slightly, then roll it up tightly and tuck under the ends.
- Transfer the loaf to a large, greased loaf tin and cover again with oiled cling film. Leave to prove for 1 hour or until doubled in size.
- Preheat the oven to 220°C (200°C fan) / 425F / gas 7.
- When the dough has risen, transfer the tin to the top shelf of the oven, then pour a small cupful of water into the base of the oven.
- Bake for 35–40 minutes or until the loaf sounds hollow underneath. Transfer the bread to a wire rack and leave to cool.

Rose water cherry cupcakes

PREPARATION TIME: **20 minutes**
COOKING TIME: **15-20 minutes**
MAKES: **12**

110 g / 4 oz / ⅔ cup self-raising flour, sifted
110 g / 4 oz / ½ cup caster (superfine) sugar
110 g / 4 oz / ½ cup butter, softened
2 large eggs
1 tbsp rose water
55 g / 2 oz / ¼ cup butter, softened
225 g / 8 oz / 2 ¼ cups icing (confectioners') sugar
1 tbsp rose syrup
12 fresh cherries

- Preheat the oven to 190°C (170°C fan) / 375F / gas 5, then line a 12-hole cupcake tray with paper cases.
- In a large mixing bowl, combine the flour, sugar, butter, eggs and rose water and whisk together until smooth. Divide the mixture between the paper cases, then transfer the tin to the oven and bake for 15-20 minutes.
- Test with a wooden toothpick. Transfer the cakes to a wire rack and leave to cool completely.
- For the frosting, beat the butter with a wooden spoon until light and fluffy, then beat in the icing sugar. Add the rose syrup, then whisk. Pipe the buttercream on each cake. Top with a cherry.

Rose water white chocolate cupcakes
Add 100 g / 3 ½ oz / ⅔ cup white chocolate chips to the cupcake mixture, stirring until evenly distributed, then bake as normal. Top with a white chocolate button.

Nutty chocolate brownies

PREPARATION TIME: **25 minutes**
COOKING TIME: **35-40 minutes**
MAKES: **9**

110 g / 4 oz dark chocolate, chopped
85 g / 3 oz / ¾ cup unsweetened cocoa powder, sifted
225 g / 8 oz / 1 cup butter
450 g / 15 oz / 2 ½ cups light brown sugar
4 large eggs
110 g / 4 oz / ⅔ cup self-raising flour
100 g / 3 ½ oz / ⅔ cup pecan nuts, chopped
100 g / 3 ½ oz / ⅔ cup walnuts, chopped
fresh strawberries to garnish

- Preheat the oven to 170°C (150°C fan) / 340F / gas 3, then oil and line a 20cm (8in) square cake tin .
- Melt the chocolate, cocoa and butter together in a saucepan, then leave to cool. Whisk together the sugar and eggs until very light and creamy.
- Pour in the chocolate mixture and sieve over the flour, then fold everything together with the chopped nuts until evenly mixed. Scrape into the tin and bake for 35-40 minutes. Cool for 10 minutes then cut into squares.

Chocolate and peanut butter brownies
Replace the walnuts and pecans with 150 g / 5 ½ oz / 1 cup chopped, roasted peanuts, then scrape the mixture into the tin and dollop teaspoons of smooth peanut butter over the top.

Orange and walnut cake

PREPARATION TIME: 15 minutes
COOKING TIME: 30 minutes
SERVES: 8

150 g / 5 ½ oz / 1 cup walnuts, chopped
150 g / 5 ½ oz / 1 cup self-raising flour, sifted
1 tsp baking powder
110 g / 4 oz / ½ cup butter, softened
2 large eggs
110 g / 4 oz / ½ cup caster (superfine) sugar
juice and zest of 1 orange
icing (confectioners') sugar to dust

- Preheat the oven to 190°C (170°C fan) / 375F / gas 5, then butter a 23 cm (9 in) round baking dish.
- Place the walnuts in a food processor and grind into a fine powder.
- In a large mixing bowl, combine the ground walnuts, flour and baking powder, then rub in the butter using your fingertips.
- In a separate bowl, beat the eggs until fluffy, then gradually beat in the sugar.
- Beat in the dry ingredients, then stir in the orange juice and zest until just combined.
- Spoon the mixture into the prepared baking tray and bake for 30 minutes. Test with a wooden toothpick; if it comes out clean, the cake is done.
- Transfer to a wire rack to cool, then dust with icing sugar to finish.

Walnut cake
Omit the orange juice and zest for a different take on this recipe.

Pineapple upside-down cake

PREPARATION TIME: 15 minutes
COOKING TIME: 35 minutes
SERVES: 8

300 g / 10 ½ oz / 2 cups self-raising flour
2 tsp baking powder
250 g / 9 oz / 1 ¼ cups caster (superfine) sugar
250 g / 9 oz / 1 ¼ cups butter, softened
5 large eggs
4 tbsp runny honey
1 can pineapple rings, drained
glacé cherries to decorate

- Preheat the oven to 170°C (150°C fan) / 340F / gas 3, then butter a 23 cm (9 in) round cake tin.
- Sieve the flour and baking powder into a large mixing bowl, then add sugar, butter and eggs. Beat the mixture until smooth and well whipped.
- Spread the honey over the base of the cake tin and arrange the pineapple rings on top, then place a cherry inside each pineapple ring.
- Spoon in the cake mixture and bake for 35 minutes. Test with a wooden toothpick; if it comes out clean, the cake is done.
- Leave the cake to cool for 20 minutes before turning out onto a serving plate.

Coffee nut muffins

PREPARATION TIME: **25 minutes**
COOKING TIME: **20-25 minutes**
MAKES: **12**

1 large egg
120 ml / 4 fl. oz / ½ cup sunflower oil
120 ml / 4 fl. oz / ½ cup milk
375 g / 12 ½ oz / 2 ½ cups self-raising flour, sifted
1 tsp baking powder
1 tsp instant espresso powder
200 g / 7 oz / ¾ cup caster (superfine) sugar
50 g / 1 ¾ oz / ⅓ cup whole almonds
50 g / 1 ¾ oz / ⅓ cup walnuts, chopped
50 g / 1 ¾ oz / ⅓ cup peanuts, chopped

- Preheat the oven to 180°C (160°C fan) / 350F / gas 4. Line a 12-hole muffin tin with paper cases.
- Beat the egg in a jug with the oil and milk until well mixed. In a large mixing bowl, mix together the flour, baking powder, espresso powder and sugar. Pour in the egg mixture and stir just enough to combine.
- Divide the mixture between the paper cases and sprinkle over the nuts. Bake for 20-25 minutes. Test with a wooden toothpick; if it comes out clean, the cakes are done. Transfer to a wire rack and leave to cool.

Coffee caramel nut muffins
Half-fill each of the paper cases with the cake mixture, dollop a teaspoon of caramel curd in the centre, then top with the remaining cake mixture and nuts. Bake as normal.

Cinnamon snaps

PREPARATION TIME: **10 minutes**
COOKING TIME: **12-15 minutes**
MAKES: **36**

75 g / 2 ½ oz / ⅓ cup butter, softened
100 g / 3 ½ oz / ⅓ cup golden syrup
225 g / 8 oz / 1 ½ cups self-raising flour
100 g / 3 ½ oz / ½ cup caster (superfine) sugar
1 tsp ground cinnamon
1 large egg, beaten

- Preheat the oven to 180°C (160°C fan) / 350F / gas 4, then line two baking trays with greaseproof paper.
- Melt the butter and golden syrup together in a saucepan. In a large bowl, mix together the flour, sugar and cinnamon, then stir in the melted butter mixture and beaten egg.
- Dollop teaspoons of the mixture onto the prepared baking trays and flatten slightly with the back of the spoon. Make sure to leave room for the biscuits to spread. Bake in batches for 12–15 minutes or until golden brown. Transfer the biscuits to a wire rack and leave to cool.

Iced cinnamon snaps
Mix a little icing (confectioners') sugar with water to make a spreadable icing. Spoon into a piping bag fitted with a small nozzle, then pipe patterns on the top of the finished cookies.

Chocolate and hazelnut shortbread

PREPARATION TIME: 20 minutes
COOKING TIME: 15-20 minutes
MAKES: 16

225 g / 8 oz / 1 ½ cups plain (all-purpose) flour
75 g / 2 ½ oz / ⅓ cup caster (superfine) sugar
150 g / 5 oz / ⅔ cup butter, cubed
50 g / 1 ¾ oz / ½ cup hazelnuts (cobnuts), finely chopped
50 g / 1 ¾ oz / ⅓ cup dark chocolate

- Preheat the oven to 180 C (160 C fan) / 350F / gas 4, then line a baking tray with greaseproof paper.
- Mix together the flour and sugar in a bowl, then use your fingertips to rub in the butter.
- Knead gently with the hazelnuts until the mixture forms a smooth dough, then roll out on a lightly floured surface to 1 cm (½ in) thickness.
- Use an oval cookie cutter to cut out 16 biscuits, then spread them out on the prepared baking tray.
- Bake the biscuits for 15–20 minutes, turning the tray round halfway through.
- Transfer the biscuits to a wire rack and leave to cool.
- Meanwhile, melt the chocolate in a bowl set over a saucepan of simmering water.
- Use a teaspoon to drizzle the melted chocolate over the cooled cookies, then leave to cool and harden before serving.

Poppy seed and hazelnut shortbread
Add 4 tbsp poppy seeds to the mixture along with the hazelnuts, kneading to ensure that they are evenly distributed, then bake as normal.

Lemon meringue pie

PREPARATION TIME: **55 minutes**
COOKING TIME: **25-30 minutes**
SERVES: **8**

2 tsp cornflour (cornstarch)
4 lemons, zest and juice
4 large eggs, beaten
225 g / 8 oz / 1 cup butter
175 g / 6 oz / ¾ cups caster (superfine) sugar

FOR THE PASTRY
100 g / 3 ½ oz / ½ cups butter, cubed
200 g / 7 oz / 1 ⅓ cups plain (all-purpose) flour

FOR THE MERINGUE
4 large egg whites
110 g / 4 oz / ½ cups caster (superfine) sugar

- Preheat the oven to 200°C (180°C fan) / 400F / gas 6.
- Make the pastry first. Using your fingertips, rub the butter into the flour in a large mixing bowl, then add just enough cold water to bind.
- Chill for 30 minutes, then roll on a lightly floured surface.
- Use the pastry to line a 23 cm (9 in) tart tin and prick the base with a fork.
- Line the pastry with greaseproof paper / baking paper and fill with baking beans or rice, then bake for 10 minutes. Remove the greaseproof paper / baking paper and beans and cook for another 8 minutes to crisp.
- Meanwhile, dissolve the cornflour in the lemon juice and place in a saucepan with the egg, butter and sugar.
- Stir constantly over a medium heat to melt the butter and dissolve the sugar. Bring to a gentle simmer, then pour the mixture into the pastry case.
- In a separate mixing bowl, whisk the egg whites until stiff, then gradually add the sugar and whisk until the mixture is thick and shiny. Spoon the meringue on top of the lemon curd, making peaks with the spoon.
- Bake for 10 minutes or until golden brown.

Lavender shortbread biscuits

PREPARATION TIME: **20 minutes**
COOKING TIME: **15-20 minutes**
MAKES: **16**

200 g / 7 oz / 1 ⅓ cup plain (all-purpose) flour
75 g / 2 ½ oz / ⅓ cup caster (superfine) sugar
1 tbsp dried lavender leaves
150 g / 5 oz / ⅔ cup butter, cubed

- Preheat the oven to 180°C (160°C fan) / 350F / gas 4, then line a baking tray with greaseproof paper.
- Mix together the flour, sugar and lavender leaves in a bowl, then rub in the butter with your fingers until it looks like fine breadcrumbs.
- Knead gently until the mixture forms a smooth dough, then roll it out to a thickness of 5 mm.
- Use a round cookie cutter to cut 16 biscuits and spread them out on the prepared baking tray.
- Bake the biscuits for 15–20 minutes, turning the tray round halfway through. Transfer the biscuits to a wire rack and leave to cool.

Lavender lemon shortbread biscuits
Lemon is a great addition to these shortbread biscuits. Add the zest of 1 lemon along with the lavender leaves and bake as instructed above.

Almond cakes

PREPARATION TIME: **20 minutes**
COOKING TIME: **12-15 minutes**
MAKES: **12**

55 g / 2 oz / ⅓ cup self-raising flour, sifted
1 tsp baking powder
55 g / 2 oz / ½ cup ground almonds
110 g / 4 oz / ½ cup caster (superfine) sugar
110 g / 4 oz / ½ cup butter, softened
2 large eggs
50 g / 1 ¾ oz / ⅓ cup flaked (slivered) almonds

- Preheat the oven to 190°C (170°C fan) / 375F / gas 5, then line a 12-hole cupcake tray with paper cases.
- In a large mixing bowl, combine the flour, baking powder, ground almonds, sugar, butter and eggs, then whisk together for 2 minutes or until smooth.
- Divide between the paper cases and sprinkle with flaked almonds.
- Bake for 12–15 minutes. Test with a wooden toothpick, if the toothpick comes out clean, the cakes are done.
- Transfer the cakes to a wire rack to cool completely before serving.

Chocolate almond cakes
Add 55 g / 2 oz / ½ cup unsweetened cocoa powder to the mixture along with the ground almonds, then stir in 100 g / 3 ½ oz / ⅔ cup chocolate chips and bake as normal.

Mixed fruit loaf

PREPARATION TIME: **2 hours 30 minutes**
COOKING TIME: **35-40 minutes**
MAKES: **1 Loaf**

55 g / 2 oz / ¼ cup butter, cubed

400 g / 14 oz / 2 ⅔ cups strong white bread flour, plus extra for dusting

½ tsp easy-blend dried yeast

4 tbsp caster (superfine) sugar

1 tsp fine sea salt

2 tsp mixed spice

100 g / 3 ½ oz / ½ cup mixed dried fruit

1 egg, beaten

- Using your fingertips, rub the butter into the bread flour in a large mixing bowl.

- Stir in the yeast, sugar, salt, spice and dried fruit, then add 280 ml warm water to the mixture and stir to combine.

- Knead the mixture on a lightly oiled surface for 10 minutes or until the dough is smooth and elastic.

- Transfer the dough to a lightly oiled bowl, cover with oiled cling film and leave to rest for 1–2 hours or until doubled in size.

- Roll the dough into a sausage shape, then turn it around and roll the other way. Tuck the ends under, transfer to a large loaf tin and leave the dough to prove for 45 minutes.

- Preheat the oven to 220°C (200°C fan) / 425F / gas 7. Slash the top of the loaf in diagonals with a sharp knife and brush with beaten egg.

- Transfer the loaf tin to the oven and bake for 35–40 minutes or until the underneath sounds hollow.

Rhubarb custard tart

PREPARATION TIME: 40 minutes
COOKING TIME: 40-50 minutes
SERVES: 8

3 sticks rhubarb, chopped
4 tbsp caster (superfine) sugar

FOR THE PASTRY
100 g / 3 ½ oz / ½ cup butter, cubed
200 g / 7 oz / 1 ⅓ cups plain (all-purpose) flour

FOR THE CUSTARD
4 large egg yolks
75 g / 2 ½ oz / ⅓ cup caster (superfine) sugar
1 tsp vanilla extract
2 tsp cornflour (cornstarch)
450 ml / 16 fl. oz / 1 ¾ cups whole milk

- Preheat the oven to 200°C (180°C fan) / 400F / gas 6.
- Put the rhubarb in a roasting tin and sprinkle with sugar. Bake for 20 minutes until tender.
- Meanwhile, make the pastry. Using your fingertips, rub the butter into the flour and add just enough cold water to bind. Chill for 30 minutes.
- Roll the pastry out on a lightly floured surface and use to line a large rectangular tart tin. Prick the base with a fork, line with baking paper and fill with baking beans or rice.
- Bake for 10 minutes, then remove the baking paper and baking beans and cook for another 8 minutes to crisp.
- Reduce the oven temperature to 170°C (150°C fan) / 340F / gas 3.
- Whisk together the custard ingredients and pour into the pastry case. Arrange the rhubarb on top.
- Bake the tart for 25–35 minutes or until the custard is just set in the centre. Leave to cool completely before serving.

Blackberry and pistachio mini muffins

PREPARATION TIME: **25 minutes**
COOKING TIME: **15-20 minutes**
MAKES: **24**

1 large egg
120 ml / 4 fl. oz / ½ cup sunflower oil
120 ml / 4 fl. oz / ½ cup milk
375 g / 12 ½ oz / 2 ½ cups self-raising flour, sifted
1 tsp baking powder
200 g / 7 oz / ¾ cup caster (superfine) sugar
200 g / 7 oz / 1 ⅓ cups blackberries
100 g / 3 ½ oz / ⅔ cup pistachios, shelled and chopped

- Preheat the oven to 180°C (160°C fan) / 350F / gas 4, then line a 24-hole mini muffin tin with paper cases.
- Beat the egg in a jug with the oil and milk until well mixed. In a large mixing bowl, mix together the flour, baking powder and sugar. Pour in the egg mixture and stir just enough to combine, then fold in the blackberries and pistachios.
- Divide the mixture between the paper cases and bake for 15–20 minutes. Test with a wooden toothpick; if it comes out clean the muffins are done. Transfer to a wire rack to cool.

Blackberry, chocolate and pistachio muffins
Add 100 g / 3 ½ / ⅔ cup chocolate chips to the mixture along with the blackberries and pistachios to make these muffins more indulgent.

Salted chocolate and walnut cookies

PREPARATION TIME: **10 minutes**
COOKING TIME: **12-15 minutes**
MAKES: **36**

225 g / 8 oz / 1 ⅓ cup light brown sugar
100 g / 3 ½ oz / ½ cup caster (superfine) sugar
175 g / 6 oz / ¾ cup butter, melted
2 tsp vanilla extract
1 egg, plus 1 egg yolk
250 g / 9 oz / 1 ⅔ cups self-raising flour
1 tsp sea salt
100 g / 3 ½ oz / ¾ cup walnuts, chopped
100 g / 3 ½ oz / ¾ cup chocolate chips

- Preheat the oven to 170°C (150°C fan) / 340F / gas 3, and line two baking trays with greaseproof paper.
- In a large mixing bowl, cream together the two sugars, butter and vanilla extract. Beat in the egg and yolk, then beat in the flour, sea salt, walnut pieces and chocolate chips. Dollop tablespoons onto the baking trays, leaving room to spread.
- Bake the cookies in batches for 12–15 minutes or until the edges start to brown, but the centres are still chewy. Transfer to a wire rack to cool.

Double chocolate and pecan cookies
Add 3 tbsp unsweetened cocoa powder with the flour for an extra chocolate hit, and replace the walnuts with the same quantity of pecans to create a different nutty flavour.

Summer berry buttercream cupcakes

PREPARATION TIME: 1 hour
COOKING TIME: 15-20 minutes
MAKES: 12

110 g / 4 oz / ⅔ cup self-raising flour, sifted
110 g / 4 oz / ½ cup caster (superfine) sugar
110 g / 4 oz / ½ cup butter, softened
2 large eggs
1 tsp vanilla extract

TO DECORATE
55 g / 2 oz / ¼ cup butter, softened
225 g / 8 oz / 2 ¼ cup icing (confectioners') sugar
1 tbsp milk
50 g / 1 ¾ oz / ⅓ cup raspberries
50 g / 1 ¾ oz / ⅓ cup blueberries
50 g / 1 ¾ oz / ⅓ cup redcurrants
mint leaves to garnish

- Preheat the oven to 190°C (170°C fan) / 375F / gas 5, then line a 12-hole cupcake tray with paper cases.
- In a large mixing bowl, combine the flour, sugar, butter, eggs and vanilla extract and whisk until smooth.
- Divide the mixture between the paper cases, then bake for 15–20 minutes. Test with a wooden toothpick; if it comes out clean, the cakes are done.
- Transfer the cakes to a wire rack and leave to cool completely.
- To make the icing, beat the butter with a wooden spoon until light and fluffy, then beat in the icing sugar a bit at a time.
- Add the milk, then whip the mixture with a whisk until smooth and light.
- Spoon the icing onto the cakes and top with the fruit and a garnish of mint leaves to finish.

Salted caramel shortcake

PREPARATION TIME: 3 hours, 20 minutes
COOKING TIME: 15-20 minutes
MAKES: 9

225 g / 8 oz / 1 ½ cups plain (all-purpose) flour
2 tbsp cocoa powder
75 g / 2 ½ oz / ⅓ cup caster (superfine) sugar
150 g / 5 oz / ⅔ cup butter, cubed
50 g / 1 ¾ oz / ¼ cup granulated sugar

FOR THE TOPPING
1 can condensed milk
1 tsp fine sea salt
200 g / 7 oz milk chocolate

- Make the caramel layer first. Place the unopened can of condensed milk in a saucepan of water and simmer for 3 hours, adding more water as necessary to ensure it doesn't boil dry. Leave the can to cool.

- Preheat the oven to 180°C (160°C fan) / 350F / gas 4, then line a 20 cm (8 in) square cake tin with greaseproof paper.

- In a large mixing bowl, mix together the flour, cocoa and sugar in a bowl, then rub in the butter with your fingertips.

- Knead gently until the mixture forms a smooth dough, then press it into the bottom of the tin in an even layer.

- Bake the shortbread for 15–20 minutes, turning the tray round halfway through. Leave to cool completely.

- Open the can of condensed milk and beat until smooth. Stir in the sea salt, then spread the caramel over the shortbread and chill for 1 hour.

- Melt the chocolate in a bowl set over a saucepan of simmering water, then spread over the caramel in an even layer.

- Chill in the fridge for 30 minutes before cutting and serving.

White chocolate caramel shortcake
Substitute the milk chocolate for white chocolate, and melt using the same method. Spread over the caramel layer and sprinkle with sea salt for an extra salty kick.

Chocolate and almond biscotti

PREPARATION TIME: **25 minutes**
COOKING TIME: **35 minutes**
MAKES: **24**

2 large eggs
55 g / 2 oz / ¼ cup butter, melted
225 g / 8 oz / 1 ½ cups self-raising flour
100 g / 3 ½ oz / ½ cup caster (superfine) sugar
75 g / 2 ¾ oz / ½ cup unsweetened cocoa powder, plus extra for dusting
100 g / 3 ½ oz / ⅔ cup blanched almonds, chopped
1 tsp sea salt

- Preheat the oven to 180°C (160°C fan) / 350F / gas 4, then line two baking trays with greaseproof paper. Beat together the eggs and butter, then stir in the flour, sugar, cocoa powder, almonds and salt.
- Make a soft dough and shape into two long rolls. Transfer to one of the baking trays and press to flatten slightly. Bake for 20 minutes, then leave to cool for 15 minutes.
- Cut the rolls across into 1 cm (½ in) thick slices and spread them out over the baking trays. Bake the biscuits for 15 minutes or until crisp.
- Transfer to a wire rack and leave to cool, then dust with cocoa powder to finish.

Chocolate-dipped biscotti
Melt 100 g / 3 ½ oz / ⅔ cup chopped dark chocolate in a bowl set over a saucepan of simmering water, then dip the baked biscotti into the chocolate and leave to set.

Cinnamon cookies

PREPARATION TIME: **10 minutes**
COOKING TIME: **12-15 minutes**
MAKES: **36**

175 g / 6 oz / ¾ cup butter, melted
225 g / 8 oz / 1 ⅓ cups light brown sugar
100 g / 3 ½ oz / ½ cup caster (superfine) sugar, plus extra for dusting
2 tsp vanilla extract
1 egg, plus 1 egg yolk
250 g / 9 oz / 1 ⅔ cups self-raising flour
2 tsp ground cinnamon, plus extra for dusting

- Preheat the oven to 170°C (150°C fan) / 340F / gas 3, then line two baking trays with greaseproof paper.
- In a large mixing bowl, cream together the two sugars, butter and vanilla extract until pale and well-whipped.
- Beat in the egg and yolk, then beat in the flour and cinnamon. Dollop tablespoons of the mixture onto the prepared baking trays, leaving room for the cookies to spread.
- Bake the cookies in batches for 12–15 minutes or until the edges start to brown, but the centres are still chewy. Transfer to a wire rack and leave to cool, then dust liberally with ground cinnamon and sugar.

Cinnamon and raisin cookies
Stir in 100 g / 3 ½ oz / ¾ cup of raisins with the flour and cinnamon to add a fruity burst.

THE COOKERY COLLECTION

Orange treacle tart

PREPARATION TIME: **45 minutes**
COOKING TIME: **50-55 minutes**
SERVES: **8**

FOR THE CANDIED ORANGES
350 g / 12 ½ oz / 1 cup golden syrup
1 orange, zest and juice
150 g / 5 ½ oz / 2 cups white breadcrumbs
1 tsp ground cinnamon
icing (confectioners') sugar to dust
400 g / 14 oz / 1 ¾ cups caster (superfine) sugar
2 oranges, sliced

FOR THE PASTRY
100 g / 3 ½ oz / ½ cup butter, cubed
200 g / 7 oz / 1 ⅓ cups plain (all-purpose) flour
1 tsp ground cinnamon

- Make the pastry first. Using your fingers, rub the butter into the flour and cinnamon in a large mixing bowl, then add just enough cold water to bind. Chill the dough for 30 minutes.
- Meanwhile, make the candied orange slices. Put the sugar in a saucepan with 200 ml water and stir over a low heat until dissolved. Add the orange slices, then simmer for 25 minutes.
- Preheat the oven to 200°C (180°C fan) / 400F / gas 6.
- Roll out the pastry on a lightly floured surface and use it to line a fluted tart tin.
- Heat the golden syrup with the orange zest and juice in a small saucepan set over a medium heat. When it turns runny, stir in the breadcrumbs and cinnamon.
- Spoon the filling into the pastry case and top with the candied orange slices.
- Bake for 25–30 minutes or until the pastry is cooked through underneath, then dust with icing sugar to finish.

White chocolate and almond loaf

PREPARATION TIME: **15 minutes**
COOKING TIME: **55 minutes**
SERVES: **8**

175 g / 6 ¼ oz / 1 ¼ cups self-raising flour
50 g / 1 ¾ oz / ½ cup ground almonds
100 g / 3 ½ oz / ½ cup butter, cubed
85 g / 3 oz / ⅓ cup caster (superfine) sugar
150 g / 5 ½ oz white chocolate, chopped
100 g / 3 ½ oz / ⅔ cup dried cranberries
1 large egg
75 ml / 2 ½ fl. oz / ⅓ cup whole milk

FOR THE WHITE CHOCOLATE GLAZE
100 g / 3 ½ oz / ⅔ cup white chocolate
3 tbsp double (heavy) cream
3 tbsp icing (confectioners') sugar
2 tbsp whole almonds
2 tbsp fresh cranberries
mint leaves to garnish

- Preheat the oven to 180°C (160°C fan) / 350F / gas 4, then line a large loaf tin with greaseproof paper.
- Sieve the flour into a mixing bowl with the ground almonds, then rub in the butter until it resembles fine breadcrumbs. Stir in the sugar, white chocolate and the dried cranberries.
- In a jug, lightly beat the egg with the milk and stir it into the dry ingredients until just combined.
- Scrape the mixture into the loaf tin and bake for 55 minutes. Test with a wooden toothpick; if it comes out clean, the cake is done. Transfer to a wire rack to cool.
- To make the glaze, melt the white chocolate and cream together in a small saucepan set over a medium heat.
- Remove from the heat, then stir in the icing sugar and drizzle the glaze over the loaf cake.
- Sprinkle over the whole almonds and cranberries, then garnish with mint leaves to finish.

White chocolate and pistachio loaf
Replace the almonds with the same amount of chopped pistachios.

Lemon shortbread biscuits

PREPARATION TIME: **20 minutes**
COOKING TIME: **15-20 minutes**
MAKES: **16**

225 g / 8 oz / 1 ½ cup plain (all-purpose) flour
75 g / 2 ½ oz / ⅓ cup caster (superfine) sugar
150 g / 5 oz / ⅔ cup butter, cubed
1 lemon, zest finely grated

- Preheat the oven to 180°C (160°C fan) / 35oF / gas 4. Line a baking tray with greaseproof paper.
- Mix together the flour and sugar in a bowl, then rub in the butter with your fingertips and add the lemon zest.
- Knead gently until the mixture forms a smooth dough, then shape into a cylinder 6 cm (2 ½ in) in diameter.
- Slice the roll into 1 cm (½ in) slices and spread them out on the prepared baking tray.
- Bake the biscuits for 15–20 minutes, turning the tray round halfway through.
- Transfer the biscuits to a wire rack and leave to cool.

Lemon and ginger shortbread
Add 1 tsp crystallised ginger pieces to the mixture along with the lemon zest to give these shortbread biscuits an extra kick.

Double chocolate and hazelnut cookies

PREPARATION TIME: **10 minutes**
COOKING TIME: **12-15 minutes**
MAKES: **36**

175 g / 6 oz / ¾ cup butter, melted
225 g / 8 oz / 1 ⅓ cup dark brown sugar
100 g / 3 ½ oz / ½ cup caster (superfine) sugar
2 tsp vanilla extract
1 egg, plus 1 egg yolk
250 g / 9 oz / 1 ⅔ cup self-raising flour
2 tbsp unsweetened cocoa powder
175 g / 6 oz / 1 ¼ cup chocolate chips
175 g / 6 oz / 1 ¼ cup hazelnuts (cobnuts), chopped

- Preheat the oven to 170°C (150°C fan) / 34oF / gas 3, then line two baking trays with greaseproof paper.
- In a large mixing bowl, cream together the two sugars, butter and vanilla extract. Beat in the egg and yolk, then beat in the flour, cocoa, chocolate chips and hazelnuts. Dollop tablespoons of the mixture onto the prepared trays, leaving room for the cookies to spread.
- Bake the cookies in batches for 12–15 minutes or until the edges start to brown, but the centres are still chewy. Transfer to a wire rack to cool.

Chocolate and pistachio cookies
Replace the hazelnuts with the same quantity of shelled, chopped pistachio nuts to add a different nutty flavour to these indulgent cookies.

Blueberry ricotta tartlets

PREPARATION TIME: **45 minutes**
COOKING TIME: **15-20 minutes**
MAKES: **6**

100 g / 3 ½ oz / ½ cup butter, cubed
200 g / 7 oz / 1 ⅓ cups plain (all-purpose) flour
55 g / 2 oz / ¼ cup caster (superfine) sugar
1 egg, beaten
250 g / 9 oz / 1 ¼ cup ricotta
2 tbsp caster (superfine) sugar
100 g / 3 ½ oz / ⅔ cup blueberries
100 g / 3 ½ oz / ⅔ cup bilberries
2 tbsp runny honey

- Preheat the oven to 200°C (180°C fan) / 400F / gas 6.
- Make the pastry first. In a large mixing bowl, rub the butter into the flour using your fingertips, then add the egg and just enough cold water to bring the dough together.
- Wrap the dough in cling film and chill for 30 minutes.
- Roll the dough out on a lightly floured surface, then cut out 6 circles and use to line 6 tartlet tins. Trim and crimp the edges.
- Prick the pastry with a fork, line with greaseproof paper and fill with baking beans or rice.
- Blind bake for 10 minutes, then remove the greaseproof paper and baking beans and cook for another 8 minutes to crisp. Transfer to a wire rack to cool.
- In a clean bowl, mix the ricotta with the sugar, then spoon into the cooled pastry cases.
- Top with the ricotta and the berries, then drizzle with a little honey to finish.

Strawberry ricotta tartlets
Replace the blueberries with 200 g / 7 oz / 1 ⅓ cup strawberries, hulled and chopped, then drizzle with honey and garnish with mint leaves to finish.

Chocolate cake squares

PREPARATION TIME: **20 minutes**
COOKING TIME: **30-35 minutes**
MAKES: **12**

150 g / 6 oz / 1 cup self-raising flour
2 tbsp unsweetened cocoa powder
2 tsp baking powder
175 g / 6 oz / ¾ cup caster (superfine) sugar
175 g / 6 oz / ¾ cup butter
3 eggs

FOR THE BUTTERCREAM
100 g / 3 ½ oz / ⅔ cup butter, softened
300 g / 10 ½ oz / 3 cups icing (confectioners') sugar
2 tbsp cocoa powder
cake sprinkles

- Preheat the oven to 180°C (160°C fan) / 350F / gas 4, then grease and line a large rectangular baking tin.
- Place all the cake ingredients into a large mixing bowl and whisk together until pale and well-whipped.
- Scrape the mixture into the tin and level the top with a spatula.
- Bake for 30–35 minutes. Test the cake with a toothpick; if it comes out clean, the cake is done.
- Transfer the cake to a wire rack to cool.
- To make the buttercream, beat the butter in a clean bowl until light and fluffy, then beat in the icing sugar a bit at a time.
- Stir in the cocoa powder and use a whisk to whip the mixture until smooth and light.
- Spread the buttercream on top of the cake, then scatter over the cake sprinkles. Cut into 12 pieces to serve.

White chocolate cake squares
For the frosting, replace the cocoa powder with 100 g / 3 ½ oz / ⅔ cup melted white chocolate, stirring into the buttercream to combine.

Buttercream cupcakes

PREPARATION TIME: **10 minutes**
COOKING TIME: **15-20 minutes**
MAKES: **12**

110 g / 4 oz / ⅔ cup self-raising flour, sifted
110 g / 4 oz / ½ cup caster (superfine) sugar
110 g / 4 oz / ½ cup butter, softened
2 large eggs
1 tsp vanilla extract

FOR THE ICING
55 g / 2 oz / ¼ cup butter, softened
225 g / 8 oz / 2 ¼ cups icing (confectioners') sugar
1 tsp vanilla essence
chocolate flakes

- Preheat the oven to 190°C (170°C fan) / 375F / gas 5, then line a 12-hole cupcake tin with paper cases.
- In a large mixing bowl, combine the flour, sugar, butter, eggs and vanilla extract and whisk until smooth.
- Divide the mixture between the paper cases, then place the tin in the oven and bake for 15–20 minutes. Test with a toothpick, then transfer the cakes to a wire rack to cool.
- For the icing, beat the butter with a wooden spoon, then beat in the icing sugar a bit at a time.
- Stir in the vanilla essence using a whisk to whip the mixture until smooth and light. Spoon the icing into a piping bag fitted with star-shaped nozzle and pipe a rosette onto each cupcake. Sprinkle with chocolate flakes to finish.

Colourful buttercream cupcakes
Stir a few drops of food dye in a colour of your choice into the buttercream mixture, then finish with candy sprinkles.

Lime and lemon pie

PREPARATION TIME: **45 minutes**
COOKING TIME: **50-55 minutes**
SERVES: **8**

300 g / 10 ½ oz / 2 cups ginger biscuits
150 g / 5 ½ oz / ⅔ cup butter, melted
2 lemons, juiced
4 limes, juiced
175 g / 6 oz / ¾ cup caster (superfine) sugar
2 tsp cornflour (cornstarch)
4 large eggs, beaten
225 g / 8 oz / ¾ cup double (heavy) cream

- Preheat the oven to 200°C (180° fan) / 400F / gas 6, then grease a round fluted baking tin.
- To make the base, blitz the ginger biscuits in a food processor until fine. In a mixing bowl, mix together the biscuit crumbs and melted butter, then press into the base and sides of the prepared baking tin. Bake for 10 minutes, then remove and leave to cool. Reduce the oven temperature to 170°C (150°C fan) / 340F / gas 3.
- In a large mixing bowl, stir together the lemon and lime juices, the sugar and cornflour to dissolve, then whisk in the eggs and cream.
- Strain the mixture into the biscuit base and bake for 25–30 minutes or until just set in the centre. Leave to cool before decorating with finely grated lime zest.

Key lime pie
Juice 6 limes for the filling. Whip 300 ml / 10 ½ fl. oz / 1 ¼ cup double (heavy) cream with 1 tbsp icing (confectioners') sugar, then add to the pie and sprinkle with lime zest to finish.

THE COOKERY COLLECTION

Cherry clafoutis

PREPARATION TIME: 40 minutes
COOKING TIME: 35-45 minutes
SERVES: 6

300 g / 10 ½ oz / 2 cups cherries, stoned
2 tbsp kirsch
75 g / 2 ½ oz / ⅓ cup butter
75 g / 2 ½ oz / ⅓ cup caster (superfine) sugar
300 ml / 10 ½ fl. oz / 1 ¼ cups whole milk
2 large eggs
50 g / 1 ¾ oz / ⅓ cup plain (all-purpose) flour
icing (confectioners') sugar to dust

- Preheat the oven to 190°C (170°C fan) / 375F / gas 5.
- Place the cherries in a bowl with the kirsch and leave to marinate for 30 minutes.
- Melt the butter in a saucepan over a low heat until it starts to smell nutty.
- Brush a little of the butter around the inside of a 20 cm (8 in) cake tin, then add a spoonful of caster sugar and shake to coat.
- In a mixing bowl, whisk together the milk and eggs with the rest of the melted butter.
- Sieve the flour into a mixing bowl with a pinch of salt, then stir in the rest of the sugar.
- Make a well in the middle of the dry ingredients and gradually whisk in the liquid, incorporating all the flour from round the outside until you have a lump-free batter.
- Arrange the cherries in the prepared baking dish, pour over the batter and transfer to the oven.
- Bake for 35–45 minutes. Test with a toothpick; if it comes out clean, the pudding is done. Sprinkle with icing sugar to finish.

Zesty ginger and carrot loaf

PREPARATION TIME: 15 minutes
COOKING TIME: 35-40 minutes
MAKES: 1 loaf

250 g / 9 oz / 1 ⅔ cup self-raising flour
2 tsp baking powder
2 tsp ground ginger
200 g / 8 ½ oz / ⅔ cup golden syrup
125 g / 4 ½ oz / ½ cup butter
125 g / 4 ½ oz / ¾ cup dark brown sugar
100 g / 3 ½ oz / ½ cup candied orange peel, chopped
zest of 1 orange
1 large carrot, grated
100 g / 3 ½ oz / ⅔ cup walnuts, finely chopped
2 large eggs, beaten
240 ml / 8 fl. oz / 1 cup milk

- Preheat the oven to 180°C (160°C fan) / 350F / gas 4, then grease and line a large loaf tin.
- In a large mixing bowl, mix together the flour, baking powder and ginger.
- Heat the golden syrup, butter, sugar, candied peel and orange zest in a small saucepan and boil gently for 2 minutes, stirring to dissolve the butter.
- Add the warm mixture to the dry ingredients, then fold in the grated carrot, walnuts, eggs and milk until combined and smooth.
- Scrape the mixture into the prepared tin and bake for 35–40 minutes. The cake is ready when a toothpick inserted in the centre comes out clean.
- Transfer the cake to a wire rack to cool completely.

Chocolate shortbread

PREPARATION TIME: 20 minutes
COOKING TIME: 15-20 minutes
MAKES: 16

230 g / 8 oz / 1 ½ cups plain (all-purpose) flour
2 tbsp cocoa powder
75 g / 2 ½ oz / ⅓ cup caster (superfine) sugar
150 g / 5 oz / ⅔ cup butter, cubed
100 g / 3 ½ oz / ⅔ cup chocolate chips
50 g / 1 ¾ oz / cup icing (confectioners') sugar

- Preheat the oven to 180°C (160°C fan) / 350F
  / gas 4. Line a baking tray with greaseproof paper.
- In a large mixing bowl, mix together the flour,
  cocoa and caster sugar, then rub in the butter
  with your fingertips.
- Stir in the chocolate chips until evenly
  distributed.
- Knead gently until the mixture forms a smooth
  dough, then shape into a cylinder 6 cm (2 ½ in)
  in diameter and roll in icing sugar.
- Slice the roll into 1 cm (½ in) slices and spread
  them out on the baking tray.
- Bake the biscuits for 15–20 minutes, turning the
  tray round halfway through.
- Transfer the biscuits to a wire rack and leave to
  completely cool.

Chocolate and pistachio shortbread
Add 150 g / 5 oz / 1 cup shelled and chopped
pistachios to the mixture along with the
chocolate chips.

Nutmeg cookies

PREPARATION TIME: 10 minutes
COOKING TIME: 12-15 minutes
MAKES: 24

75 g / 2 ½ oz / ⅓ cup butter, softened
100 g / 3 ½ oz / ⅓ cup golden syrup
225 g / 8 oz / 1 ½ cups self-raising flour
100 g / 3 ½ oz / ½ cup golden caster (superfine) sugar
1 tsp nutmeg, freshly grated
1 large egg, beaten

- Preheat the oven to 180°C (160°C fan) / 350F
  / gas 4, then line two baking trays with
  greaseproof paper.
- Melt the butter and golden syrup together in
  a saucepan set over a low heat.
- In a large mixing bowl, mix together the flour,
  sugar and nutmeg, then stir in the melted butter
  mixture and the beaten egg.
- Dollop tablespoons of the mixture onto the
  prepared baking trays, leaving room for the
  cookies to spread.
- Bake in batches for 12–15 minutes or until
  golden brown.
- Transfer the biscuits to a wire rack and leave
  to cool and crisp.

Nutmeg and lemon cookies
Add the zest of 1 lemon to the mixture and stir
to combine before baking as normal. Sprinkle a
little lemon zest over the finished cookies for an
extra zesty flavour.

Chocolate chip quinoa cookies

PREPARATION TIME: **40 minutes**
COOKING TIME: **20-25 minutes**
MAKES: **36**

150 g / 5 ½ oz / 1 ½ cups quinoa flakes
100 g / 3 ½ oz / ⅔ cup porridge oats
125 g / 4 ½ oz / ¾ cup stoneground wholemeal flour
1 tsp baking powder
175 g / 6 oz / ¾ cup butter
150 g / 5 1/2 oz / ¾ cup soft brown sugar
2 tbsp raw quinoa
150 g / 5 ½ oz / 1 cup chocolate chips
75 g / 2 ¾ oz / ½ cup dried cranberries
75 g / 2 ¾ oz / ½ cup walnuts, chopped

- In a large mixing bowl, mix together the quinoa flakes, oats, flour and baking powder.
- In a separate bowl, cream together the butter with the sugar, then beat in the dry ingredients.
- Fold in the quinoa, chocolate chips, cranberries and walnuts, then bring the dough together chill for 30 minutes.
- Preheat the oven to 180°C (160°C fan) / 350F / gas 4, then line two baking trays with greaseproof paper.
- Shape the dough into small balls, then arrange them on the prepared baking trays and press down slightly.
- Bake for 20–25 minutes or until cooked through and golden brown.
- Transfer the biscuits to a wire rack and leave to cool completely.

Quinoa and fruit cookies
Replace the chocolate chips with the same quantity of raisins and chopped dates, to give these cookies a chewy texture and fruity flavour.

Sweet plum tart

PREPARATION TIME: **2 hours**
COOKING TIME: **30-40 minutes**
SERVES: **8**

150 g / 5 ½ oz / 1 ½ cups ground almonds
150 g / 5 ½ oz / ⅔ cup butter, softened
150 g / 5 ½ oz / ⅔ cup caster (superfine) sugar
2 large eggs
2 tbsp plain (all-purpose) flour
900 g / 2 lb plums, stoned and halved
3 tbsp runny honey
Icing (confectioners') sugar to dust

FOR THE PASTRY
100 g / 3 ½ oz / ½ cup butter, cubed
200 g / 7 oz / 1 ⅓ cups plain (all-purpose) flour
50 g / 1 ¾ oz / ¼ cup caster (superfine) sugar

- Preheat the oven to 200°C (180°C fan) / 400F / gas 6.
- Make the pastry first. Using your fingertips, rub the butter into the flour in a large mixing bowl until the mixture resembles fine breadcrumbs.
- Stir in the sugar and add enough cold water to bring the pastry together into a pliable dough.
- Chill the dough for 30 minutes, then roll out on a lightly floured surface. Use the pastry to line a 23cm (9in) round baking tin.
- In a clean bowl, whisk together the almonds, butter, sugar, eggs and flour until smoothly whipped, then spoon the mixture into the pastry case.
- Arrange the plums on top, brush with honey and bake for 25 minutes.
- Transfer to a wire rack to cool slightly, then dust with icing sugar to finish.

Gingerbread stars

PREPARATION TIME: **1 hour, 15 minutes**
COOKING TIME: **8-10 minutes**
MAKES: **36**

100 g / 3 ½ oz / ½ cup caster (superfine) sugar
100 g / 3 ½ oz / ½ cup butter, softened
2 tsp ground ginger
1 large egg, beaten
300 g / 10 ½ oz / 2 cups plain (all-purpose) flour
icing (confectioners') sugar to dust

- In a large mixing bowl, cream together the sugar, butter and ginger until pale and well-whipped.
- Beat in the egg, then beat in the flour.
- Bring the mixture together into a ball, then wrap in cling film and chill for 45 minutes.
- Preheat the oven to 190°C (170°C fan) / 375F / gas 5, then line two baking trays with greaseproof paper.
- Roll out the dough on a lightly floured surface to 5 mm thick. Use a star-shaped cutter to cut out 36 biscuits, using the off-cuts as necessary.
- Transfer the biscuits to the prepared baking trays in batches and bake for 8–10 minutes or until cooked through and golden brown.
- Transfer the biscuits to a wire rack and leave to cool completely before dusting with icing sugar.

Chocolate gingerbread stars
Add 2 tbsp unsweetened cocoa powder and 100 g / 3 ½ oz / ⅔ cup chocolate chips to the mixture along with the ginger and stir until combined. Dust with cocoa powder to finish.

Chocolate and ice cream cookie

PREPARATION TIME: **20 minutes**
COOKING TIME: **12-15 minutes**
MAKES: **18**

225 g / 8 oz / 1 ⅓ cup dark brown sugar
100 g / 3 ½ oz / ½ cup caster (superfine) sugar
175 g / 6 oz / ¾ cup butter, melted
2 tsp vanilla extract
1 egg, plus 1 egg yolk
250 g / 9 oz / 1 ⅔ cups self-raising flour
2 tbsp unsweetened cocoa powder
1 litre / 1 pt 15 fl. oz / 4 cup vanilla ice cream

- Remove the ice cream from the freezer for 15 minutes to allow it to soften slightly. Preheat the oven to 170°C (150°C fan) / 340F / gas 3, then line two baking trays with greaseproof paper.
- Cream together the two sugars, butter and vanilla extract until pale and well-whipped. Beat in the egg and yolk, then beat in the flour and cocoa powder. Dollop 36 tablespoons of the mixture onto the prepared baking trays, leaving room for the cookies to spread.
- Bake the cookies in batches for 12–15 minutes or until the edges start to brown, but the centres are still chewy. Transfer to a wire rack to cool.
- To serve, dollop teaspoons of ice cream onto 18 of the cookies, then top with another cookie.

Chocolate chip and pistachio cookie
Stir 175 g / 6 oz / 1 ¼ cups chocolate chips into the cookie mixture before baking, and use pistachio flavoured ice cream instead of vanilla to sandwich your double chocolate cookies.

Gooseberry pudding

PREPARATION TIME: **10 minutes**
COOKING TIME: **35-45 minutes**
SERVES: **6**

75 g / 2 ½ oz / ⅓ cup butter
75 g / 2 ½ oz / ⅓ cup caster (superfine) sugar
300 ml / 10 ½ fl. oz / 1 ¼ cups whole milk
2 large eggs
50 g / 1 ¾ oz / ⅓ cup plain (all-purpose) flour
2 tbsp ground almonds
300 g / 10 ½ oz / 2 cups gooseberries

- Preheat the oven to 190°C (170°C fan) / 375F / gas 5.
- Melt the butter over a low heat until it starts to smell nutty.

- Brush a little of the butter around the inside of a round pie dish, then add a spoonful of caster sugar and shake to coat.
- In a mixing bowl, whisk together the milk and eggs with the rest of the butter.
- Sieve the flour into a separate, large mixing bowl, then add a pinch of salt and stir in the ground almonds and the rest of the sugar.
- Make a well in the middle of the dry ingredients and gradually whisk in the liquid, incorporating all the flour from round the outside until you have a lump-free batter.
- Arrange the gooseberries in the prepared pie dish, pour over the batter and transfer to the oven immediately.
- Bake the pudding for 35–45 minutes. Test with a wooden toothpick; if it comes out clean, the pudding is done.

Chocolate and buttercream biscuits

PREPARATION TIME: 1 hour, 15 minutes
COOKING TIME: 25-30 minutes
MAKES: 36

150 g / 5 ½ oz / ⅔ cup caster (superfine) sugar
350 g / 12 oz / 1 ½ cup butter, softened
1 tsp vanilla extract
300 g / 10 ½ oz / 2 cup plain (all-purpose) flour
2 tbsp unsweetened cocoa powder
150 g / 5 ½ oz / 1 ½ cup ground almonds

FOR THE BUTTERCREAM
110 g / 4 oz / ½ cup butter, softened
225 g / 8 oz / 2 ¼ cup icing (confectioners') sugar
2 tbsp milk

- In a large mixing bowl, cream together the sugar, butter and vanilla extract, then stir in the flour, cocoa and ground almonds.
- Using your hands, shape the mixture into a ball and wrap in cling film. Refrigerate for 45 minutes.
- Preheat the oven to 140°C (120°C fan) / 275F / gas 1, then line two baking sheets with greaseproof paper.
- When the dough is cool, roll out on a lightly floured surface to about 5 mm thick. Cut out 72 small circles, using the off-cuts.
- Transfer the biscuits to the prepared trays in batches and bake for 25–30 minutes.
- Leave the biscuits to cool on a wire rack.
- To make the buttercream, beat the butter with a wooden spoon until light and fluffy, then beat in the icing sugar.
- Whisk in the milk for 2 minutes or until smooth and well-whipped.
- Use the buttercream to sandwich two biscuits.

Lavender lemon loaf cake

PREPARATION TIME: **10 minutes**
COOKING TIME: **55 minutes**
MAKES: **1 Loaf**

300 g / 10 ½ oz / 2 cups self-raising flour
2 tsp baking powder
250 g / 9 oz / 1 ¼ cups caster (superfine) sugar
250 g / 9 oz / 1 ¼ cups butter, softened
5 large eggs
zest of 2 lemons, finely grated
1 tbsp dried lavender leaves
3 tbsp runny honey
lavender sprigs to garnish

- Preheat the oven to 170°C (150°C fan) / 340F / gas 3. Line a large loaf tin with greaseproof paper.
- Sieve the flour and baking powder into a large mixing bowl and add the sugar, butter and eggs.
- Beat the mixture until smooth and well-whipped, then fold in the lemon zest and lavender leaves.
- Scrape the mixture into the loaf tin and bake for 55 minutes. Test the cake with a wooden toothpick; if it comes out clean, the cake is done.
- Transfer the cake to a wire rack and brush over the honey while the cake is still warm, allowing it to run down the sides. Garnish with sprigs of lavender to finish.

Lemon thyme loaf cake
Replace the lavender leaves with the same quantity of dried thyme leaves, then garnish with sprigs of thyme to give this cake a different, fragrant flavour.

Pear and caramel tarte Tatin

PREPARATION TIME: **10 minutes**
COOKING TIME: **20-25 minutes**
SERVES: **8**

125 g / 4 ½ oz / ½ cup caster (superfine) sugar
50 g / 1 ¾ oz / ¼ cup butter
1 tsp ground ginger
6 pears, peeled, cored and halved
250 g / 9 oz all-butter puff pastry
vanilla pod, to garnish

- Preheat the oven to 220°C (200°C fan) / 425F / gas 7. Heat the sugar in an ovenproof frying pan set over a medium-high heat, stirring constantly, until the sugar turns a caramel colour. Add the butter and ground ginger, then stir to combine.
- Place the pears in the caramel sauce, stirring to coat, then cook over a low heat for 5 minutes or until the pears start to soften. Remove from the heat and arrange the pears in the pan, cut side up, then leave to cool a little.
- Roll out the pastry on a lightly floured surface and cut out a circle the same size as the frying pan. Lay over the pears and tuck in the edges, then transfer the pan to the oven and bake for 25 minutes.
- Cool for 10 minutes. Carefully turn the tart out onto the plate. Garnish with a vanilla pod and serve warm.

Pear and chocolate tarte Tatin
While the tart is cooking, melt 100 g / 3 ½ oz / ⅔ cup dark chocolate in a bowl set over a saucepan of simmering water. Drizzle the melted chocolate over the tarte Tatin to serve.

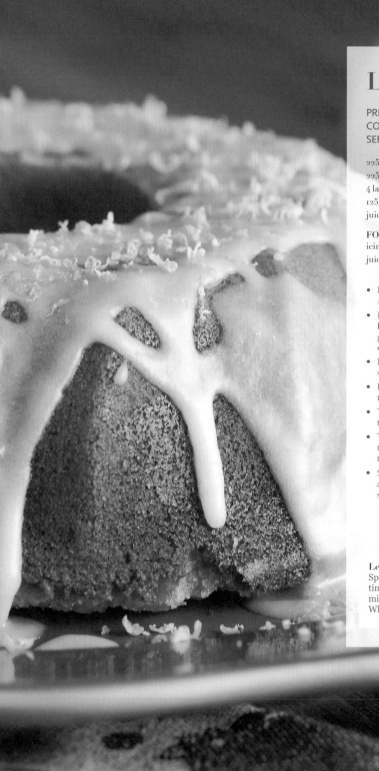

Lemon bundt cake

PREPARATION TIME: 5 minutes
COOKING TIME: 45 minutes
SERVES: 8-10

225 g / 8 oz / 1 cup butter, softened
225 g / 8 oz / 1 cup caster (superfine) sugar
4 large eggs, beaten
125 g/ 4 ½ oz / ¾ cup self-raising flour
juice and zest of 1 lemon

FOR THE ICING
icing (confectioners') sugar to dust
juice and zest of 1 lemon

- Preheat the oven to 180°C (160°C fan) / 350F / gas 4, then grease a bundt tin.
- In a large mixing bowl, cream together the butter and sugar until well-whipped, then gradually whisk in the eggs, beating well after each addition.
- Fold in the flour, lemon juice and zest, then scrape the mixture into the prepared tin.
- Bake for 45 minutes. Test the cake with a toothpick; if it is clean, the cake is done.
- Turn the cake out onto a wire rack and leave to cool.
- To make the icing, mix the icing sugar with the lemon juice. Add a little water to make a thick, spreadable icing.
- Spoon the icing onto the top of the cake, allowing it to drip down the sides, then sprinkle over the lemon zest to finish.

Lemon curd bundt cake
Spoon half of the cake mixture into the bundt tin, then spoon lemon curd in the centre of the mixture and top with the remaining cake mix. When sliced, the cake will ooze lemon curd.

Apple, walnut and honey tarts

PREPARATION TIME: **30 minutes**
COOKING TIME: **20 minutes**
MAKES: **6**

225 g / 8 oz puff pastry
150 g / 5 ½ oz / 1 ½ cups ground walnuts
150 g / 5 ½ oz / ⅔ cup butter, softened
150 g / 5 ½ oz / ⅔ cup caster (superfine) sugar
2 large eggs
2 tbsp plain (all-purpose) flour
4 eating apples, cored and sliced
4 tbsp runny honey
2 tbsp chopped walnuts
1 tsp ground cinnamon

- Preheat the oven to 200°C (180°C fan) / 400F / gas 6.
- Roll out the pastry on a lightly floured surface, then use the pastry to line 6 round tartlet cases.
- Prick the pastry with a fork, line with greaseproof paper and fill with baking beans or rice.
- Blind bake for 10 minutes, then remove the paper and baking beans.
- In a large mixing bowl, whisk together the ground walnuts, butter, sugar, eggs and flour until smooth, then spoon the mixture into the pastry cases.
- Arrange the apple slices on top and bake for 20 minutes or until the tart is cooked through and the pastry is crisp underneath.
- Heat the honey until very runny and stir in the walnuts, then drizzle it over the hot tarts. Sprinkle ground cinnamon over to finish.

Apple, almond and honey tarts
Replace the ground walnuts with the same quantity of ground almonds, then stir 2 tbsp flaked (slivered) almonds into the honey to drizzle over the tartlets.

Strawberry cream tartlets

PREPARATION TIME: 15 minutes
COOKING TIME: 25-35 minutes
MAKES: 12

110 g / 4 oz / ½ cup butter, cubed and chilled
225 g / 8 oz / 1 ½ cups plain (all-purpose) flour
300 ml / 10 ½ fl. oz / 1 ¼ cup double (heavy) cream
300 g / 10 ½ oz / 2 cups strawberries, halved
fresh mint leaves to garnish

- Preheat the oven to 200°C (180°C fan) / 400F / gas 6.
- In a large mixing bowl, rub the butter into the flour with your fingertips until the mixture resembles fine breadcrumbs.
- Stir in just enough cold water to bring the pastry together into a pliable dough.
- Roll out the pastry on a lightly floured surface, then cut out 12 circles and use them to line a 12-hole tartlet tray (or individual tartlet cases).
- Bake for 15–20 minutes or until the pastry is crisp. Transfer to a wire rack to cool.
- In a clean bowl, whip the cream until it thickens and has a smooth texture.
- Divide the whipped cream between the cooled pastry cases, then top with sliced strawberries and some fresh mint leaves to garnish.

Strawberry mess tartlets
To make easy Eton mess style tartlets, buy some ready-made meringues and break into pieces. Stir into the double cream and strawberries (you could also use raspberries), then spoon into the pastry cases.

Pear and honey cake

PREPARATION TIME: 10 minutes
COOKING TIME: 30-35 minutes
MAKES: 12

300 g / 10 ½ oz / 2 cups self-raising flour
2 tsp baking powder
250 g / 9 oz / 1 ¼ cups caster (superfine) sugar
250 g / 9 oz / 1 ¼ cups butter, softened
5 large eggs
4 tbsp runny honey
2 large pears, peeled and chopped
100 g / 3 ½ oz / 1 cup icing (confectioners') sugar
pink candy pieces to decorate

- Preheat the oven to 170°C (150°C fan) / 340F / gas 3, then butter a 23 cm (9 in) round cake tin.
- Sieve the flour and baking powder into a large mixing bowl, then add sugar, butter, eggs and honey. Beat the mixture until smooth and well whipped.
- Arrange the chopped pears in the base of the prepared cake tin, then spoon over the mixture.
- Bake for 35 minutes. Test with a wooden toothpick. Transfer to a wire rack to cool.
- To make the icing, mix the icing sugar with enough water to make a spreadable icing. Use a spoon to drizzle the icing over the cake, then sprinkle over the candy pieces to finish.

Pear and golden syrup cake
Replace the honey with 4 tbsp golden syrup to give this cake a richer flavour, then bake and ice as normal.

Fig and honey muffins

PREPARATION TIME: 25 minutes
COOKING TIME: 20-25 minutes
MAKES: 12

1 large egg
120 ml / 4 fl. oz / ½ cup sunflower oil
120 ml / 4 fl. oz / ½ cup milk
100 g / 3 ½ oz / ⅓ cup runny honey
375 g / 12 ½ oz / 2 ½ cups self-raising flour, sifted
1 tsp baking powder
100 g / 3 ½ oz / ½ cup caster (superfine) sugar
4 fresh figs, chopped
icing (confectioners') sugar to dust.

- Preheat the oven to 180°C (160°C fan) / 350F / gas 4, then grease 12 fluted muffin cases (or line a 12-hole muffin tin with paper cases).
- Beat the egg in a jug with the oil, milk and honey until well mixed.
- In a large mixing bowl, mix together the flour, baking powder and sugar.
- Pour in the egg mixture and stir just enough to combine.
- Divide the mixture between the muffin cases and press the chopped figs into the tops.
- Bake for 20 – 25 minutes. Test the muffins with a wooden toothpick; if it comes out clean, they are done.
- Transfer the muffins to a wire rack and leave to cool completely, then dust liberally with icing sugar to finish.

Chocolate gateau with cherries

PREPARATION TIME: 10 minutes
COOKING TIME: 45-50 minutes
SERVES: 10-12

110 g / 4 oz / ⅔ cup self-raising flour
2 tbsp unsweetened cocoa powder
1 tsp baking powder
110 g / 4 oz / ½ cup caster (superfine) sugar
110 g / 4 oz / ½ cup butter
2 large eggs

FOR THE BUTTERCREAM
100 g / 3 ½ oz / ⅔ cup butter, softened
300 g / 10 ½ oz / 3 cups icing (confectioners') sugar
2 tbsp cocoa powder
3 tbsp chocolate flakes
100 g / 3 ½ oz / ⅔ cup fresh cherries

- Preheat the oven to 180°C (160°C fan) / 350F / gas 4, then grease and line a 23cm (9in) round cake tin.
- In a large mixing bowl, whisk together all the cake ingredients until fully combined.
- Scrape the mixture into the prepared tin and bake for 30–35 minutes. Test the cake with a toothpick; if it comes out clean, the cake is done.
- Transfer the cake to a wire rack to cool completely, then use a serrated knife to slice the cake in half horizontally.
- To make the buttercream, beat the butter in a clean bowl until light and fluffy, then beat in the icing sugar a bit at a time.
- Stir in the cocoa powder and use a whisk to whip the mixture until smooth and light.
- Use half of the buttercream to sandwich together the cakes, then spread the rest over the top and sides of the cake.
- Sprinkle chocolate flakes over the top of the cake, then pile the cherries on top to finish. Serve a cherry on top of each slice of cake.

Pumpkin and raisin loaf cake

PREPARATION TIME: **15 minutes**
COOKING TIME: **55 minutes**
MAKES: **1 loaf**

225 g / 8 oz / 1 cup pumpkin purée
2 eggs
120 ml / 4 fl. oz / ½ cup sunflower oil
75 ml / 2 fl. oz / ¼ cup water
300 g / 10 ½ oz / 1 ⅓ cup caster (superfine) sugar
300 g / 10 ½ oz / 2 cup self-raising flour
2 tsp baking powder
1 tsp ground cinnamon
100 g / 3 ½ oz / ⅔ cup raisins, chopped
100 g / 3 ½ oz / ⅔ cup walnuts, chopped
icing (confectioners') sugar to dust

- Preheat the oven to 190°C (170°C fan) / 375F / gas 5, then grease a large loaf tin.
- In a mixing bowl, mix together the pumpkin purée, eggs, oil, water and sugar until well mixed.
- Sieve the flour into a separate bowl, then stir in the baking powder, cinnamon, raisins and walnuts. Add to the pumpkin mixture and stir until just combined. Scrape the mixture into the prepared loaf tin and bake for 55 minutes.
- Test the cake with a wooden toothpick. Transfer to a wire rack to cool, then dust with icing sugar.

Pumpkin loaf cake
Remove the raisins and walnuts from the cake mixture to simplify this cake, instead adding 100 g / 3 ½ oz / ⅔ cup pumpkin seeds to the mixture. Bake as normal.

Blueberry and lemon curd tartlets

PREPARATION TIME: **45 minutes**
COOKING TIME: **15-20 minutes**
MAKES: **6**

100 g / 3 ½ oz / ½ cup butter, cubed
200 g / 7 oz / 1 ⅓ cup plain (all-purpose) flour
1 egg, beaten
4 eggs
4 unwaxed lemons, zest and juice
200 g / 7 oz / 1 ⅓ cup caster (superfine) sugar
100 g / 3 ½ oz / ½ cup butter, cubed
1 tsp cornflour (cornstarch)
200 g / 7 oz / 1 cup blueberries
icing (confectioners') sugar to dust

- Make the pastry first. In a large mixing bowl, rub the butter into the flour using your fingertips, then add just enough cold water to bind. Chill for 30 minutes.
- Preheat the oven to 200°C (180°C fan) / 400F / gas 6.
- Roll out the pastry on a lightly floured surface and use it to line 6 tartlet cases, rerolling the trimmings as necessary.
- Prick the pastry with a fork, line with greaseproof paper and fill with baking beans or rice. Bake for 10 minutes, then remove the greaseproof paper and baking beans. Brush the inside of the cases with beaten egg and cook for another 8 minutes. Transfer to a wire rack to cool.
- Whisk the eggs in a saucepan, then add the rest of the curd ingredients and set over a medium heat. Whisk continuously until the mixture thickens, then lower the heat and whisk for another minute. Spoon the curd into the pastry, allow to cool slightly, then top with the blueberries and dust with icing sugar to finish.

Raspberry and lemon curd tartlets
Raspberries are a great accompaniment for lemon – replace the blueberries with the same quantity of raspberries for a zingy flavour.

Apple cider loaf cake

PREPARATION TIME: 10 minutes
COOKING TIME: 55 minutes
SERVES: 8

300 g / 10 ½ oz / 2 cups self-raising flour
2 tsp baking powder
250 g / 9 oz / 1 ½ cups light brown sugar
250 g / 9 oz / 1 ¼ cups butter, softened
4 large eggs
100 ml / 3 ½ fl. oz / ⅓ cup dry cider
2 eating apples, cored and chopped
2 tsp ground cinnamon

- Preheat the oven to 170°C (150°C fan) / 340F / gas 3, then line a large loaf tin with greaseproof paper.
- Sieve the flour and baking powder into a large mixing bowl, then add the rest of the ingredients.
- Beat the mixture with a whisk for 4 minutes or until smooth and well-whipped.
- Scrape the mixture into the prepared loaf tin and bake for 55 minutes. Test the cake with a toothpick; if it comes out clean, the cake is done.
- Transfer the cake to a wire rack and leave to cool.

Plum galette

PREPARATION TIME: 15 minutes
COOKING TIME: 25-35 minutes
SERVES: 6

110 g / 4 oz / ½ cup butter, cubed and chilled
250 g / 9 oz /1 ⅔ cup plain (all-purpose) flour
450 g / 1 lb plums, halved and stoned
450g / 1 lb / 1 ¼ cup plum jam (jelly)
golden caster (superfine) sugar for dusting

- Preheat the oven to 200°C (180°C fan) / 400F / gas 6.
- In a large mixing bowl, rub the butter into the flour using your fingertips until the mixture resembles fine breadcrumbs.
- Stir in just enough cold water to bring the pastry together into a pliable dough.
- Roll out the pastry on a lightly floured surface into a large circle.
- Arrange the halved plums in the pastry case and spoon over the jam.
- Fold the edges of the dough up and over the plums, so that a circle of filling is visible. Dust with golden caster sugar.
- Bake for 25–35 minutes or until the pastry is crisp and the jam has melted around the plums.

Apricot galette
Replace the plums with the same quantity of apricots, then spoon over apricot jam and bake as normal.

Honey cake with cherries

PREPARATION TIME: **10 minutes**
COOKING TIME: **35-40 minutes**
SERVES: **8-10**

300 g / 10 ½ oz / 2 cups self-raising flour
2 tsp baking powder
125 g / 4 ½ oz / ½ cup caster (superfine) sugar
125 g / 4 ½ oz / ⅓ cup runny honey
250 g / 9 oz / 1 ¼ cup butter, softened
5 large eggs
75 g / 2 ½ oz / ½ cup cherries, halved and stoned
icing (confectioners') sugar to dust

- Preheat the oven to 170°C (150°C fan) / 340F / gas 3, then line a 23cm (9in) round cake tin with greaseproof paper.
- Sieve the flour and baking powder into a large mixing bowl, then add the sugar, honey, butter and eggs.
- Whisk the mixture until smooth, then stir in the cherries until evenly distributed.
- Bake for 35–40 minutes. Test the cake with a toothpick; if it comes out clean, the cake is done.
- Transfer the cake to a wire rack and leave to cool completely, then dust with icing sugar to finish.

Honey cake with raspberries
Replace the cherries with double the amount of fresh raspberries to add a sharp sweetness to this honey cake.

Sticky chocolate brownies

PREPARATION TIME: **25 minutes**
COOKING TIME: **35-40 minutes**
MAKES: **9**

100 g / 3 ½ oz / ⅔ cup milk chocolate, chopped
100 g / 3 ½ oz / ⅔ cup unsweetened cocoa powder, sifted
225 g / 8 oz / 1 cup butter
450 g / 15 oz / 2 ½ cups light brown sugar
4 large eggs
1 tbsp golden syrup
110 g / 4 oz / ⅔ cup self-raising flour
100 g / 3 ½ oz / ⅔ cup chocolate chips

- Preheat the oven to 170°C (150°C fan) / 340F / gas 3, then oil and line a 20cm (8in) square cake tin.
- Melt the chocolate, cocoa and butter together in a saucepan, then leave to cool a little.
- In a large mixing bowl, whisk together the sugar, eggs and golden syrup until very light and creamy.
- Pour in the chocolate mixture, then sieve over the flour and fold everything together with the chocolate chips until evenly mixed.
- Scrape into the prepared tin and bake for 35–40 minutes or until the outside is set, but the centre is still chewy. Leave the brownie to cool completely before cutting into nine squares.

Sticky chocolate orange brownies
Add 1 tsp orange flower water to give these brownies a classic chocolate-orange flavouring.

Nutty cookies

PREPARATION TIME: 15 minutes
COOKING TIME: 20-25 minutes
MAKES: 24

125 g / 4 ½ oz / ½ cup butter, cubed
125 g / 4 ½ oz / ¾ cup plain (all-purpose) flour
125 g / 4 ½ oz / ½ cup caster (superfine) sugar
3 large egg yolks
75 g / 2 ½ oz / ⅔ cup ground almonds
75 g / 2 ½ oz / ⅔ cup walnuts, finely chopped
75 g / 2 ½ oz / ⅔ cup hazelnuts (cobnuts), finely chopped
1 tsp ground cinnamon

- Preheat the oven to 180°C (160°C fan) / 350F / gas 4, then line a baking tray with greaseproof paper.
- In a large mixing bowl, rub the butter into the flour with your fingertips, then add the sugar with a pinch of salt.
- Beat the egg yolks and stir into the dry ingredients with the ground almonds, walnuts, hazelnuts and cinnamon.
- Bring the mixture together into a soft dough and dollop tablespoons of the mixture onto the prepared baking tray.
- Bake the biscuits for 20–25 minutes or until they turn golden brown.
- Transfer the biscuits to a wire rack and leave to cool.

Banoffee tart

PREPARATION TIME: **45 minutes**
COOKING TIME: **25 minutes**
SERVES: **6**

FOR THE PASTRY
100 g / 3 ½ oz / ½ cup butter, cubed
200 g / 7 oz / 1 ⅓ cups plain (all-purpose) flour
50 g / 1 ¾ oz / ¼ cup dark brown sugar

FOR THE FILLING
1 can condensed milk
2 bananas, sliced
300 ml / 10 ½ fl. oz / 1 ¼ cup double (heavy) cream
50 g / 1 ¾ oz / ⅓ cup chocolate, finely grated

- Make the caramel first. Place the unopened can of condensed milk in a saucepan of water and simmer for 3 hours, add water as necessary then leave to cool.

- To make the pastry, rub the butter into the flour using your fingertips until the mixture resembles breadcrumbs.
- Stir in the sugar and add enough cold water to bring the pastry together into a dough.
- Chill the dough for 30 minutes, then roll out on a lightly floured surface. Use the pastry to line a fluted baking tin.
- Prick the base with a fork, line with baking paper and fill with baking beans or rice.
- Bake for 10 minutes, then remove the baking paper and baking beans.
- Spread the slightly cooled caramel into the pastry case, then top with sliced banana.
- In a clean bowl, whip the cream until it thickens and has a smooth texture.
- Spoon the whipped cream over the bananas, then sprinkle grated chocolate over the tart to finish.

Baked pecan mini muffins

PREPARATION TIME: **25 minutes**
COOKING TIME: **15-20 minutes**
MAKES: **24**

1 large egg
120 ml / 4 fl. oz / ½ cup sunflower oil
120 ml / 4 fl. oz / ½ cup milk
1 tsp vanilla extract
375 g / 12 ½ oz / 2 ½ cups self-raising flour, sifted
1 tsp baking powder
200 g / 7 oz / 1 ¼ cups soft brown sugar
55 g / 2 oz / ½ cup ground almonds
75 g / 2 ½ oz / ⅔ cup pecan nuts

- Preheat the oven to 180°C (160°C fan) / 350F / gas 4, then grease a 24-hole mini muffin tray (or line two 12-hole cupcake trays with mini paper cases).
- Beat the egg in a jug with the oil, milk and vanilla extract until well mixed. In a large mixing bowl, mix together the flour, baking powder, sugar and ground almonds, then pour in the egg mixture and stir just enough to combine.
- Divide the mixture between the moulds and press one or two pecan nuts into each cupcake. Bake for 15–20 minutes. Test with a wooden toothpick. Transfer to a wire rack to cool.

Chocolate pecan mini muffins
To give these muffins a more indulgent flavour, add 2 tbsp unsweetened cocoa powder to the cake mixture instead of the vanilla extract, then add 100 g / 3 ½ oz / ⅔ cup white chocolate chips and bake as normal.

Date and oatmeal cookies

PREPARATION TIME: **10 minutes**
COOKING TIME: **12-15 minutes**
MAKES: **36**

225 g / 8 oz / 1 ⅓ cup light brown sugar
100 g / 3 ½ oz / ½ cup caster (superfine) sugar
175 g / 6 oz / ¾ cup butter, melted
2 tsp vanilla extract
1 egg, plus 1 egg yolk
250 g / 9 oz / 1 ⅔ cups self-raising flour
100 g / 3 ½ oz / 1 cup porridge oats
100 g / 3 ½ oz / ½ cup dates, stoned and finely chopped

- Preheat the oven to 170°C (150°C fan) / 340F / gas 3, then line two baking trays with greaseproof paper. In a large mixing bowl, cream together the two sugars, butter and vanilla extract until pale and well-whipped. Beat in the egg and yolk, then beat in the flour, porridge oats and dates until the ingredients are evenly distributed.
- Dollop tablespoons of the mixture onto the prepared baking trays, leaving room to spread. Bake in batches for 12–15 minutes or until the edges start to brown. Cool on a wire rack.

Date, cherry and oatmeal cookies
Add 100 g / 3 ½ oz / ⅔ cup of chopped glacé cherries to the mixture along with the oats and dates, to give these cookies an extra fruity flavour.

THE COOKERY COLLECTION

EVERYDAY COOKING | **BAKING**

Blueberry cake

PREPARATION TIME: 15 minutes
COOKING TIME: 35 minutes
SERVES: 8

300 g / 10 ½ oz / 2 cups self-raising flour
2 tsp baking powder
250 g / 9 oz / 1 ¼ cups caster (superfine) sugar
250 g / 9 oz / 1 ¼ cups butter, softened
5 large eggs
4 tbsp runny honey
200 g / 7 oz / 1 ⅓ cup blueberries
icing (confectioners') sugar to dust

- Preheat the oven to 170°C (150°C fan) / 340F / gas 3, then butter a 23 cm (9 in) round cake tin.
- Sieve the flour and baking powder into a large mixing bowl, then add sugar, butter and eggs. Beat the mixture until smooth and well-whipped.
- Spread the honey over the base of the cake tin and arrange the blueberries on top.
- Spoon in the cake mixture and bake for 35 minutes. Test with a wooden toothpick; if it comes out clean, the cake is done.
- Leave the cake to cool for 20 minutes before turning out onto a serving plate and dusting with icing sugar.

Blackberry cake
If blackberries are in season, they make a great substitution for the blueberries – why not try half and half?

Redcurrant muffins

PREPARATION TIME: **25 minutes**
COOKING TIME: **15-20 minutes**
MAKES: **12**

100 g / 3 ½ oz / ⅔ cup self-raising flour, sifted
100 g / 3 ½ oz / ½ cup caster (superfine) sugar
100 g / 3 ½ oz / ½ cup butter, softened
3 large eggs
100 g / 3 ½ oz / ⅔ cup redcurrants
icing (confectioners') sugar to dust

- Preheat the oven to 190°C (170°C fan) / 375F / gas 5, then line a 12-hole muffin tray with paper cases.
- In a large mixing bowl, combine the flour, sugar, butter and eggs and whisk together until smooth. Fold in the redcurrants.
- Divide the mixture between the cupcake cases, then transfer to the oven and bake for 15–20 minutes. Test with a wooden toothpick; if it comes out clean, the cakes are done.
- Transfer the cakes to a wire rack and leave to cool completely, then dust with icing sugar to finish.

Redcurrant and white chocolate muffins
Add 75 g / 2 ¾ oz / ⅓ cup chopped white chocolate to the mixture with the redcurrants to give these muffins an extra sweet flavour.

Ginger shortbread

PREPARATION TIME: 20 minutes
COOKING TIME: 15-20 minutes
MAKES: 16

225 g / 8 oz / 1 ½ cups plain (all-purpose) flour
2 tsp ground ginger
75 g / 2 ½ oz / ⅓ cup caster (superfine) sugar, plus extra for dusting
150 g / 5 oz / ⅔ cup butter, cubed

- Preheat the oven to 180°C (160°C fan) / 350F / gas 4. Line a baking tray with greaseproof paper.
- In a large mixing bowl, mix together the flour, ginger and sugar, then use your fingertips to rub in the butter.
- Knead gently until the mixture forms a smooth dough, then roll out on a lightly floured surface 1 cm (½ in) thickness. Cut into squares.
- Spread the shortbread biscuits out on the prepared baking tray and bake for 15–20 minutes, turning the tray round halfway through baking.
- Transfer the biscuits to a wire rack and leave to cool, then dust with sugar to finish.

Lemon ginger shortbread
Add the zest of 1 lemon to the shortbread mixture along with the ginger, to give these biscuits a hint of citrus.

Plum and chocolate loaf cake

PREPARATION TIME: 15 minutes
COOKING TIME: 55 minutes
SERVES: 8

225 g / 8 oz / 1 ½ cups self raising flour
100 g / 3 ½ oz / ½ cup butter, cubed
85 g / 3 oz / ⅓ cup caster (superfine) sugar
4 plums, stoned and chopped
100 g / 3 ½ oz / ⅔ cup chocolate chips
1 large egg
75 ml / 2 ½ fl. oz / ⅓ cup whole milk

- Preheat the oven to 180°C (160°C fan) / 350F / gas 4. Line a large loaf tin with greaseproof paper.
- Sieve the flour into a large mixing bowl, then rub in the butter with your fingertips until it resembles fine breadcrumbs. Stir in the sugar, plums and chocolate chips.
- In a separate bowl, lightly beat the egg with the milk, then stir it into the dry ingredients until just combined.
- Scrape the mixture into the prepared loaf tin and bake for 55 minutes. Test with a wooden toothpick; if it comes out clean, the cake is done.
- Transfer the cake to a wire rack and leave to cool.

Plum and honey loaf cake
Remove the chocolate chips from the cake mixture. Stir in 3 tbsp runny honey with the egg and milk, then bake as normal.

Melt-in-the-middle chocolate puddings

PREPARATION TIME: 50 minutes
COOKING TIME: 8 minutes
MAKES: **6**

2 tbsp unsweetened cocoa powder
150 g / 6 oz milk chocolate, chopped
150 g / 6 oz / ⅔ cup butter, chopped
85 g / 3 oz / ⅓ cup caster (superfine) sugar
3 large eggs
3 egg yolks
1 tbsp plain (all-purpose) flour

- Oil 6 ramekins and dust the insides with cocoa.
- Melt the chocolate, butter and sugar in a small saucepan set over a medium heat, stirring to dissolve the sugar.
- Leave to cool a little, then beat in the eggs and egg yolks, and fold in the flour.
- Divide the mixture between the ramekins and chill for 30 minutes.
- Preheat the oven to 180°C (160°C fan) / 350F / gas 4 and heat a baking tray.
- Transfer the ramekins to the heated baking tray and bake in the oven for 8 minutes.
- Leave the fondants to cool for 2 minutes, then serve.

Carrot, orange and walnut cake

PREPARATION TIME: 25 minutes
COOKING TIME: 30-35 minutes
SERVES: 8-10

175 g / 6 oz / 1 cup soft light brown sugar
2 large eggs
150 ml / 5 fl. oz / ⅔ cup sunflower oil
175 g / 6 oz / 1 ¼ cups stoneground wholemeal flour
3 tsp baking powder
2 tsp ground cinnamon
200 g / 7 oz / 1 ⅔ cups carrots, finely grated
1 orange, zest finely grated
100 g / 3 ½ oz / ¾ cup walnuts, chopped

FOR THE FROSTING
225 g / 8 oz / 1 cup cream cheese
110 g / 4 oz / ½ cup butter, softened
225 g / 8 oz / 2 ¼ cups icing (confectioners') sugar
1 tsp vanilla extract

- Preheat the oven to 190°C (170°C fan) / 375F / gas 5, then line two 23cm (9in) round cake tins with greaseproof paper.
- In a large mixing bowl, whisk the sugar, eggs and oil.
- Fold in the flour, baking powder and cinnamon, followed by the carrots, orange zest and walnuts, reserving some of the zest and nuts for the frosting.
- Divide the mixture between the tins and bake for 30–35 minutes. Test the cakes with a toothpick; if it comes out clean, the cakes are done.
- Transfer the cakes to a wire rack to cool.
- To make the icing, beat the cream cheese and butter together with a wooden spoon until light and fluffy, then beat in the icing sugar a bit at a time.
- Add the vanilla extract, then whisk the mixture until smooth and light.
- Spread a third of the frosting over one of the cakes, then sprinkle with some of the zest and nuts. Top with the second cake.
- Spread the rest of the frosting over the top of the cake, then sprinkle with the remaining orange zest and nuts to finish.

Fig and almond tarts

PREPARATION TIME: **45 minutes**
COOKING TIME: **35 minutes**
MAKES: **6**

150 g / 5 ½ oz / 1 ½ cups ground almonds
250 g / 9 oz / 1 cup butter, softened
200 g / 7 oz / ¾ cup caster (superfine) sugar
2 large eggs
200 g / 7 oz / 1 ⅓ cups plain (all-purpose) flour
6 fresh figs, chopped
2 tbsp flaked (slivered) almonds
icing (confectioners') sugar to dust

- Preheat the oven to 200°C (180°C fan) / 400F /
  gas 6. Using your fingertips, rub 100 g of the
  butter into the flour (leaving a handful to
  one side) until the mixture resembles fine
  breadcrumbs. Stir in 50 g of the sugar
  and add water.
- Chill the dough for 30 minutes, then roll out
  on a lightly floured surface. Use the pastry to
  line 6 tartlet cases. Prick the base with a fork,
  line with greaseproof paper and fill with baking
  beans or rice.
- Bake for 10 minutes, then remove the paper and
  beans. Bake for 8 more minutes to crisp.
- Whisk together the almonds, eggs, the rest
  of the butter, sugar and flour until smoothly
  whipped. Spoon the mixture into the pastry
  cases, then arrange the figs on top and sprinkle
  with flaked almonds.
- Bake for 15 minutes and sprinkle with icing sugar.

Apricot and almond tarts
Replace the figs with 200 g / 7 oz sliced apricots,
then top with honey and flaked almonds.

Fruit scones

PREPARATION TIME: **15 minutes**
COOKING TIME: **10 minutes**
MAKES: **10**

350 g / 12 oz / 2 ⅓ cup self-raising flour
1 tsp baking powder
75 g / 2 ½ oz / ⅓ cup butter, cubed
50 g / 1 ¾ oz / ¼ cup golden caster (superfine) sugar,
plus extra for dusting
100 g / 3 ½ oz / ⅔ cup raisins
150 ml / 5 fl. oz / ⅔ cup milk
2 large eggs, beaten
raspberry jam (jelly) to serve

- Preheat the oven to 220°C (200°C fan) / 425F
  / gas 7, then grease a baking tray.
- Sieve the flour and baking powder into a large
  mixing bowl, then rub in the butter using your
  fingers until it resembles fine breadcrumbs.
- Stir in the sugar and raisins, then add the milk
  and most of the beaten egg. Stir to bring the
  dough together. Knead gently on a lightly floured
  surface, then roll out to about 2 cm (1 in) thick
  and cut out 10 rounds using a circular cutter.
- Arrange the scones on the prepared baking tray
  and bake for 10 minutes or until risen and gold.
- Transfer to a wire rack to cool, then sprinkle
  with the remaining sugar.

Cherry scones
Halve the quantity of raisins and add 75 g / 2 ¾ oz
/ ⅔ cup chopped glacé cherries to the mixture.

EVERYDAY COOKING | **BAKING**

Apricot and honey tarte Tatin

PREPARATION TIME: 10 minutes
COOKING TIME: 20-25 minutes
SERVES: 8

2 tbsp butter, softened and cubed
4 tbsp runny honey
1 vanilla pod, seeds scraped out
10 fresh apricots, halved
250 g / 9 oz all-butter puff pastry

- Preheat the oven to 220°C (200°C fan) / 425F / gas 7.
- Heat the butter and honey in a large ovenproof frying pan set over a medium-low heat until melted, then stir in the vanilla seeds.

- Arrange the apricots in the pan with the honey mixture, cut-side up.
- Roll out the pastry on a lightly floured surface and cut out a circle the same size as the frying pan.
- Lay the pastry over the apricots and tuck in the edges, then transfer the pan to the oven and bake for 25 minutes or until the pastry is golden brown and cooked through.
- Allow to cool for 10 minutes, then run a knife around the edge of the pan to loosen the tart. Place a large plate over the top of the frying pan and carefully turn the tart out onto the plate. Serve warm.

Fig and honey tarte Tatin
Replace the apricots with 8 quartered figs, arranging them in the frying pan and baking as normal.

Chocolate truffle loaf

PREPARATION TIME: **15 minutes**
COOKING TIME: **40-50 minutes**
SERVES: **8-10**

600 g / 1 lb 5 oz / 2 ¾ cups cream cheese
150 ml / 5 fl. oz / ⅔ cup soured cream
175 g / 6 oz / ¾ cup caster (superfine) sugar
2 large eggs
1 egg yolk
2 tbsp plain (all-purpose) flour
2 tbsp cocoa powder
200 g / 7 oz / 1 ⅓ cups dark chocolate (minimum 60 % cocoa solids), melted

- Preheat the oven to 180°C (160°C fan) / 350F / gas 4, then grease and line a large loaf tin with greaseproof paper.
- Put all the ingredients in a large mixing bowl and whisk together until smooth.
- Scrape the mixture into the loaf tin and level the top with a palette knife.
- Put the tin in a large roasting tin and pour around enough boiling water to come half way up the side of the loaf tin.
- Bake the cake for 40–50 minutes or until the centre is only just set.
- Leave to cool completely in the tin, then chill for 2 hours before turning out and serving.

Almond biscotti

PREPARATION TIME: **25 minutes**
COOKING TIME: **35 minutes**
MAKES: **24**

2 large eggs
55 g / 2 oz / ¼ cup butter, melted
225 g / 8 oz / 1 ½ cups self-raising flour
100 g / 3 ½ oz / ½ cup caster (superfine) sugar
100 g / 3 ½ oz / ⅔ cup blanched almonds

- Preheat the oven to 180°C (160°C fan) / 350F / gas 4, then line two baking trays with greaseproof paper.
- Beat together the eggs and butter, then stir in the flour, sugar and almonds.
- Make a soft dough and shape into two long rolls.
- Transfer the rolls to one of the baking trays and press to flatten slightly.
- Bake for 20 minutes or until golden, then leave to cool for 15 minutes.
- Cut the rolls across into 1 cm (½ in) thick slices and spread them out over the baking trays.
- Bake the biscuits for 15 minutes or until golden and crisp.
- Transfer the biscuits to a wire rack and leave to cool completely.

Almond and pistachio biscotti
Reduce the quantity of blanched almonds to 50 g and add 50 g of chopped pistachios to the mix for an extra nutty flavour.

Chocolate loaf cake

PREPARATION TIME: **10 minutes**
COOKING TIME: **45-50 minutes**
MAKES: **1 loaf**

100 g / 3 ½ oz / ⅔ cup self-raising flour
1 tsp baking powder
2 tbsp cocoa powder
150 g / 5 ½ oz / ⅔ cup caster (superfine) sugar
150 g / 5 ½ oz / ⅔ cup butter
3 large eggs
100 g / 3 ½ oz / ⅔ cup dark chocolate (minimum 60 % cocoa solids), chopped

- Preheat the oven to 180°C (160°C fan) / 350F / gas 4, then grease a large loaf tin .
- Sieve the flour, baking powder and cocoa into a large mixing bowl, then add the sugar, butter and eggs and whisk until pale and well-whipped.
- Fold in the chocolate, then spoon into the prepared loaf tin and bake for 45–50 minutes.
- Test the cake with a toothpick; if it comes out clean, the cake is done.
- Transfer the cake to a wire rack to cool.

Chocolate fudge loaf cake
Stir 100 g / 3 ½ / ⅔ cup chopped fudge pieces into the cake mixture, the press some into the top of the cake before baking.

Lemon and lime madeleines

PREPARATION TIME: 1 hour, 30 minutes
COOKING TIME: 10-15 minutes
MAKES: 12

110 g / 4 oz / ½ cup butter
55 g / 2 oz / ⅓ cup plain (all-purpose) flour
1 lemon, zest finely grated
1 lime, zest finely grated
55 g / 2 oz / ½ cup ground almonds
110 g / 4 oz / 1 cup icing (confectioners') sugar, plus extra to dust
3 large egg whites

- Heat the butter in a small saucepan set over a low heat until it starts to foam.
- In a large mixing bowl, combine the flour, lemon and lime zest, ground almonds and icing sugar, then whisk in the egg whites.
- Pour the cooled, melted butter into the bowl and whisk into the mixture.
- Leave the cake mixture to rest in the fridge for 1 hour.
- Preheat the oven to 170°C (150°C fan) / 340F / gas 3, then oil and flour a 12-hole Madeleine mould.
- Spoon the mixture into the moulds, then transfer the tin to the oven and bake for 10–15 minutes.
- Test with a wooden toothpick; if it comes out clean, the Madeleines are done.
- Transfer the Madeleines to a wire rack to cool, then dust with icing sugar to finish.

Pear and ginger upside-down cake

PREPARATION TIME: **15 minutes**
COOKING TIME: **35 minutes**
SERVES: **8**

300 g / 10 ½ oz / 2 cups self-raising flour
2 tsp baking powder
2 tsp ground ginger
250 g / 9 oz / 1 ¼ cups dark brown sugar
250 g / 9 oz / 1 ¼ cups butter, softened
5 large eggs
100 g / 3 ½ oz / ⅔ cup dates, stoned and finely chopped
150 g / 5 ½ oz / ½ cup runny honey
4 pears, peeled, cored and sliced
crystallised ginger pieces to decorate

- Preheat the oven to 170°C (150°C fan) / 340F / gas 3. Grease a 23 cm (9 in) round cake tin.

- Sieve the flour, baking powder and ground ginger into a large mixing bowl, then add the sugar, butter and eggs. Beat the mixture until smooth and well-whipped.

- Fold in the dates until evenly distributed.

- Spread the honey over the base of the cake tin and arrange the pears on top.

- Spoon in the cake mixture and bake for 35 minutes. Test with a wooden toothpick; if it comes out clean, the cake is done.

- Transfer the cake to a wire rack to cool, then sprinkle with crystallised ginger pieces.

Strawberry jam biscuits

PREPARATION TIME: **1 hour, 15 minutes**
COOKING TIME: **25-30 minutes**
MAKES: **36**

150 g / 5 ½ oz / ⅔ cup caster (superfine) sugar
350 g / 12 oz / 1 ½ cup butter, softened
1 tsp vanilla extract
300 g / 10 ½ oz / 2 cups plain (all-purpose) flour
150 g / 5 ½ oz / 1 ½ cups ground almonds
200 g / 7 oz / ⅔ cup strawberry jam (jelly)
icing (confectioners') sugar to dust

- In a large mixing bowl, cream together the sugar, butter and vanilla extract until pale and well-whipped, then stir in the flour and ground almonds. Bring the mixture together with your hands and shape into a ball. Wrap in cling film and refrigerate for 45 minutes.
- Preheat the oven to 140°C (120°C fan) / 275F / gas 1, then line two baking trays with greaseproof paper. Roll out the dough on a lightly-floured surface to about 5 mm thickness. Use a flower-shaped cutter to cut out 72 biscuits.
- Use a smaller flower-shaped cutter to cut a hole out of the centre of 36 biscuits, then prick them with a fork. Transfer the biscuits to the prepared trays in batches and bake for 25–30 minutes, then place on a wire rack and leave to cool.
- Spread a teaspoon of jam on the plain biscuits and top with a holey biscuit. Dust liberally with icing sugar.

Apricot jam biscuits
Replace the strawberry jam with apricot for a different fruity flavour.

Iced almond shortbread stars

PREPARATION TIME: **20 minutes**
COOKING TIME: **15-20 minutes**
MAKES: **20**

175 g / 6 oz / 1 ¼ cups plain (all-purpose) flour
55 g / 2 oz / ½ cup ground almonds
75 g / 2 ½ oz / ⅓ cup caster (superfine) sugar
150 g / 5 oz / ⅔ cup butter, cubed
4 tbsp icing (confectioners') sugar

- Preheat the oven to 180°C (160°C fan) / 350F / gas 4, then line a baking tray with greaseproof paper.
- In a large mixing bowl, mix together the flour, ground almonds and sugar, then use your fingertips to rub in the butter.
- Knead gently on a lightly floured surface until the mixture forms a smooth dough.
- Roll the dough to a 1 cm (½ in) thickness and use a star-shaped cutter to cut out 20 star shapes, using the off-cuts if necessary.
- Bake the biscuits for 15–20 minutes, turning the tray round halfway through.
- Transfer the biscuits to a wire rack and leave to cool. Mix the icing sugar with just enough water to form a thick icing. Spoon it into a piping bag and pipe to cover the tops of the stars.

Almond and star anise shortbread stars
Add ½ tsp ground star anise to the shortbread mixture, along with the zest of ½ an orange. This will give these cookies a more festive feel, although they're perfect for any occasion.

Pecan pie

PREPARATION TIME: 20 minutes
COOKING TIME: 55 minutes
SERVES: 8

75 g / 2 ½ oz / ⅓ cup butter
100 g / 3 ½ oz / ½ cup golden caster (superfine) sugar
350 g / 12 ½ oz / 1 cup golden syrup
3 eggs, beaten
½ tsp vanilla extract
300 g / 10 ½ oz / 2 ½ cups pecans

FOR THE PASTRY
200 g / 7 oz / 1 ⅓ cups plain (all-purpose) flour
100 g / 3 ½ oz / ½ cup butter, cubed and chilled

- Preheat the oven to 200°C (180°C fan) / 400F / gas 6.
- Make the pastry first. Sieve the flour into a large mixing bowl, then rub in the butter using your fingertips until the mixture resembles fine breadcrumbs.
- Stir in just enough cold water to bring the pastry together into a pliable dough, then chill for 30 minutes.
- Roll out the pastry on a lightly floured surface and use it to line a round tart tin. Prick the base with a fork, line with greaseproof paper and fill with baking beans or rice.
- Bake for 10 minutes, then remove the greaseproof paper and baking beans and cook for another 8 minutes to crisp. Transfer to a wire rack to cool.
- In a large mixing bowl, beat the butter and sugar together, then beat in the golden syrup.
- Gradually add the eggs, then stir in the vanilla extract and pecans.
- Pour the mixture into the pastry case and bake for 30–35 minutes.

Raspberry meringue roulade

PREPARATION TIME: **20 minutes**
COOKING TIME: **15 minutes**
SERVES: **8**

4 large egg whites
a pinch of cream of tartar
200 g / 7 oz / ¾ cup caster (superfine) sugar
300 ml / 10 ½ fl. oz / 1 ¼ cups double (heavy) cream
200 g / 7 oz / 1 ⅓ cups raspberries
icing (confectioners') sugar for dusting
mint leaves to garnish

- Preheat the oven to 180°C (160°C fan) / 350F / gas 4, then line a Swiss roll tin with greaseproof paper.
- In a large mixing bowl, whisk the egg whites with the cream of tartar until stiff, then whisk in the caster sugar a tablespoon at a time.
- Spread the mixture onto the Swiss roll tray in an even layer with a palette knife and bake for 15 minutes. Leave to cool completely.
- In a clean bowl, whip the double cream with a whisk until it just holds its shape.
- Sprinkle a large sheet of greaseproof paper with icing sugar and turn the meringue out onto it.
- Spread the meringue with cream and sprinkle over most of the raspberries, then roll it up, using the greaseproof paper to help you.
- Sprinkle the remaining raspberries over the top of the roulade, dust with icing sugar and garnish with mint leaves to finish.

Strawberry meringue roulade
Strawberries work equally well with this roulade, especially paired with the whipped cream. Simply replace the raspberries with the same quantity of hulled and halved strawberries.

Coconut and lemon cake

PREPARATION TIME: 10 minutes
COOKING TIME: 45-55 minutes
SERVES: 8-10

225 g / 8 oz / 1 cup butter, softened
225 g / 8 oz / 1 cup caster (superfine) sugar
4 large eggs, beaten
225 g / 4 ½ oz / 1 ½ cups self-raising flour
juice of 1 lemon
2 tbsp lemon curd
100 g / 3 ½ oz / 1 cup desiccated coconut
50 g / 3 ½ oz / ⅓ cup redcurrants and blackberries

- Preheat the oven to 180°C (160°C fan) / 350F / gas 4, then grease and line a 23 cm (9 in) round cake tin with greaseproof paper.
- In a large mixing bowl, cream together the butter and sugar, then gradually whisk in the eggs, beating well after each addition. Fold in the flour, then scrape the mixture into the tin.
- Bake the cake for 45–55 minutes. Test the cake with a toothpick; if it comes out clean, the cake is done. Transfer to a wire rack, brush with lemon juice and leave to cool. Spread a thin layer of lemon curd on the top and sides of the cake, then sprinkle over the desiccated coconut. Top with the fruit to finish.

Almond and lemon curd cake
Reduce the self-raising flour by 50 g and replace with ground almonds, then replace the desiccated coconut with flaked (slivered) almonds to finish the cake.

Iced nutmeg biscuits

PREPARATION TIME: 10 minutes
COOKING TIME: 12-15 minutes
MAKES: 36

75 g / 2 ½ oz / ⅓ cup butter, softened
100 g / 3 ½ oz / ⅓ cup golden syrup
225 g / 8 oz / 1 ½ cups self-raising flour
100 g / 3 ½ oz / ½ cup golden caster (superfine) sugar
2 tsp nutmeg, freshly grated
1 large egg, beaten
4 tbsp icing (confectioners') sugar
1 tsp nutmeg, freshly grated

- Preheat the oven to 180°C (160°C fan) / 350F / gas 4, then line two baking trays with greaseproof paper. Melt the butter and golden syrup together in a saucepan set over a low heat.
- In a large mixing bowl, combine the flour, sugar and half the nutmeg, then stir in the melted butter mixture and the beaten egg. Dollop teaspoons of the mixture onto the prepared baking trays, leaving room for the biscuits to spread.
- Bake in batches for 12–15 minutes or until golden brown. Transfer to a wire rack and leave to cool.
- To make the icing, mix the icing sugar and remaining nutmeg together, then add enough water to form a thick icing. Spoon it into a piping bag and pipe patterns on the top of each biscuit.

Iced nutmeg and hazelnut biscuits
Add 50 g / 1 ¾ oz / ½ cup roughly chopped hazelnuts (cobnuts) to the mixture along with the nutmeg and stir unevenly evenly distributed. Bake as normal to give these cookies an extra nutty flavour.

Apricot and nut fruit cake

PREPARATION TIME: 15 minutes
COOKING TIME: 55 minutes
MAKES: 1 loaf

225 g / 8 oz / 1 ½ cups self-raising flour
100 g / 3 ½ oz / ½ cup butter, cubed
100 g / 3 ½ oz / ½ cup light brown sugar
100 g / 3 ½ oz / ½ cup sultanas
150 g / 5 ½ oz / ¾ cup dried apricots, chopped
100 g / 3 ½ oz / ½ cup glacé cherries, halved
150 g / 5 ½ oz / ¾ cup mixed nuts, chopped
zest of 1 orange
1 large egg
75 ml / 2 ½ fl. oz / ⅓ cup whole milk

- Preheat the oven to 180°C (160°C fan) / 350F / gas 4. Line a large loaf tin with greaseproof paper.
- Sieve the flour into a large mixing bowl, then rub in the butter using your fingertips until it resembles fine breadcrumbs.
- Stir in the sugar, sultanas, apricots, cherries, mixed nuts and orange zest.
- In a jug, lightly beat the egg with the milk, then stir it into the dry ingredients until it is just combined.
- Scrape the mixture into the loaf tin and bake for 55 minutes. Test the cake with a toothpick; if it comes out clean, the cake is done.
- Transfer the cake to a wire rack and leave to cool completely.

Chocolate and hazelnut torte

PREPARATION TIME: 15 minutes
COOKING TIME: 25-30 minutes
SERVES: 8

2 large eggs, separated

150 g / 5 ½ oz / ⅔ cup caster (superfine) sugar

75 g / 2 ½ oz / ⅓ cup butter

2 tbsp unsweetened cocoa powder, plus extra for dusting

100 g / 3 ½ oz dark chocolate (minimum 60% cocoa solids), chopped

200 g / 7 oz / 1 ⅔ cups hazelnuts (cobnuts), finely chopped

- Preheat the oven to 180°C (160°C fan) / 350F / gas 4, then line a 23cm (9in) round cake tin with greaseproof paper.
- In a large mixing bowl, whisk together the egg yolks and sugar until smooth.
- Place the butter, cocoa powder and chocolate in a saucepan and melt over a medium heat.
- Fold the melted ingredients into the egg yolk mixture, then stir in 150 g of the hazelnuts.
- In a separate bowl, whip the egg whites until they form stiff peaks, then fold into the cake mixture.
- Scrape the mixture into the prepared tin, being careful to retain as many air bubbles as possible, and bake for 25–30 minutes or until the centre is just set.
- Transfer to a wire rack to cool, then dust liberally with cocoa powder and arrange the remaining hazelnuts in a circular shape on top of the torte.

Fig and white chocolate loaf

PREPARATION TIME: **15 minutes**
COOKING TIME: **55 minutes**
MAKES: **1 loaf**

225 g / 8 oz / 1 ½ cups self-raising flour
100 g / 3 ½ oz / ½ cup butter, cubed
85 g / 3 oz / ⅓ cup caster (superfine) sugar
10 fresh figs, chopped
1 large egg
75 ml / 3 ½ fl. oz / ⅓ cup whole milk
100 g / 3 ½ oz / ⅔ cup white chocolate
3 tbsp double (heavy) cream
3 tbsp icing (confectioners') sugar
2 tbsp flaked (slivered) almonds

- Preheat the oven to 180°C (160°C fan) / 350F / gas 4, then line a large loaf tin with greaseproof paper.
- Sieve the flour into a large mixing bowl, then rub in the butter with your fingertips until it resembles fine breadcrumbs. Stir in the sugar and ⅔ of the chopped figs.
- In a separate bowl, lightly beat the egg with the milk, then stir it into the dry ingredients until just combined.
- Scrape the mixture into the loaf tin and bake for 55 minutes. Test the cake with a toothpick; if it comes out clean, the cake is done. Transfer to a wire rack to cool.
- To make the glaze, melt the white chocolate and cream together in a small saucepan set over a medium heat. Stir in the icing sugar, then drizzle over the loaf cake.
- Top with the remaining chopped figs and sprinkle with flaked almonds to serve.

Fig and lemon loaf
Add the zest of 1 lemon to the cake mixture. For the glaze, omit the white chocolate and double cream, then mix the icing sugar with the juice of 1 lemon, stirring in a little water if necessary.

Cranberry brownies

PREPARATION TIME: **25 minutes**
COOKING TIME: **35-40 minutes**
MAKES: **9**

110 g / 4 oz milk chocolate, chopped
85 g / 3 oz / ¾ cup cocoa powder, sifted
225 g / 8 oz / 1 cup butter
450 g / 15 oz / 2 ½ cups light brown sugar
4 large eggs
110 g / 4 oz / ⅔ cup self-raising flour
100 g / 3 ½ oz / ⅔ cup dried cranberries
100 g / 3 ½ oz / ⅔ cup walnuts, chopped
icing (confectioners') sugar to dust

- Preheat the oven to 170°C (150°C fan) / 340F / gas 3, then grease and line a square baking tin.
- Melt the chocolate, cocoa and butter together in a saucepan set over a medium-low heat, then leave to cool a little.
- In a large mixing bowl, whisk together the sugar and eggs until very light and creamy.
- Pour in the chocolate mixture and sieve over the flour, then fold everything together with the cranberries and walnuts until well mixed.
- Scrape into the tin and bake for 35–40 minutes. Test with a wooden toothpick; if it comes out clean, the brownie is done. Transfer to a wire rack to cool, then sprinkle with icing sugar and cut into 9 squares to serve.

Chocolate biscuit brownies
Replace the cranberries and walnuts with broken up biscuit pieces to give an extra crunch.

Banana and chocolate spring rolls

PREPARATION TIME: **25 minutes**
COOKING TIME: **12-15 minutes**
MAKES: **20**

225 g / 8 oz filo pastry
100 g / 3 ½ oz / ½ cup butter, melted
200 g / 7 oz dark chocolate (minimum 60 % cocoa solids), finely chopped
1 banana, sliced
1 egg, beaten
2 tbsp dark chocolate, grated

- Preheat the oven to 180°C (160° fan) / 350F / gas 4, then grease a large baking tray.
- Cut the filo pastry sheets in half. Take one halved sheet and brush with melted butter.
- Sprinkle a tablespoon of chopped chocolate and a few banana slices along the centre.
- Fold over one side of the pastry sheet, then fold over the top and bottom. Continue rolling until the spring roll is sealed.
- Place on the prepared baking tray, then repeat with the rest of the filo sheets.
- Brush the spring rolls with beaten egg and bake for 12–15 minutes or until crisp and golden brown.
- Sprinkle with grated chocolate and serve warm.

Chocolate and walnut spring rolls
Roughly chop 100 g / 3 ½ oz / ⅔ cup walnuts and sprinkle over the chocolate instead of the bananas, for a nutty taste.

Apple and cinnamon pie

PREPARATION TIME: **45 minutes**
COOKING TIME: **35-45 minutes**
SERVES: **8**

125 g / 4 ½ oz / ½ cup caster (superfine) sugar
2 tbsp plain (all-purpose) flour
1 tsp ground cinnamon
900 g / 2 lb Bramley apples, peeled and chopped
1 egg, beaten

FOR THE PASTRY
300 g / 11 oz / 2 cups plain (all-purpose) flour
150 g / 5 ½ oz / ⅔ cup butter, chilled
1 tsp caster (superfine) sugar, for dusting

- Make the pastry first. Sieve the flour into a large mixing bowl. Dip the chilled butter in the flour, then grate it into the bowl and mix.
- Add enough cold water to bring it together into a pliable dough, then chill for 30 minutes.
- Preheat the oven to 190°C (170°C fan) / 375F / gas 5. Grease a 23 cm (9 in) round pie tin.
- Mix together the sugar, flour and ground cinnamon, then stir in the apples.
- Roll out half the pastry on a lightly floured surface and use it to line the pie tin.
- Spoon the apples into the pastry case and brush around the top of the pastry with beaten egg.
- Roll out the other half of the pastry and cut into strips. Arrange the pastry strips over the apples in a lattice and press down around the outside to seal. Crimp the edges and trim away any excess pastry.
- Brush with beaten egg, sprinkle with sugar and bake for 35–45 minutes. The pastry should be crisp and golden brown on top and starting to shrink away from the edges.

Pear and cinnamon pie
Replace the apples with the same quantity of pears (cored, peeled and chopped) then bake as normal for a different fruity flavour.

Chocolate ganache cupcakes

PREPARATION TIME: **20 minutes**
COOKING TIME: **15-20 minutes**
MAKES: **12**

110 g / 4 oz / ⅔ cup self-raising flour, sifted
110 g / 4 oz / ½ cup caster (superfine) sugar
2 tbsp cocoa powder
110 g / 4 oz / ½ cup butter, softened
2 large eggs
100 ml / 3 ½ fl. oz / ½ cup double (heavy) cream
100 g / 3 ½ oz / ⅔ cup dark chocolate, chopped
1 tbsp butter, softened

- Preheat the oven to 190°C (170°C fan) / 375F / gas 5, then line a 12-hole cupcake tray with paper cases.
- In a large mixing bowl, combine the flour, sugar, cocoa, butter and eggs and whisk together until smooth. Divide the mixture between the paper cases, then transfer the tray to the oven and bake for 15–20 minutes. Test with a wooden toothpick; if it comes out clean, the cakes are done. Transfer the cakes to a wire rack to cool.
- Heat the cream to simmering point, then pour it over the chocolate and stir until smooth. Blend in the butter. When the ganache has cooled to a spreadable consistency, spread it on top of the cakes with a palette knife.

Chocolate and ginger ganache cupcakes
Add 1 tsp ground ginger and 2 tbsp crystallised ginger to the cake mixture along with the cocoa, then bake as normal.

Chocolate chip blondies

PREPARATION TIME: **25 minutes**
COOKING TIME: **35-40 minutes**
MAKES: **9**

100 g / 3 ½ oz / ⅔ cup white chocolate, chopped
225 g / 8 oz / 1 cup butter
450 g /15 oz / 2 ½ cups caster (superfine) sugar
4 large eggs
110 g / 4 oz / ⅔ cup self-raising flour
100 g / 3 ½ oz / ⅔ cup chocolate chips

- Preheat the oven to 170°C (150°C fan) / 340F / gas 3, then oil and line a 20cm (8in) square cake tin .
- Melt the chocolate and butter together in a saucepan set over a medium heat, then leave to cool a little.
- In a large mixing bowl, whisk together the sugar and eggs until very light and creamy.
- Pour in the chocolate mixture and sieve over the flour, then fold everything together until evenly mixed.
- Scrape into the tin and sprinkle over the chocolate chips.
- Bake for 35–40 minutes or until the outside is set, but the centre is still quite chewy.
- Leave the blondie to cool completely before cutting into 9 squares.

Chocolate chip raspberry blondies
Add 100 g / 3 ½ oz / ⅔ cup fresh raspberries to the blondie mixture along with the sugar, then bake as normal.

THE COOKERY COLLECTION

Indulgent chocolate and berry cake

PREPARATION TIME: 10 minutes
COOKING TIME: 30-35 minutes
SERVES: 10-12

150 g / 6 oz / 1 cup self-raising flour
3 tbsp unsweetened cocoa powder
2 tsp baking powder
175 g / 6 oz / ¾ cup caster (superfine) sugar
175 g / 6 oz / ¾ cup butter
3 eggs

FOR THE GANACHE
100 ml / 3 ½ fl. oz / ⅔ cup double (heavy) cream
100 g / 3 ½ oz / ⅔ cup milk chocolate, chopped
50 g / 1 ¾ oz / ⅓ cup blueberries
50 g / 1 ¾ oz / ⅓ cup blackberries
1 plum, de-stoned and sliced

- Preheat the oven to 180°C (160°C fan) / 350F / gas 4, then grease and line a 23cm (9in) round cake tin.
- In a large mixing bowl, whisk together all the cake ingredients until fully combined.
- Scrape the mixture into the prepared cake tin and bake for 30–35 minutes.
- Test the cake with a toothpick; if it comes out clean, the cake is done.
- Transfer the cake to a wire rack to cool.
- Heat the cream in a small saucepan set over a medium heat and bring to a simmer. Pour it over the chocolate and stir until smooth.
- Pour the slightly cooled chocolate glaze over the cakes, allowing it to drip down the sides.
- Put the cake in the fridge for 1 hour to set, then decorate with blueberries, blackberries and sliced plum.

Ginger muffins

PREPARATION TIME: 15 minutes
COOKING TIME: 20-25 minutes
MAKES: 12

1 large egg
120 ml / 4 fl. oz / ½ cup sunflower oil
120 ml / 4 fl. oz / ½ cup milk
375 g / 12 ½ oz / 2 cups self-raising flour, sifted
1 tsp baking powder
2 tsp ground ginger
200 g / 7 oz / ¾ cup caster (superfine) sugar
1 tbsp sesame seeds
ground nutmeg to dust

- Preheat the oven to 180°C (160°C fan) / 350F / gas 4, then grease a 12-hole muffin tin.
- Beat the egg in a jug with the oil and milk until mixed.
- In a large mixing bowl, mix together the flour, baking powder, ground ginger and sugar. Pour in the egg mixture and stir just enough to combine.
- Divide the mixture between the moulds and sprinkle with sesame seeds.
- Bake for 20–25 minutes. Test the muffins with a wooden toothpick; if it comes out clean, the muffins are done.
- Transfer the muffins to a wire rack and leave to cool completely, then dust with ground nutmeg to serve.

Spiced carrot loaf cake

PREPARATION TIME: 10 minutes
COOKING TIME: 55 minutes
SERVES: 8

300 g / 10 ½ oz / 2 cups self-raising flour
2 tsp baking powder
½ tsp ground cinnamon
½ tsp ground nutmeg
250 g / 9 oz / 1 ¼ cups butter, softened
75 g / 2 ½ oz / ½ cup dark brown sugar
4 large eggs
200 g / 7 oz / 1 ⅓ cup carrots, finely grated
225 g / 8 oz / 2 ¼ cup cream cheese
150 g / 5 ½ oz / 1 ½ cups icing (confectioners') sugar
1 tsp vanilla extract
50 g / 1 ¾ oz / ⅓ cup walnuts, chopped

- Preheat the oven to 170°C (150°C fan) / 340F / gas 3. Line a large loaf tin with greaseproof paper.
- Sieve the flour and baking powder into a mixing bowl, then stir in the cinnamon and nutmeg.
- In a separate bowl, beat together the butter and sugar, then beat in the eggs and grated carrot. Gradually whisk in the flour mixture until smooth. Spoon into the prepared tin.
- Bake for 55 minutes. Test the cake with a toothpick. Transfer to a wire rack to cool.
- Meanwhile, whisk together the cream cheese, icing sugar and vanilla extract. Spoon the frosting on, then sprinkle with chopped walnuts.

> **Spiced carrot and ginger loaf**
> Add 1 tsp ground ginger to the cake mixture, then sprinkle the frosting with walnuts and 2 tbsp crystallised ginger pieces.

Oat and cranberry cookies

PREPARATION TIME: 10 minutes
COOKING TIME: 12-15 minutes
MAKES: 36

225 g / 8 oz / 1 ⅓ cup dark brown sugar
100 g / 3 ½ oz / ½ cup caster (superfine) sugar
175 g / 6 oz / ¾ cup butter, melted
2 tsp vanilla extract
1 egg, plus 1 egg yolk
250 g / 9 oz / 1 ⅔ cups self-raising flour
100 g / 3 ½ oz / 1 cup oats
100 g / 3 ½ oz / ½ cup dried cranberries

- Preheat the oven to 170°C (150°C fan) / 340F / gas 3, then line two baking trays with greaseproof paper.
- In a large mixing bowl, cream together the two sugars, butter and vanilla extract until pale and well-whipped. Beat in the egg and yolk, then beat in the flour, oats and cranberries.
- Dollop tablespoons of the mixture onto the prepared baking trays, leaving room for the cookies to spread. Bake in batches for 12–15 minutes or until the edges are starting to brown, but the centres are still chewy. Transfer to a wire rack to cool.

> **Oat, raisin and cranberry cookies**
> Add 100 g / 3 ½ oz / ½ cup raisins to the mixture along with the cranberries, beating to make sure the ingredients are evenly distributed. Bake as normal for an extra fruity flavour.

Chocolate tart with cherries

PREPARATION TIME: 25 minutes
COOKING TIME: 10-18 minutes
SERVES: 8-10

250 ml / 9 fl. oz / 1 cup double (heavy) cream
250 g / 9 oz / 1 ⅔ cups dark chocolate, chopped
55 g / 2 oz / ¼ cup butter, softened
100 g / 3 ½ oz / ⅔ cup fresh cherries, to garnish

FOR THE PASTRY
200 g / 7 oz / 1 ⅓ cups plain (all-purpose) flour
55 g / 2 oz / ¼ cups caster (superfine) sugar
2 tbsp cocoa powder
100 g / 3 ½ oz / ½ cup butter, cubed
1 egg, beaten

Chocolate, pistachio and cherry tart
Add 100 g / 3 ½ oz / 1 cup shelled and
chopped pistachios to the tart mixture after
the butter has been blended in, then leave
to set and decorate with the cherries, and
a sprinkling of pistachios.

- Preheat the oven to 200°C (180°C fan) / 400F / gas 6.
- Make the pastry first. In a large mixing bowl, combine the flour, sugar and cocoa powder, then rub in the butter using your fingertips.
- Add the egg and just enough cold water to bind.
- Wrap the dough in cling film and chill for 30 minutes.
- Roll the pastry out on a lightly floured surface. Use the pastry to line a 23 cm (9 in) fluted tin and trim the edges.
- Prick the pastry with a fork, line with baking paper and fill with baking beans or rice.
- Bake for 10 minutes, then remove the baking paper and baking beans and cook for another 8 minutes to crisp. Transfer to a wire rack to cool.
- Heat the cream in a saucepan over a medium heat to simmering point, then pour it over the chocolate and stir until smooth.
- Add the butter and blend it in with a stick blender, then pour over the pastry base.
- Leave the ganache to cool for 2 hours. Pile the cherries on top to serve.

Banana and walnut spiced loaf

PREPARATION TIME: 10 minutes
COOKING TIME: 55 minutes
MAKES: 1 loaf

3 very ripe bananas
110 g / 4 oz / ½ cup soft light brown sugar
2 large eggs
120 ml / 4 fl. oz / ½ cup sunflower oil
225 g / 8 oz / 1 ½ cup plain (all-purpose) flour
1 tsp bicarbonate of (baking) soda
½ tsp ground ginger
½ tsp ground cinnamon
½ tsp mixed spice
75 g / 2 ½ oz / ⅔ cup walnuts, chopped

- Preheat the oven to 170°C (150°C fan) / 340F / gas 3, then line a loaf tin with greaseproof paper.
- In a large mixing bowl, mash the bananas roughly with a fork, then whisk in the sugar, eggs and oil.
- Sieve the flour and bicarbonate of soda into the bowl, then add the spices and most of the chopped walnuts. Stir just enough to evenly mix all the ingredients together.
- Scrape the mixture into the loaf tin and sprinkle over the remaining walnuts.
- Bake for 55 minutes. Test the cake with a toothpick; if it comes out clean, the cake is done.
- Transfer the cake to a wire rack and leave to cool completely.

Blood orange upside-down cake

PREPARATION TIME: **15 minutes**
COOKING TIME: **35 minutes**
SERVES: **8**

300 g / 10 ½ oz / 2 cups stoneground wholemeal flour
2 tsp baking powder
250 g / 9 oz / 1 ¼ cup caster (superfine) sugar
250 g / 9 oz / 1 ¼ cup butter, softened
5 large eggs
1–2 blood oranges, sliced

- Preheat the oven to 170°C (150°C fan) / 340F / gas 3, then butter a 23 cm (9 in) round cake tin.
- Sieve the flour and baking powder into a large mixing bowl and add the sugar, butter and eggs. Beat the mixture until smooth and well-whipped.
- Arrange the orange slices in the bottom of the tin and spoon the cake mixture on top.
- Bake for 35 minutes or until a skewer is inserted and comes out clean.
- Leave the cake to cool for 20 minutes before turning out onto a serving plate.

Spiced blood orange upside-down cake
Add 1 tsp allspice to the cake mixture along with the caster sugar, to give this cake an extra kick.

Cinnamon oatmeal cookies

PREPARATION TIME: **10 minutes**
COOKING TIME: **12-15 minutes**
MAKES: **36**

225 g / 8 oz / 1 ⅓ cup dark brown sugar
100 g / 3 ½ oz / 1 ½ cup caster (superfine) sugar
175 g / 6 oz / ¾ cup butter, melted
2 tsp vanilla extract
1 egg, plus 1 egg yolk
250 g / 9 oz / 1 ⅔ cups self-raising flour
2 tsp ground cinnamon
100 g / 3 ½ oz / 1 cup oats

- Preheat the oven to 170°C (150°C fan) / 340F / gas 3, then line two baking trays with greaseproof paper.
- In a large mixing bowl, cream together the two sugars, butter and vanilla extract until pale and well-whipped. Beat in the egg and yolk, then beat in the flour, cinnamon and oats.
- Dollop tablespoons of the mixture onto the prepared baking trays, leaving room for the cookies to spread.
- Bake the cookies in batches for 12–15 minutes or until the edges are starting to brown, but the centres are still chewy. Transfer to a wire rack and leave to cool.

Cinnamon and raisin oatmeal cookies
Add 100 g / 3 ½ oz / ⅔ cup of raisins to the mixture along with the oats and stir.

Banana, carrot and ginger loaf

PREPARATION TIME: 10 minutes
COOKING TIME: 55 minutes
MAKES: 1 loaf

3 very ripe bananas
110 g / 4 oz / ½ cup soft light brown sugar
2 large eggs
120 ml / 4 fl. oz / ½ cup sunflower oil
75 g / 2 2/3 oz / ½ cup stoneground wholemeal flour
50 g / 1 ¾ oz / ½ cup porridge oats
2 tsp baking powder
100 g / 3 ½ oz / 1 cup carrot, grated
100 g / 3 ½ oz / ⅔ cup walnuts, finely chopped
1 tsp ground ginger

- Preheat the oven to 170°C (150°C fan) 340F / gas 3, then line a large loaf tin with greaseproof paper.
- In a large mixing bowl, mash the bananas roughly with a fork, then whisk in the sugar, eggs and oil.
- Sieve the flour, oats and baking powder into the bowl, then add the grated carrot, walnuts and ground ginger. Stir just enough to evenly mix all the ingredients together.
- Scrape the mixture into the loaf tin and bake for 55 minutes.
- Test the cake with a toothpick: if it comes out clean, the cake is done.
- Transfer the cake to a wire rack and leave to cool completely.

Classic coffee cake

PREPARATION TIME: 10 minutes
COOKING TIME: 35-40 minutes
SERVES: 12

200 g / 7 oz / 1 ⅓ cups self-raising flour
200 g / 7 oz / ¾ cup caster (superfine) sugar
200 g / 7 oz / ¾ cup butter
4 eggs
1 tsp baking powder
1 tbsp instant espresso powder

FOR THE BUTTERCREAM
200 g / 7 oz / ¾ cup butter, softened
400 g / 14 oz / 4 cups icing (confectioners') sugar
1 tbsp instant espresso powder

- Preheat the oven to 180°C (160°C fan) / 350F / gas 4, then grease and line two 23cm (9in) round cake tins.
- Put all the cake ingredients in a large mixing bowl and whisk them together until pale and well-whipped.
- Divide the mixture between the prepared cake tins and bake for 35–40 minutes. Test the cakes with a toothpick; if it comes out clean, the cakes are done.
- Transfer the cakes to a wire rack to cool completely.
- To make the buttercream, whisk the butter until soft, then gradually add the icing sugar and espresso powder. Whisk until smooth.
- Use a third of the buttercream to sandwich the two cakes together, then spread the rest over the top to finish.

Cinnamon shortbread

PREPARATION TIME: **20 minutes**
COOKING TIME: **12-15 minutes**
MAKES: **16**

150 g / 5 ½ oz / 1 cup plain (all-purpose) flour
1 tbsp ground cinnamon
75 g / 2 ½ oz / ⅓ cup caster (superfine) sugar
150 g / 5 oz / ⅔ cup butter, cubed

* Preheat the oven to 180°C (160°C fan) / 350F / gas 4. Line a baking tray with greaseproof paper.
* In a large mixing bowl, mix together the flour, ground cinnamon and sugar, then rub in the butter with your fingertips.
* Knead gently until the mixture forms a smooth dough, then roll out on a lightly floured surface to 5 mm thick.
* Use a cookie cutter to cut out 16 biscuits and spread them out on the baking tray, leaving room for the biscuits to spread.
* Bake the biscuits for 12–15 minutes, turning the tray round halfway through.
* Transfer the biscuits to a wire rack to cool.

Coconut shortbread
Replace the ground cinnamon with 55 g / 2 oz / ½ cup desiccated coconut, leaving some to sprinkle over the shortbread when it's ready.

Gluten-free sponge

PREPARATION TIME: **10 minutes**
COOKING TIME: **45-50 minutes**
SERVES: **12**

150 g / 5 ¼ oz / 1 cup gluten-free self-raising flour
150 g / 5 ½ oz / ⅔ cup caster (superfine) sugar
150 g / 5 ½ oz / ⅔ cup butter
3 eggs
2 tsp baking powder
1 tsp vanilla extract
icing (confectioners') sugar to dust

* Preheat the oven to 180°C (160° fan) / 350F / gas 4, then grease and line a 23cm (9in) round cake tin with greaseproof paper.
* Put all the cake ingredients in a large mixing bowl and whisk them together until pale and well-whipped.
* Scrape the mixture into the tin and level the top with a spatula.
* Bake for 45–50 minutes. Test the cake with a wooden toothpick; if it comes out clean, the cake is done.
* Transfer the cake to a wire rack to cool completely, then dust with icing sugar to finish.

Gluten-free chocolate sponge
Add 55 g / 2 oz / ½ cup unsweetened cocoa powder to the cake mixture, stirring to combine, then bake as normal.

THE COOKERY COLLECTION

Wholemeal chocolate muffins

PREPARATION TIME: 25 minutes
COOKING TIME: 20-25 minutes
MAKES: 12

1 large egg
120 ml / 4 fl. oz / ½ cup sunflower oil
120 ml / 4 fl. oz / ½ cup milk
200 g / 7 oz / 1 ⅓ cups self-raising flour, sifted
175 g / 6 oz / 1 ¼ cups stoneground wholemeal flour
2 tbsp cocoa powder
2 tsp baking powder
200 g / 7 oz / ¾ cup dark brown sugar
150 g / 5 ½ oz dark chocolate (minimum 60% cocoa solids), grated

- Preheat the oven to 180°C (160°C fan) / 350F / gas 4, then line a 12-hole muffin tray with paper cases.
- Beat the egg in a jug with the oil and milk until well mixed.
- In a large mixing bowl, mix together the flours, cocoa, baking powder, sugar and chocolate. Pour in the egg mixture and stir just enough to combine.
- Divide the mixture between the paper cases and bake for 20–25 minutes.
- Test with a wooden toothpick; if it comes out clean, the cakes are done.
- Transfer the muffins to a wire rack and leave to cool completely.

Pumpkin pie

PREPARATION TIME: **40 minutes**
COOKING TIME: **1 hour 10 minutes**
SERVES: **10**

600 g / 1 lb 5 oz pumpkin, peeled, deseeded and cubed
2 large eggs
150 ml / 5 ½ fl. oz / ⅔ cup maple syrup
150 ml / 5 ½ fl. oz / ⅔ evaporated milk
1 tsp mixed spice

FOR THE PASTRY
200 g / 7 oz / 1 ⅓ cups plain (all-purpose) flour
55 g / 2 oz / ¼ cup caster (superfine) sugar
100 g / 3 ½ oz / ½ cup butter, cubed
1 egg, beaten

- Preheat the oven to 200°C (180°C fan) / 400F / gas 6.
- Start making the pastry first. Add the flour and sugar to a large mixing bowl, then rub in the butter using your fingertips. Add the egg with just enough cold water to bring the mixture together. Wrap the dough in cling film and chill for 30 minutes.
- When the dough is cooled, roll out on a lightly floured surface, and use to line a 23 cm (9 in) baking tin. Prick the base with a form, then line with greaseproof paper and fill with baking beans or rice.
- Bake for 10 minutes, then remove the greaseproof paper and baking beans and cook for another 8 minutes to crisp.
- Meanwhile, put the pumpkin in a roasting tin, cover with foil and bake for 30 minutes.
- Drain any excess liquid, then purée the pumpkin in a food processor. Add the eggs, maple syrup, evaporated milk and spice, then pulse until smoothly combined.
- Reduce the oven temperature to 180°C (160°C fan) / 350F / gas 4.
- Pour the pumpkin mixture into the pastry case and bake for 30–40 minutes or until just set in the centre. Leave to cool completely before slicing.

Pumpkin and walnut pie
Add 100 g / 3 ½ oz / ⅔ cup finely chopped walnuts to the filling mixture after it's been in the food processor, then bake as normal.

Cranberry loaf cake

PREPARATION TIME: **10 minutes**
COOKING TIME: **55 minutes**
SERVES: **8**

300 g / 10 ½ oz / 2 cups self-raising flour
2 tsp baking powder
250 g / 9 oz / 1 ½ cups light brown sugar
250 g / 9 oz / 1 ¼ cups butter, softened
4 large eggs
200 g / 7 oz / 1 ⅓ cups fresh cranberries

* Preheat the oven to 170°C (150°C fan) / 340F / gas 3. Line a large loaf tin with greaseproof paper.
* Sieve the flour and baking powder into a large mixing bowl, then add the rest of the ingredients.
* Beat the mixture with a whisk for 4 minutes or until smooth and well-whipped.
* Scrape the mixture into the prepared loaf tin and bake for 55 minutes. Test the cake with a toothpick; if it comes out clean, the cake is done.
* Transfer the cake to a wire rack and leave to cool completely.

Cranberry and apple loaf cake
Apple makes a tasty accompaniment for cranberries. Core, peel and finely chop 1 Bramley apple and stir into the mixture with the cranberries, then bake as normal.

Apricot cupcakes

PREPARATION TIME: **10 minutes**
COOKING TIME: **15-20 minutes**
MAKES: **12**

110 g / 4 oz / ⅔ cup self-raising flour, sifted
110 g / 4 oz / ½ cup caster (superfine) sugar
110 g / 4 oz / ½ cup butter, softened
2 large eggs
1 tsp vanilla extract
100 g / 3 ½ oz / ⅔ cup dried apricots, chopped
icing (confectioners') sugar to dust

* Preheat the oven to 190°C (170°C fan) / 375F / gas 5 and line a 12-hole cupcake tin with paper cases.
* In a large mixing bowl, combine the flour, sugar, butter, eggs and vanilla extract and whisk together for 2 minutes or until smooth.
* Stir in the apricot pieces until evenly distributed.
* Divide the mixture between the paper cases, then bake for 15–20 minutes.
* Test with a wooden toothpick; if it comes out clean, the cakes are done.
* Transfer the cakes to a wire rack and leave to cool completely, then dust liberally with icing sugar to serve.

Apricot jam cupcakes
Half-fill the paper cases with the cake mixture, then spoon a teaspoon of apricot jam (jelly) into the centre of the cases. Top with the remaining cake mixture and bake as normal.

Fruit and nut chocolate tart

PREPARATION TIME: 25 minutes
COOKING TIME: 10-18 minutes
SERVES: 8

250 ml / 9 fl. oz / 1 cup double (heavy) cream
250 g / 9 oz / 1 ⅔ cups dark chocolate (minimum 60 % cocoa solids), chopped
55 g / 2 oz / ¼ up butter, softened
100 g / 3 ½ oz / ⅔ cup walnuts, chopped
100 g / 3 ½ oz / ⅔ cup peanuts, chopped
50 g / 1 ¾ oz / ⅓ cup raisins
50 g / 1 ¾ oz / ⅓ cup dried cranberries

FOR THE PASTRY
100 g / 3 ½ oz / ½ cup butter, cubed
200 g / 7 oz / 1 ⅓ cups plain (all-purpose) flour
55 g / 2 oz / ¼ cup light brown sugar
1 egg, beaten

- Preheat the oven to 200°C (180°C fan) / 400F / gas 6.
- Make the pastry first. In a large mixing bowl, rub the butter into the flour and sugar using your fingertips, until the mixture resembles fine breadcrumbs.
- Add the egg and just enough cold water to bring the dough together.
- Wrap the dough in cling film and chill for 30 minutes, then roll out on a lightly floured surface.
- Use the pastry to line a 23 cm (9 in) tart tin and trim the edges.
- Prick the base with a fork, line with greaseproof paper and fill with baking beans or rice.
- Bake for 10 minutes, then remove the greaseproof paper and baking beans and cook for another 8 minutes to crisp. Transfer to a wire rack to cool.
- Heat the cream in a small saucepan over a medium heat to a simmer, then pour it over the chocolate and stir until smooth, then beat in the butter.
- Stir in most of the nuts and fruit, reserving some to decorate the top.
- Pour the ganache into the pastry case, level the top with a palette knife, then sprinkle over the remaining fruit and nuts.
- Leave the ganache to cool and set for at least 2 hours before cutting and serving.

Rich chocolate caramel tart

PREPARATION TIME: **3 hours, 25 minutes**
COOKING TIME: **10-18 minutes**
SERVES: **8**

1 can condensed milk
250 ml / 9 fl. oz / 1 cup double (heavy) cream
250 g / 9 oz dark chocolate (minimum 60 % cocoa solids), chopped
55 g / 2 oz / ¼ cup butter, softened
100 g / 3 ½ oz / ⅔ cup pistachios, shelled and chopped

FOR THE PASTRY
100 g / 3 ½ oz / ½ cup butter, cubed
200 g / 7 oz / 1 ⅓ cup plain (all-purpose) flour
55 g / 2 oz / ¼ cup caster (superfine) sugar
1 egg, beaten

- Make the caramel first. Place the unopened can of condensed milk in a saucepan of water and simmer for 3 hours, adding more water as necessary to ensure it doesn't boil dry. Leave the can to cool.

- Preheat the oven to 200°C (180°C fan) / 400F / gas 6.

- To make the pastry, rub the butter into the flour and sugar using your fingertips until the mixture resembles fine breadcrumbs. Add the egg with just enough cold water to combine.

- Wrap the dough in cling film and chill for 30 minutes, then roll out on a lightly floured surface. Use the pastry to line a 23 cm (9 in) tart tin and trim the edges.

- Prick the pastry with a fork, line with greaseproof paper and fill with baking beans or rice.

- Bake for 10 minutes, then remove the greaseproof paper and baking beans and cook for another 8 minutes to crisp.

- Heat the cream to simmering point, then pour it over the chocolate and stir until smooth. Add the butter and beat until very smooth.

- Pour the caramel into the pastry case, then top with the chocolate and level the top with a palette knife. Leave to cool and set, then sprinkle with chopped pistachios around the edge to finish.

Raspberry muffins

PREPARATION TIME: 10 minutes
COOKING TIME: 15-20 minutes
MAKES: 12

110 g / 4 oz / ⅔ cup self-raising flour, sifted
110 g / 4 oz / ½ cup caster (superfine) sugar
110 g / 4 oz / ½ cup butter, softened
2 large eggs
1 tsp vanilla extract
75 g / 2 ½ oz / ⅓ cup fresh raspberries

- Preheat the oven to 190°C (170°C fan) / 375F / gas 5, then line a 12-hole muffin tin with paper cases.
- In a large mixing bowl, combine the flour, sugar, butter, eggs and vanilla and whisk until smooth.
- Fold in the raspberries until evenly distributed.
- Divide the mixture between the moulds, then transfer the muffin tin to the oven and bake for 15–20 minutes.
- Test with a wooden toothpick; if it comes out clean, the cakes are done.
- Transfer the cakes to a wire rack and leave to cool completely.

Strawberry and mint muffins
Replace the raspberries with the same quantity of fresh strawberries, hulled and halved, then add a handful of finely chopped mint leaves to the cake mixture along with the fruit to give these muffins a summery flavour.

Apple, pecan and cinnamon loaf

PREPARATION TIME: 10 minutes
COOKING TIME: 55 minutes
SERVES: 8

300 g / 10 ½ oz / 2 cups self-raising flour
2 tsp ground cinnamon
2 tsp baking powder
250 g / 9 oz / 1 ⅓ cups caster (superfine) sugar
250 g / 9 oz / 1 ¼ cups butter, softened
5 large eggs
2 eating apples, cored and chopped
100 g / 3 ½ oz / ⅔ cup pecans, chopped

- Preheat the oven to 170°C (150C fan) / 340F / gas 3, then line a large loaf tin with greaseproof paper.
- Sieve the flour, cinnamon and baking powder into a large mixing bowl, then add the sugar, butter and eggs.
- Beat the mixture with a whisk for 4 minutes or until smooth and well-whipped.
- Fold in the chopped apples and scrape the mixture into the loaf tin. Sprinkle over the chopped pecans in an even layer.
- Bake for 55 minutes. Test the cake with a toothpick; if it comes out clean, the cake is done.
- Transfer the cake to a wire rack and leave to cool completely.

Pear, pecan and ginger loaf
Replace the cinnamon with the same quantity of ginger, and the apples with 2 cored and chopped pears, then bake as normal.

Pear, almond and vanilla tart

PREPARATION TIME: 45 minutes
COOKING TIME: 25 minutes
SERVES: 8

150 g / 5 ½ oz / 1 ½ cups ground almonds
150 g / 5 ½ oz / ⅔ cup butter, softened
150 g / 5 ½ oz / ⅔ cup caster (superfine) sugar
2 large eggs
2 tbsp plain (all-purpose) flour
4 pears, cored and thinly sliced
1 tbsp runny honey

FOR THE PASTRY
200 g / 7 oz / 1 ⅓ cups plain (all-purpose) flour
55 g / 2 oz / ¼ cup caster (superfine) sugar
100 g / 3 ½ oz / ½ cup butter, cubed
1 egg, beaten

- Preheat the oven to 200°C (180°C fan) / 400F / gas 6.
- Make the pastry first. Add the flour and sugar to a large mixing bowl, then rub in the butter using your fingertips.
- Add the egg with just enough cold water to bring the mixture together.
- Wrap the dough in cling film and chill for 30 minutes, then roll out on a lightly floured surface.
- Use the pastry to line a 23 cm (9 in) baking tin and trim the edges. Prick the base with a fork, line with greaseproof paper and fill with baking beans or rice.
- Bake for 10 minutes, then remove the greaseproof paper and baking beans and cook for another 8 minutes to crisp.
- In a large mixing bowl, whisk together the almonds, butter, sugar, eggs and flour until smoothly whipped, then spoon the mixture into the pastry case.
- Arrange the pear slices on top and bake the tart for 25 minutes or until the frangipane is cooked through. Brush the pears with honey to finish.

Apple, almond and vanilla tart
Replace the pears with 4 eating apples, cored and thinly sliced. Arrange the apple slices on top of the frangipane and bake as normal.

Rhubarb and strawberry crumble

PREPARATION TIME: **20 minutes**
COOKING TIME: **25 minutes**
SERVES: **8**

500 g / 17 ½ oz / 2 ½ cups rhubarb, chopped
75 g / 2 ¾ oz / ⅓ cup caster (superfine) sugar
225 g / 8 oz / 1 ¼ cups strawberries, hulled and
sliced, plus extra to garnish

FOR THE CRUMBLE
150 g / 5 oz / ⅔ cup butter
100 g / 3 ½ oz / ⅔ cup plain (all-purpose) flour
50 g / 1 ¾ oz / ½ cup porridge oats
75 g / 2 ½ oz / ½ cup light brown sugar

- Preheat the oven to 200°C (180°C fan) / 400F
  / gas 6.
- Rinse the rhubarb and shake off any excess
  water. Place in a baking tray with the sugar,
  toss to coat, then roast for 15 minutes.
- Add the strawberries and roast for a further
  5 minutes.
- Meanwhile, in a large mixing bowl, rub the
  butter into the flour using your fingertips,
  then stir in the oats and sugar.
- Take handfuls of the topping and squeeze it
  into a clump, then crumble over the rhubarb
  and strawberries.
- Bake the crumble for 25 minutes until the
  crumble is golden brown. Leave to cool for 20
  minutes, then garnish with strawberries and
  serve warm.

Rhubarb and apple crumble
Bring two classic flavours together with this
fruity combination. Replace the strawberries
with 500 g / 17 ½ oz / 2 ½ cups chopped eating
apples, then roast both fruits together for 15
minutes. Bake with the crumble as normal.

Light orange loaf cake

PREPARATION TIME: **10 minutes**
COOKING TIME: **35-40 minutes**
MAKES: **1 loaf**

150 g / 5 ½ oz / 1 cup self-raising flour
150 g / 5 ½ oz / ⅔ cup caster (superfine) sugar
150 g / 5 ½ oz / ⅔ cup butter
3 eggs
1 tsp baking powder
1 tbsp orange zest
50 ml / 1 ¾ fl. oz / ¼ cup orange juice
icing (confectioners') sugar to dust
orange slices to decorate

• Preheat the oven to 180°C (160°C fan) /350F / gas 4, then grease and line a large loaf tin with greaseproof paper.
• In a large mixing bowl, combine the flour, sugar, butter, eggs, baking powder and orange zest and whisk together until pale and well-whipped.
• Scrape the mixture into the tin and level the top with a palette knife.
• Bake for 35–40 minutes. Test with a wooden toothpick. Transfer to a wire rack, then brush over the orange juice while it's still warm. When cool, dust with icing sugar and decorate with orange slices.

Light orange and honey loaf
Heat 2 tbsp runny honey in a saucepan with the orange juice, then brush over while warm.

Ginger bread

PREPARATION TIME: **15 minutes**
COOKING TIME: **35-40 minutes**
MAKES: **1 loaf**

250 g / 9 oz / 1 ⅔ cups self-raising flour
1 tsp bicarbonate of (baking) soda
2 tsp ground ginger
200 g / 8 ½ oz / ⅔ cup golden syrup
125 g / 4 ½ oz / ½ cup butter
125 g / 4 ½ oz / ¾ cup dark brown sugar
2 large eggs, beaten
240 ml / 8 fl. oz / 1 cup milk

• Preheat the oven to 180°C (160°C fan) / 350F / gas 4, then grease and line a large loaf tin .
• Sieve the flour, bicarbonate of soda and ginger into a mixing bowl.
• In a small saucepan, heat the golden syrup, butter and brown sugar, then boil for 2 minutes, stirring to dissolve the sugar.
• Pour the heated mixture into the dry ingredients, then fold in the eggs and milk until the mixture is smooth.
• Transfer the mixture into the prepared tin and bake for 35–40 minutes. Test the centre of the cake with a toothpick; if it comes out clean, the cake is done. Transfer to a wire rack to cool.

Raisin and walnut ginger bread
Add 100 g / 3 ½ oz / ¾ cup chopped walnuts and the same quantity of raisins to the mixture along with the eggs and milk, then bake as before.

Almond cookies

PREPARATION TIME: **15 minutes**
COOKING TIME: **15-20 minutes**
MAKES: **24**

2 large egg whites
175 g / 6 oz / 1 ¾ cup ground almonds
100 g / 3 ½ oz / 1 cup icing (confectioners') sugar
75 g / 2 ½ oz / ⅓ cup caster (superfine) sugar
1 tbsp amaretto liqueur

- Preheat the oven to 170°C (150°C fan) / 325F / gas 3, then oil a large baking tray.
- Using a clean bowl, whisk the egg whites into stiff peaks, then fold in the almonds, icing sugar, caster sugar and amaretto liqueur.
- Spoon the mixture into a piping bag fitted with a large plain nozzle and pipe small circles onto the baking tray.
- Bake for 15–20 minutes or until golden brown and crisp, then transfer to a wire rack to cool.

Cherry and cranberry tart

PREPARATION TIME: 40 minutes
COOKING TIME: 35-40 minutes
SERVES: 8

150 g / 14 oz / 2 ⅔ cups fresh cranberries
200 g / 7 oz / 1 ½ cups cherries, chopped
200 g / 7 oz / ¾ cup caster (superfine) sugar

FOR THE PASTRY

100 g / 3 ½ oz / ½ cup butter, cubed
200 g / 7 oz / ⅓ cup plain (all-purpose) flour
50 g / 1 ¾ oz / ¼ cup caster (superfine) sugar
1 large egg, beaten

- Preheat the oven to 200°C (180°C fan) / 400F / gas 6.
- Make the pastry first. In a large mixing bowl, rub the butter into the flour using your fingertips until the mixture resembles fine breadcrumbs. Stir in the sugar and add enough cold water to bring the pastry together into a pliable dough.
- Chill for 30 minutes, then roll out on a lightly floured surface. Use the pastry to line a 25 cm (9 in) round, fluted tart case and trim the edges, leaving a 1 cm (½ in) overhang to allow for shrinkage. Leave some aside for lattice strips, if required.
- Prick the pastry all over with a fork, line with greaseproof paper and fill with baking beans or rice. Bake the case for 10 minutes, then remove the greaseproof paper and baking beans.
- Brush the inside with the beaten egg and return to the oven for 8 minutes or until golden and crisp. Transfer to a wire rack to cool.
- Meanwhile, put most of the cranberries and cherries in a large saucepan with 100 ml water and bring to a simmer.
- Cook for 10 minutes until the fruit has softened, then add the sugar and stir well to dissolve.
- Boil for 8 minutes, then pour the mixture into the pastry case and sprinkle with the remaining fruit. Leave to cool and thicken before serving.

Lemon and poppy seed cakes

PREPARATION TIME: **1 hour**
COOKING TIME: **15-20 minutes**
MAKES: **12**

110 g / 4 oz / ⅔ cup self-raising flour, sifted
110 g / 4 oz caster / ½ cup (superfine) sugar
110 g / 4 oz / ½ cup butter, softened
2 large eggs
1 lemon, zest finely grated
1 tbsp poppy seeds

- Preheat the oven to 190°C (170°C fan) / 375F / gas 5, then line a 12-hole cupcake tin with paper cases.
- Combine the flour, sugar, butter, eggs, lemon zest and poppy seeds in a large mixing bowl and whisk together until smooth.
- Divide the mixture between the paper cases, then transfer the tin to the oven and bake for 15–20 minutes.
- Test with a wooden toothpick; if it comes out clean, the cakes are done.
- Transfer the cakes to a wire rack and leave to cool completely.

Lemon and thyme cakes
Thyme complements the zesty kick of lemon perfectly; pick the leaves from 2 sprigs of fresh thyme and stir into the mixture along with the lemon zest.

Chocolate and almond brownies

PREPARATION TIME: **25 minutes**
COOKING TIME: **35-40 minutes**
MAKES: **9**

110 g / 4 oz milk chocolate, chopped
85 g / 3 oz / ¾ cup unsweetened cocoa powder, sifted
225 g / 8 oz / 1 cup almond butter
400 g /14 oz / 2 ⅓ cups light brown sugar
50 g / 1 ¾ oz / ⅓ cup ground almonds
4 large eggs
110 g / 4 oz / ⅔ cup self-raising flour
100 g / 3 ½ oz / ⅔ cup almonds, chopped

- Preheat the oven to 170°C (150°C fan) / 340F / gas 3, then oil and line a 20cm (8in) square cake tin .
- Melt the chocolate, cocoa and butter together in a saucepan, then leave to cool a little.
- In a large mixing bowl, whisk together the sugar and eggs until very light and creamy.
- Pour in the chocolate mixture and sieve over the flour, then fold everything together until evenly mixed. Scrape into the prepared tin and press the almonds into the top of the brownie.
- Bake for 35–40 minutes or until the outside is set, but the centre is still quite chewy.
- Leave the brownie to cool completely before cutting into 9 squares.

Chocolate, orange and almond brownies
Add the zest of 1 orange to the cake mixture along with the chocolate to give these brownies a hint of citrus.

Fruit cake

PREPARATION TIME: 15 minutes
COOKING TIME: 55 minutes
MAKES: 1 loaf

225 g / 8 oz / ½ cups self-raising flour
100 g / 3 ½ oz / ½ cup butter, cubed
100 g / 3 ½ oz / ½ cup caster (superfine) sugar
100 g / 3 ½ oz / ⅔ cup mixed dried fruit
8 glacé cherries, quartered
1 tsp grated lemon zest
1 large egg
75 ml / 2 ½ fl. oz / ⅓ cups whole milk
icing (confectioners') sugar to dust

- Preheat the oven to 180°C (160°C fan) / 350F / gas 4, then line a large loaf tin with greaseproof paper.
- Sieve the flour into a large mixing bowl, then rub in the butter using your fingertips until it resembles fine breadcrumbs.
- Stir in the sugar, dried fruit, cherries and lemon zest.
- In a jug, lightly beat the egg with the milk, then stir it into the dry ingredients until just combined.
- Scrape the mixture into the prepared loaf tin and bake for 55 minutes. Test the cake with a wooden toothpick; if it comes out clean, the cake is done.
- Transfer the cake to a wire rack and leave to cool completely, then dust with icing sugar to finish.

Spiced fruit cake
Remove the lemon zest, then stir 1 tsp ground cinnamon and 1 tsp ground ginger into the mixture along with the dried fruit.

Lemon surprise cupcakes

PREPARATION TIME: 1 hour
COOKING TIME: 15-20 minutes
MAKES: 12

110 g / 4 oz / ⅔ cup self-raising flour, sifted
110 g / 4 oz / ¾ cup caster (superfine) sugar
110 g / 4 oz / ½ cup butter, softened
2 large eggs
1 lemon, zest finely grated
2 tbsp lemon curd

FOR THE BUTTERCREAM
55 g / 2 oz / ¼ cup butter, softened
225 g / 8 oz / 2 ¼ cup icing (confectioners') sugar
1 tbsp lemon juice
few drops of yellow food dye
lemon slices to garnish

- Preheat the oven to 190°C (170°C fan) / 375F / gas 5, then line a 12-hole cupcake tin with paper cases.
- In a large mixing bowl, combine the flour, sugar, butter, eggs and lemon zest and whisk together until smooth.
- Half-fill the paper cases with the mixture, then spoon a little lemon curd in the centre of each case. Top with the remaining mixture.
- Bake for 15 – 20 minutes. Test the cakes with a wooden toothpick; if it comes out clean, the cakes are done.
- Transfer the cakes to a wire rack and leave to cool completely.
- To make the buttercream, beat the butter with a wooden spoon until light and fluffy, then beat in the icing sugar a bit at a time.
- Add the lemon juice and a few drops of lemon food dye, then use a whisk to whip the mixture for 2 minutes or until smooth and light. Spoon the buttercream into a piping bag fitted with a star-shaped nozzle.
- Pipe a rosette around the top of each cupcake, the decorate with lemon slices to finish.

Double chocolate button cookies

PREPARATION TIME: **10 minutes**
COOKING TIME: **12-15 minutes**
MAKES: **36**

225 g / 8 oz / 1 ⅓ cup dark brown sugar
100 g / 3 ½ oz / ½ cup caster (superfine) sugar
175 g / 6 oz / ¾ cup butter, melted
2 tsp vanilla extract
1 egg, plus 1 egg yolk
250 g / 9 oz / 1 ⅔ cup self-raising flour
2 tbsp unsweetened cocoa powder
175 g / 6 oz / 1 ¼ cup chocolate chips
36 white chocolate buttons

- Preheat the oven to 170°C (150°C fan) / 340F / gas 3, then line two baking trays with greaseproof paper. In a large mixing bowl, cream together the two sugars, butter and vanilla extract until pale and well-whipped.
- Beat in the egg and yolk, then beat in the flour, cocoa and chocolate chips. Dollop tablespoons of the mixture onto the prepared baking trays, leaving room for the cookies to spread.
- Press a white chocolate button into the top of each cookie. Bake in batches for 12–15 minutes until the outsides are crispy, but the centres are still chewy. Transfer to a wire rack to cool.

Double chocolate cherry cookies
Chocolate and cherry are a classic pairing. Replace the white chocolate buttons with glacé cherries, pressing one into each cookie before baking.

Raspberry and lemon loaf

PREPARATION TIME: **15 minutes**
COOKING TIME: **55 minutes**
MAKES: **1 loaf**

225 g / 8 oz / 1 ½ cups self raising flour
100 g / 3 ½ oz / ½ cup butter, cubed
85 g / 3 oz / ⅓ cup caster (superfine) sugar
150 g / 5 ¼ oz / 1 cup raspberries
zest of 1 lemon
1 large egg
75 ml / 2 ½ fl. oz / ⅓ cup whole milk

- Preheat the oven to 180°C (160°C fan) / 350F / gas 4, then line a large loaf tin with greaseproof paper.
- Sieve the flour into a large mixing bowl, then rub in the butter using your fingertips until it resembles fine breadcrumbs. Stir in the sugar, raspberries and lemon zest.
- In a jug, lightly beat the egg with the milk and stir it into the dry ingredients until it is just combined.
- Scrape the mixture into the loaf tin and bake for 55 minutes. Test with a wooden toothpick; if it comes out clean, the cake is done.
- Transfer the cake to a wire rack and leave to cool.

Raspberry and rose water loaf
Replace the lemon zest with 1 tbsp rose water to give this cake a fragrant, floral flavour.

Pear and chocolate sponge

PREPARATION TIME: 10 minutes
COOKING TIME: 30-35 minutes
SERVES: 8

100 g / 3 ½ oz / ⅔ cup self-raising flour, sifted
100 g / 3 ½ oz / ⅔ cup ground almonds
2 tbsp unsweetened cocoa powder
150 g / 5 ½ oz / 1 cup caster (superfine) sugar
150 g / 5 ½ oz / 1 cup butter, softened
2 large eggs
2 pears, peeled, cored and diced
icing (confectioners') sugar to dust

- Preheat the oven to 190°C (170°C fan) / 375F / gas 5, then grease and line a 23 cm (9 in) round baking tin.
- In a large mixing bowl, combine the flour, almonds, cocoa powder, sugar, butter and eggs, then whisk together until smooth.
- Fold in the chopped pears. Spoon into the baking tin and bake for 30–35 minutes.
- Test with a wooden toothpick; if it comes out clean, the cake is done.
- Transfer the cake to a wire rack and leave to cool completely. Dust with icing sugar.

Gluten and dairy-free banana loaf cake

PREPARATION TIME: **10 minutes**
COOKING TIME: **55 minutes**
MAKES: **1 loaf**

3 very ripe bananas
110 g / 4 oz / ½ cup caster (superfine) sugar
2 large eggs
120 ml / 4 fl. oz / ½ cup sunflower oil
175 g / 6 oz / 1 ¼ cups rice flour
2 tsp baking powder
50 g / 1 ¾ oz / ⅓ cup ground almonds
1 tsp cinnamon
50 g / 1 ¾ oz / ⅓ cup walnuts, chopped

- Preheat the oven to 170°C (150°C fan) / 340F / gas 3. Line a large loaf tin with greaseproof paper.
- In a large mixing bowl, mash the bananas with a fork. Whisk in the sugar, eggs and oil.
- Sieve the rice flour and baking powder into the bowl, then add the ground almonds, cinnamon and chopped walnuts. Stir to evenly mix all the ingredients together.
- Scrape the mixture into the loaf tin and bake for 55 minutes. Test with a wooden toothpick; if it comes out clean, the cake is done.
- Transfer the cake to a wire rack and leave to cool completely.

Rum and raisin
loaf cake

PREPARATION TIME: **15 minutes**
COOKING TIME: **55 minutes**
MAKES: **1 loaf**

225 g / 8 oz / 1 ½ cups self-raising flour
100 g / 3 ½ oz / ½ cup butter, cubed
85 g / 3 oz / ⅓ cup caster (superfine) sugar
150 g / 5 ½ oz / ¾ cup raisins
1 large egg
2 tbsp rum
3 tbsp milk
icing (confectioners') sugar to dust

- Preheat the oven to 180°C (160°C fan) / 350F
  / gas 4, then line a large loaf tin with
  greaseproof paper.
- Sieve the flour into a mixing bowl and rub in the
  butter with your fingertips until it resembles fine
  breadcrumbs. Stir in the sugar and raisins.
- In a jug, lightly beat the egg with the rum and
  milk, then stir it into the dry ingredients until
  just combined. Scrape the mixture into the loaf
  tin and bake for 55 minutes. Test with a wooden
  toothpick; if it comes out clean, the cake is done.
- Transfer the cake to a wire rack and leave to cool,
  then dust with icing sugar to finish.

Rum, chocolate and raisin loaf
Add 100 g / 3 ½ oz / ⅔ cup milk chocolate chips
to the mixture along with the sugar and raisins,
stirring until evenly distributed.

Orange and chocolate
shortbread

PREPARATION TIME: **20 minutes**
COOKING TIME: **12-15 minutes**
MAKES: **20**

175 g / 6 oz / 1 ¼ cups plain (all-purpose) flour
1 orange, zest finely grated
75 g / 2 ½ oz / ⅓ cup caster (superfine) sugar
150 g / 5 oz / ⅔ cup butter, cubed
50 g / 1 ¾ oz / ⅓ cup dark chocolate

- Preheat the oven to 180°C (160°C fan) / 350F / gas
  4, then line a baking tray with greaseproof paper.
- In a large mixing bowl, mix together the flour,
  orange zest and sugar in a bowl, then use your
  fingertips to rub in the butter.
- Knead gently until the mixture forms a smooth
  dough, then roll out on a lightly floured surface
  to 5 mm thick. Use a circular cookie cutter to
  cut out 20 biscuits and spread them out on the
  prepared baking tray.
- Bake the biscuits for 12–15 minutes, turning
  the tray round halfway through. Transfer the
  biscuits to a wire rack and leave to cool.
- Melt the chocolate in a bowl set over a saucepan
  of simmering water. Use a teaspoon to drizzle
  melted chocolate over the shortbread biscuits,
  leaving to cool and harden before serving.

Chocolate orange cinnamon shortbread
Add 1 tsp ground cinnamon to the mixture along
with the orange zest to give this shortbread a
spiced flavour.

Double choc cookies

PREPARATION TIME: 10 minutes
COOKING TIME: 12-15 minutes
MAKES: 36

225 g / 8 oz / 1 ⅓ cup dark brown sugar
100 g / 3 ½ oz / ½ cup caster (superfine) sugar
175 g / 6 oz / ¾ cup butter, melted
2 tsp vanilla extract
1 egg, plus 1 egg yolk
250 g / 9 oz / 1 ⅔ cups self-raising flour
2 tbsp unsweetened cocoa powder
175 g / 6 oz / 1 ¼ cups chocolate chips

- Preheat the oven to 170°C (150°C fan) / 340F / gas 3, then line two baking trays with greaseproof paper.
- In a large mixing bowl, cream together the sugars, butter and vanilla extract until pale and well-whipped.
- Beat in the egg and yolk, then the flour, cocoa and chocolate chips until the mixture is fully combined.
- Dollop tablespoons of the mixture onto the prepared baking trays, leaving plenty of room for them to spread.
- Bake the cookies in batches for 12–15 minutes or until the edges start to brown, but the centres are still chewy.
- Transfer to a wire rack and leave to cool.

Double chocolate cinnamon cookies
Add 2 tbsp ground cinnamon with the flour and cocoa powder to add extra depth of flavour to these cookies.

Lemon and poppy seed loaf

PREPARATION TIME: 10 minutes
COOKING TIME: 35-40 minutes
MAKES: 1 loaf

150 g / 5 ½ oz / 1 cup self-raising flour
150 g / 5 ½ oz / ⅔ cup caster (superfine) sugar
150 g / 5 ½ oz / ⅔ cup butter
3 eggs
1 tsp baking powder
1 tsp vanilla extract
2 tbsp poppy seeds
juice and zest of 1 lemon

- Preheat the oven to 180°C (160°C fan) / 350F / gas 4, then grease and line a small loaf tin.
- Place all the ingredients in a large mixing bowl, then whisk until pale and well-whipped.
- Transfer the mixture to the prepared tin and level the top with a spatula.
- Bake for 35–40 minutes. The cake is ready when a toothpick inserted in the centre comes out clean.
- Transfer the cake to a wire rack to cool completely.

Lemon meringue cupcakes

PREPARATION TIME: **10 minutes**
COOKING TIME: **20-25 minutes**
MAKES: **12**

110 g / 4 oz / ⅔ cup self-raising flour, sifted
1 tsp baking powder
110 g / 4 oz / ½ cup caster (superfine) sugar
110 g / 4 oz / ½ cup butter, softened
2 large eggs
zest of 1 lemon, finely grated
4 large egg whites
110 g / 4 oz / ½ cup caster (superfine) sugar

- Preheat the oven to 190°C (170°C fan) / 375F / gas 5, then line a 12-hole cupcake tray with paper cases. In a large mixing bowl, combine the flour, baking powder, sugar, butter and eggs and whisk together until smooth. Stir in the lemon zest.

- Divide between the paper cases and bake for 20–25 minutes. Test with a wooden toothpick, and move to a wire rack to cool.

- To make the meringue topping, whisk the egg whites in a clean bowl until stiff, then gradually whisk in half the sugar until the mixture is shiny.

- Fold in the remaining sugar, then spoon the meringue into a piping bag fitted with a star-shaped nozzle and pipe a swirl on top of the cakes. Heat the grill, then place under the grill until the meringue starts to turn gold.

Raspberry meringue cupcakes
Add 100 g / 3 ½ oz / ⅔ cup fresh raspberries to the cupcake mixture, stirring to combine, before baking as normal.

Iced orange loaf cake

PREPARATION TIME: **15 minutes**
COOKING TIME: **45 minutes**
MAKES: **1 loaf**

225 g / 8 oz / 1 cup butter, softened
225 g / 8 oz / 1 cup caster (superfine) sugar
1 orange, zest finely grated
55 g / 1 oz / ⅓ cup candied orange peel
4 large eggs, beaten
225 g / 8 oz / 1 ½ cups self-raising flour
100 g / 3 ½ oz / ½ cup icing (confectioners') sugar
orange slices

- Preheat the oven to 180°C (160°C fan) / 350F / gas 4, then grease and line a large loaf tin with greaseproof paper. In a large mixing bowl, cream together the butter, sugar and orange zest and peel until well-whipped. Gradually whisk in the eggs, beating well after each addition.

- Sieve the flour into the mixture, the fold it all together until combined. Scrape the mixture into the tin and bake for 45 minutes. Test the loaf with a toothpick; if it comes out clean, the loaf cake is done. Move to a wire rack to cool.

- Stir the icing sugar with enough cold water to make a thick, runny icing, then drizzle over the loaf cake and top with orange slices to finish.

Orange and poppy seed loaf
Add 2 tbsp poppy seeds to the mixture along with the orange zest and peel, then bake and ice as normal.

Chocolate torte

PREPARATION TIME: 25 minutes
COOKING TIME: 40-50 minutes
SERVES: 8

150 g / 5 ½ oz dark chocolate (minimum 60 % cocoa solids), chopped

110 g / 4 oz / ¾ cup plain (all-purpose) flour

1 tsp baking powder

110 g / 4 oz / ¾ cup butter

110 g / 4 oz / ¾ cup caster (superfine) sugar

4 large eggs, separated

75 g / 2 ¾ oz / ¾ cup ground almonds

FOR THE ICING

150 g / 5 ½ oz dark chocolate (minimum 60 % cocoa solids), chopped

150 ml / 5 fl. oz / ⅔ cup double (heavy) cream

1 tbsp apricot jam (jelly)

- Preheat the oven to 170°C (150°C fan) / 340F, gas 3, then oil and line a 23 cm (9 in) round cake tin.
- Melt the chocolate in a bowl set over a saucepan of simmering water, then remove from the heat.
- Sieve the flour and baking powder into a large mixing bowl, then add the butter, sugar and egg yolks. Whisk until the mixture has a smooth consistency, then beat in the melted chocolate.
- In a separate bowl, whisk the egg whites to soft peaks, then fold into the chocolate mixture.
- Scrape into the tin and bake for 40–50 minutes or until the outside is set and the centre is springy. Allow to cool for 10 minutes, then turn out onto a wire rack to cool completely.
- To make the icing, melt the chocolate in a bowl set over a saucepan of simmering water, then remove from the heat and stir through the cream.
- Warm the apricot jam, then brush over the cake and pour over the icing. Leave to set for 2–3 hours before serving.

Blueberry carrot muffins

PREPARATION TIME: **25 minutes**
COOKING TIME: **15-20 minutes**
MAKES: **24**

1 large egg
120 ml / 4 fl. oz / ½ cup sunflower oil
60 ml / 2 fl. oz / ¼ cup milk
375 g / 12 ½ oz / 2 ½ cups self-raising flour, sifted
1 tsp baking powder
200 g / 7 oz / ¾ cup caster (superfine) sugar
1 tsp ground cinnamon
200 g / 7 oz / 1 ⅓ cups carrots, finely grated
200 g / 7 oz / 1 ⅓ cups blueberries

- Preheat the oven to 180°C (160°C fan) / 35oF / gas 4, then line a 24-hole cupcake tray with paper cases.
- Beat the egg in a jug with the oil and milk until well mixed.
- Sieve the flour, baking powder, sugar and ground cinnamon into a large mixing bowl, stirring to combine.
- Pour in the egg mixture and stir just enough to combine, then fold in the grated carrots and most of the blueberries.
- Divide the mixture between the paper cases, top with the remaining blueberries and bake for 15–20 minutes.
- Test with a wooden toothpick; if it comes out clean, the cakes are done.
- Transfer the muffins to a wire rack and leave to cool completely.

Summer berry tarts

PREPARATION TIME: 45 minutes
COOKING TIME: 18 minutes
MAKES: 6

200 g / 7 oz / 1 ⅓ cups plain (all-purpose) flour
100g / 3 ½ oz / ½ cup butter, cubed
1 egg, beaten
450 g / 1 lb / 2 cups mascarpone
100 g / 3 ½ oz / 1 cup icing (confectioners') sugar
1 tsp vanilla extract
12 strawberries, halved
1 kiwi, sliced
50 g / 1 ¾ oz / ⅓ cup blueberries
50 g / 1 ¾ oz / ⅓ cup blackberries
50 g / 1 ¾ oz / ⅓ cup raspberries
2 tbsp runny honey

- Preheat the oven to 200°C (180°C fan) / 400F / gas 6. Using your fingertips, rub the butter into the flour and add just enough cold water to bind.
- Chill for 30 minutes, then roll out on a lightly floured surface. Use the pastry to line 6 tartlet cases. Prick the base with a fork, line with baking paper and fill with baking beans or rice. Bake for 10 minutes, then remove the baking paper and baking beans. Brush the inside of the pastry cases with beaten egg and cook for another 8 minutes to crisp.
- In a large mixing bowl, whisk the mascarpone with the icing sugar and vanilla extract until smooth. Spoon into the cooled pastry cases and level with a palette knife. Stir the fruit and honey together and arrange on top to finish.

Nutty berry tarts
Add 75 g / 2 ¾ oz / ⅓ cup chopped mixed nuts to the topping along with the fruit.

Coconut cookies

PREPARATION TIME: 10 minutes
COOKING TIME: 12-15 minutes
MAKES: 36

225 g / 8 oz / 1 ⅓ cup light brown sugar
100 g / 3 ½ oz / ½ cup caster (superfine) sugar
175 g / 6 oz / ¾ cup butter, melted
2 tsp vanilla extract
1 egg, plus 1 egg yolk
250 g / 9 oz / 1 ⅔ cups self-raising flour
100 g / 3 ½ oz / 1 cup desiccated coconut, plus extra for dusting

- Preheat the oven to 170°C (150°C fan) / 340F / gas 3, then line two baking trays with greaseproof paper. In a large mixing bowl, cream together the two sugars, butter and vanilla extract until pale and well-whipped. Beat in the egg and yolk, then beat in the flour and desiccated coconut.
- Dollop tablespoons of the mixture onto the prepared baking trays, leaving room for the cookies to spread. Bake the cookies in batches for 12–15 minutes or until the edges start to brown, but the centres are still chewy. Transfer to a wire rack to cool, then dust with desiccated coconut.

Coconut and pine nut cookies
Sprinkle 100 g / 3 ½ oz / ¾ cup pine nuts over the biscuits before transferring to the oven. They should begin to brown and caramelise when the biscuits are done, and will add a nutty crunch to these sweet biscuits.

Cranberry and pistachio biscotti

PREPARATION TIME: 25 minutes
COOKING TIME: 35 minutes
MAKES: 24

2 large eggs
55 g / 2 oz / ¼ cup butter, melted
225 g / 8 oz / 1 ½ cups self-raising flour
100 g / 3 ½ oz / ½ cup caster (superfine) sugar
100 g / 3 ½ oz / ⅔ cup dried cranberries
100 g / 3 ½ oz / ⅔ cup pistachios,
shelled and chopped

- Preheat the oven to 180°C (160°C fan) / 350F / gas 4, then line two baking trays with greaseproof paper.
- In a large mixing bowl, beat together the eggs and butter, then stir in the flour, sugar, cranberries and pistachios.
- Make a soft dough and then shape into two long rolls.
- Transfer the rolls to one of the baking trays and press to flatten slightly.
- Bake for 20 minutes or until golden, then leave to cool for 15 minutes.
- Cut the rolls across into 1 cm thick slices and spread them out over the baking trays.
- Bake the biscuits for 15 minutes or until golden and crisp.
- Transfer the biscuits to a wire rack and leave to cool completely.

Chocolate-dipped pistachio biscotti
Melt 150 g / 5 ½ oz dark chocolate in a bowl set over a medium heat, then dip one end of the bake biscotti into the chocolate. Leave to set before serving.

Banana, chocolate and cashew loaf

PREPARATION TIME: **10 minutes**
COOKING TIME: **55 minutes**
MAKES: **1 loaf**

3 very ripe bananas
110 g / 4 oz / ⅓ cup caster (superfine) sugar
2 large eggs
120 ml / 4 fl. oz / ½ cup sunflower oil
225 g / 8 oz / 1 ½ cup plain (all-purpose) flour
1 tsp bicarbonate of (baking) soda
75 g / 2 ½ oz / ½ cup dark chocolate
75 g / 2 ½ oz / ½ cup cashew nuts

- Preheat the oven to 170°C (150°C fan) / 340F / gas 3. Line a large loaf tin with greaseproof paper.
- In a large mixing bowl, mash the bananas roughly with a fork, then whisk in the sugar, eggs and oil.
- Sieve the flour and bicarbonate of soda into the bowl.
- Break most of the chocolate into chunks, reserving some for decoration. Stir into the banana mixture along with most of the cashew nuts until evenly distributed.
- Scrape the mixture into the loaf tin and bake for 55 minutes. Test the cake with a toothpick; if it comes out clean, the cake is done.
- Transfer the cake to a wire rack and leave to cool completely.
- Grate the remaining chocolate over the top of the cake and sprinkle with the remaining cashew nuts.

Banana and double chocolate loaf cake
Add 2 tbsp unsweetened cocoa powder to the mixture along with the flour, then stir in 75 g / 2 ½ oz / ½ cup white chocolate with the dark chocolate to give this cake a more indulgent chocolate flavour.

Rose and almond shortbread biscuits

PREPARATION TIME: **20 minutes**
COOKING TIME: **15-20 minutes**
MAKES: **20**

175 g / 6 oz / 1 ¼ cup plain (all-purpose) flour
55 g / 2 oz / ½ cup ground almonds
75 g / 2 ½ oz / ⅓ cup caster (superfine) sugar
150 g / 5 oz / ⅔ cup butter, cubed
1 tsp rose water

- Preheat the oven to 180°C (160° fan) / 350F / gas 4, then line a baking tray with greaseproof paper.
- In a large mixing bowl, mix together the flour, ground almonds and sugar, then use your fingertips to rub in the butter and rose water.
- Knead gently on a lightly floured surface until the mixture forms a smooth dough.
- Divide the dough into 20 balls, transfer to the prepared baking tray and use the back of a spoon to flatten the biscuits slightly.
- Bake the biscuits for 15–20 minutes, turning the tray round halfway through.
- Transfer the biscuits to a wire rack and leave to cool.

Almond and orange flower shortbread
To give these biscuits a different floral flavour, replace the rose water with 1 tsp orange flower water and bake as normal.

Apple crumble

PREPARATION TIME: **10 minutes**
COOKING TIME: **35-40 minutes**
SERVES: **8**

450 g / 1 lb Bramley apples, peeled and chopped
50 g / 1 ¾ oz / ¼ cup caster (superfine) sugar
1 tsp ground cinnamon
1 tbsp cornflour (cornstarch)

FOR THE CRUMBLE
150 g / 5 oz / ⅔ cup butter
100 g / 3 ½ oz / ⅔ cup plain (all-purpose) flour
50 g / 1 ¾ oz / ½ cup ground almonds
75 g / 2 ½ oz / ½ cup light brown sugar

- Preheat the oven to 200°C (180°C fan) / 400F / gas 6.
- In a large mixing bowl, mix together the chopped apple, sugar, cinnamon and cornflour. Spoon the mixture into a baking dish.
- To make the crumble topping, rub the butter into the flour using your fingertips, then stir in the almonds and sugar.
- Take handfuls of the topping and squeeze it into a clump, then crumble it over the apple.
- Bake the tart for 35–40 minutes until the crumble is golden brown. Leave to cool for 20 minutes before serving.

Apple and blackberry crumble
Add 100 g / 3 ½ oz / 1 cup blackberries to the apple mixture, stirring to combine, then spoon into the dish and top with crumble.

THE COOKERY COLLECTION

Summer fruit tart

PREPARATION TIME: 20 minutes
COOKING TIME: 25 minutes
SERVES: 6

150 g / 5 ½ oz / 1 ½ cups ground almonds
150 g / 5 ½ oz / ⅔ cup butter, softened
150 g / 5 ½ oz / ⅔ cup caster (superfine) sugar
2 large eggs
2 tbsp plain (all-purpose) flour
4 tbsp apricot jam (jelly)
200 g / 7 oz / 1 ⅓ cups strawberries
100 g / 3 ½ oz / ⅔ cup blueberries
mint leaves to garnish

FOR THE PASTRY
200 g / 7 oz / 1 ⅓ cups plain (all-purpose) flour
100 g / 3 ½ oz / ½ cup butter, cubed
50 g / 1 ¾ oz / ¼ cups caster (superfine) sugar

- Preheat the oven to 200°C (180°C fan) / 400F / gas 6.
- To make the pastry, rub the butter into the flour using your fingertips until the mixture resembles fine breadcrumbs.
- Stir in the sugar and add enough cold water to bring the pastry together into a pliable dough. Chill the dough for 30 minutes.
- Roll the dough out on a lightly floured surface and use it to line a 23 cm (9 in) round tart case. Prick the base with a fork, line with greaseproof paper and fill with baking beans or rice.
- Bake for 10 minutes, then remove the paper and beans. Return to the oven for 8 minutes to crisp.
- Whisk together the almonds, butter, sugar, eggs and flour until smoothly whipped and spoon the mixture into the pastry case.
- Scatter the fruit over the top and press into the mixture slightly.
- Bake the tart for 25 minutes or until the frangipane is cooked through. Leave to cool completely, then garnish with mint leaves.

Sponge fingers

PREPARATION TIME: 20 minutes
COOKING TIME: 10-15 minutes
MAKES: 45-50

4 large eggs
125 g / 4 ½ oz / ½ cup caster (superfine) sugar
1 tsp vanilla extract
cream of tartar
115 g / 4 oz / ¾ cup plain (all-purpose) flour
zest of 1 lemon, finely grated
icing (confectioners') sugar to dust

- Preheat the oven to 190°C (170°C fan) / 375F / gas 5, then grease and line two baking trays with greaseproof paper.

- First, separate the eggs. Place the yolks in a large mixing bowl, then add half of the sugar and the vanilla extract. Whisk until thick and pale.

- In a separate bowl, whisk the egg whites with the cream of tartar until the mixture reaches the soft peak stage. Gradually whisk in the remaining sugar.

- Sieve the flour over the yolk mixture, then fold in the egg white mixture and lemon zest with a metal spoon.

- Spoon the mixture into a piping bag fitted with a large plain nozzle. Pipe 10 cm (4 in) lines onto the prepared baking trays, leaving room for the biscuits to spread.

- Bake the biscuits for 10–15 minutes.

- Transfer to a wire rack and leave to cool completely, then dust with icing sugar to serve.

Cream puffs

PREPARATION TIME: **20 minutes**
COOKING TIME: **25-30 minutes**
MAKES: **12**

150 g / 5 ½ oz / ¾ cup butter, cubed
225 g / 8 oz / 1 ½ cups plain (all-purpose) flour
1 tsp fine sea salt
4 large eggs
300 ml / 10 ½ fl. oz / 1 ¼ whipped cream
icing (confectioners') sugar to dust

- Preheat the oven to 200°C (180°C fan) / 400F / gas 6, then grease a baking tray.
- Heat the butter in a saucepan with 300 ml of water until it starts to boil. Remove from the heat and pour in the flour and salt, then beat until smooth. Transfer to a bowl to cool for a few minutes. Beat in the eggs, one at a time, until the mixture is smooth and shiny.
- Spoon the mixture into a piping bag, then pipe 12 balls of pastry onto the prepared baking tray.
- Transfer to the oven, then pour a small cupful of water into the base of the oven and close the door. Bake for 25–30 minutes, or until golden brown. Transfer to a wire rack to cool, then cut in half, fill with whipped cream and sandwich together. Dust with icing sugar to finish.

Strawberry cream puffs
Spoon a little strawberry jam (jelly) into centre of the cream puffs before the whipped cream, then top with halved strawberries. Sandwich together, dust with icing sugar and garnish with more strawberries.

Almond and coconut sponge cookies

PREPARATION TIME: **10 minutes**
COOKING TIME: **10-15 minutes**
MAKES: **45-50**

4 large eggs
125 g / 4 ½ oz / ½ cup caster (superfine) sugar
1 tsp vanilla extract
a pinch cream of tartar
100 g / 3 ½ oz / ⅔ cup plain (all-purpose) flour
1 tbsp ground almonds
2 tbsp desiccated coconut

- Preheat the oven to 190°C (170°C fan) / 375F / gas 5, then grease and line two baking trays with greaseproof paper. Separate the eggs, then transfer the yolks to a bowl with half the sugar and the vanilla extract. Whisk until very thick.
- In a separate bowl, whisk the egg whites with the cream of tartar until they reach the soft peak stage. Gradually whisk in the remaining sugar.
- Sieve the flour over the egg yolk mixture, then fold in the egg whites with the almonds and coconut, keeping as much air in the mixture as possible. Dollop teaspoons of the mixture onto the baking tray, using the back of the spoon to spread them out slightly. Bake the biscuits for 10–15 minutes or until firm to the touch.

Almond sponge cookies
Replace the plain flour with the same quantity of almond flour, and substitute the desiccated coconut with the same quantity of flaked (slivered) almonds to give these sponges an extra nutty flavour.

Cinnamon spice loaf cake

PREPARATION TIME: 10 minutes
COOKING TIME: 35-40 minutes
SERVES: 8

150 g / 5 ¼ oz / 1 cup self-raising flour
2 tsp baking powder
150 g / 5 ½ oz / ⅔ cup caster (superfine) sugar
150 g / 5 ½ oz / ⅔ cup butter
3 eggs
1 tsp ground cinnamon
1 tsp ground ginger
½ tsp freshly grated nutmeg
50 g / 1 ¾ oz / ⅓ cup dark chocolate

- Preheat the oven to 180°C (160°C fan) / 350F / gas 4, then grease and line a small loaf tin with greaseproof paper.
- In a large mixing bowl, whisk together the flour, baking powder, sugar, butter, eggs and spices until pale and well-whipped.
- Scrape the mixture into the prepared loaf tin and level the top with a palette knife.
- Bake for 35–40 minutes. Test with a wooden toothpick; if it is clean, the cake is done.
- Transfer the cake to a wire rack to cool.
- Meanwhile, melt the chocolate in a bowl set over a saucepan of simmering water. Drizzle over the cooled cake to finish.

Ginger spice loaf cake
Remove the cinnamon and add 1 tbsp crystallised ginger to the cake mixture along with the ground ginger, then sprinkle a few pieces over the top of the cake before baking. Drizzle with melted chocolate as normal.

Chocolate chip muffins

PREPARATION TIME: **25 minutes**
COOKING TIME: **20-25 minutes**
MAKES: **12**

1 large egg
120 ml / 4 fl. oz / ½ cup sunflower oil
120 ml / 4 fl. oz / ½ cup milk
375 g / 12 ½ oz / 2 ½ cups self-raising flour, sifted
1 tsp baking powder
200 g / 7 oz / ¾ cup caster (superfine) sugar
150 g / 5 ½ oz / 1 cup chocolate chips

- Preheat the oven to 180°C (160°C fan) / 350F / gas 4, then line a 12-hole muffin tin with paper cases.
- Beat the egg in a jug with the oil and milk until well mixed.
- In a large mixing bowl, combine the flour, baking powder, sugar and chocolate chips.
- Pour in the egg mixture and stir just enough to combine.
- Divide the mixture between the paper cases and bake for 20–25 minutes.
- Test with a wooden toothpick; if it comes out clean, the cakes are done.
- Transfer the muffins to a wire rack and leave to cool completely..

Bundt cake

PREPARATION TIME: **5 minutes**
COOKING TIME: **45 minutes**
SERVES: **8-10**

225 g / 8 oz / 1 cup butter, softened
225 g / 8 oz / 1 cup caster (superfine) sugar
4 large eggs, beaten
125 g / 4 ½ oz / ¾ cup self-raising flour
icing (confectioners') sugar to dust

- Preheat the oven to 180°C (160°C fan) / 350F / gas 4, then grease a bundt tin.
- In a large mixing bowl, cream together the butter and sugar until well-whipped, then gradually whisk in the eggs, beating after each addition.
- Fold in the flour, then scrape the mixture into the prepared tin.
- Bake for 45 minutes. Test the cake with a toothpick; if it comes out clean, the cake is done.
- Turn the cake out onto a wire rack and leave to cool, the dust with icing sugar to finish.

Bundt cake with lemon
Add the zest and juice of 1 lemon to the cake mixture after the flour to give this simple bundt cake a citrus burst.

Mini chocolate cupcakes

PREPARATION TIME: **35 minutes**
COOKING TIME: **10-15 minutes**
MAKES: **36**

110 g / 4 oz / 1 cup self-raising flour, sifted
110 g / 4 oz / ½ cup caster (superfine) sugar
110 g / 4 oz / ½ cup butter, softened
2 tbsp cocoa powder
2 large eggs
1 tsp vanilla extract

FOR THE BUTTERCREAM
110 g / 4 oz / ½ butter, softened
225 g / 8 oz / 2 ¼ cups icing (confectioners') sugar
1 tbsp cocoa powder
2 tbsp milk
sugar sweets to decorate

- Preheat the oven to 190°C (170°C fan) / 375F / gas 5, then line a 36-hole cupcake tin with mini paper cases (use more than one tin if necessary).
- In a large mixing bowl, combine all the cake ingredients and whisk together until smooth. Divide the mixture between the paper cases and bake for 10–15 minutes.
- Test with a wooden toothpick. Transfer the cakes to a wire rack and leave to cool completely. To make the buttercream, beat the butter with a wooden spoon until light and fluffy, then beat in the icing sugar and cocoa powder a bit at a time. Use a whisk to incorporate the milk, then whisk until smooth.
- Spoon the mixture into a piping bag fitted with a small, star-shaped nozzle, then pipe small rosettes over the tops of the cakes and sprinkle with sugar sweets to finish.

Mini vanilla cupcakes
Remove the cocoa powder from the cake mixture. For the buttercream, replace the cocoa powder with 1 tsp vanilla extract, then stir in a little food dye to give the frosting a little colour.

Mini white chocolate loaf cakes

PREPARATION TIME: 10 minutes
COOKING TIME: 15-20 minutes
MAKES: 12

110 g / 4 oz / ⅔ cup self-raising flour, sifted
110 g / 4 oz / ½ cup caster (superfine) sugar
110 g / 4 oz / ½ cup butter, softened
2 large eggs
1 tsp vanilla extract
crispy chocolate balls to decorate

FOR THE FROSTING
110 g / 3 ¾ oz / ½ cup butter
110 g / 3 ¾ oz / ½ cup cream cheese, softened
1 tsp vanilla extract
100 g / 3 ½ oz / ⅔ cup white chocolate chips
150 g / 5 ¼ oz / ½ cup icing (confectioners') sugar

- Preheat the oven to 190°C (170°C fan) / 375F / gas 5, then oil a 12-hole silicone mini loaf cake mould.
- In a large mixing bowl, combine the flour, sugar, butter, eggs and vanilla and whisk until smooth.
- Divide the mixture between the moulds, then transfer the mould to the oven and bake for 15–20 minutes. Test with a wooden toothpick; if it comes out clean, the cakes are done.
- Transfer the cakes to a wire rack and leave to cool completely.
- To make the frosting, beat the butter in a clean bowl until smooth, then beat in the cream cheese.
- Melt the white chocolate chips in a bowl set over a pan of simmering water, stirring constantly. Add to the butter mixture and beat until fully incorporated.
- Gradually add the icing sugar until combined. Scrape the frosting into a piping bag and pipe onto the cooled cakes. Sprinkle with chocolate balls to finish.

Lemon curd tart

PREPARATION TIME: 55 minutes
COOKING TIME: 10-28 minutes
SERVES: 8

2 tsp cornflour (cornstarch)
4 lemons, zest and juice
4 large eggs, beaten
225 g / 8 oz / 1 cup butter
175 g / 6 oz / ¾ cup caster (superfine) sugar
icing (confectioners' sugar to dust

FOR THE PASTRY
200 g / 7 oz / 1 ⅓ cups plain (all-purpose) flour
55 g / 2 oz / ¼ cup caster (superfine) sugar
100 g / 3 ½ oz / ½ cup butter, cubed
1 egg, beaten

- Preheat the oven to 200°C (180°C fan) / 400F / gas 6.
- Make the pastry first. Add the flour and sugar to a large mixing bowl, then rub in the butter using your fingertips.
- Add the egg with just enough cold water to bring the mixture together.
- Wrap the dough in cling film and chill for 30 minutes, then roll out on a lightly floured surface.
- Use the pastry to line a 23 cm (9 in) baking tin and trim the edges.
- Prick the base with a fork, line with baking paper and fill with baking beans or rice.
- Bake for 10 minutes, then remove the baking paper and baking beans and cook for another 8 minutes to crisp.
- Meanwhile, dissolve the cornflour in the lemon juice and put it in a saucepan with the rest of the ingredients.
- Stir constantly over a medium heat to melt the butter and dissolve the sugar, and continue stirring until the mixture thickens and bubbles.
- Spoon the curd into the pastry case and level the top with a palette knife.
- Leave to cool, then dust with icing sugar to finish.

Poppy seed shortbread biscuits

PREPARATION TIME: 20 minutes
COOKING TIME: 15-20 minutes
MAKES: 16

225 g / 8 oz / 1 ½ cup plain (all-purpose) flour
75 g / 2 ½ oz / ⅓ cup caster (superfine) sugar
1 tbsp poppy seeds
1 tbsp white sesame seeds
150 g / 5 oz / ⅔ cup butter, cubed

- Preheat the oven to 180°C (160° fan) / 35oF / gas 4, then line a baking tray with greaseproof paper.
- In a large mixing bowl, mix together the flour, sugar and seeds, then use your fingertips to rub in the butter.
- Knead gently until the mixture forms a smooth dough, then roll it into a log, 7 cm (2 ¾ in) in diameter.
- Cut the log into 1 cm (½ in) slices and spread the shortbread biscuits out on the prepared baking tray.
- Bake for 15–20 minutes, turning the tray round halfway through.
- Transfer the biscuits to a wire rack and leave to cool completely.

Lemon and poppy seed shortbread
Replace the sesame seeds with more poppy seeds and add the finely grated zest of 1 lemon to the mixture along with the poppy seeds, then bake as normal.

Vanilla cream muffins

PREPARATION TIME: 10 minutes
COOKING TIME: 20-25 minutes
MAKES: 12

1 large egg
120 ml / 4 fl. oz / ½ cup sunflower oil
120 ml / 4 fl. oz / ½ cup milk
375 g / 12 ½ oz / 2 ½ cups self-raising flour, sifted
1 tsp baking powder
200 g / 7 oz / ¾ cup caster (superfine) sugar
1 tsp vanilla extract
300 ml / 10 ½ fl. oz / 1 ¼ cup double (heavy) cream

- Preheat the oven to 180°C (160°C fan) / 35oF / gas 4, then line a 12-hole muffin tray with paper cases. Beat the egg in a jug with the oil and milk until well mixed.
- In a large mixing bowl, mix together the flour, baking powder and sugar. Pour in the egg mixture and vanilla extract, then stir.
- Divide the mixture between the cases and bake for 20–25 minutes. Test with a wooden toothpick; if it comes out clean, the muffins are done.
- Transfer the muffins to a wire rack and leave to cool completely.
- In a clean bowl, whip the cream until it thickens and has a smooth texture, then spoon into a piping bag fitted with a star-shaped nozzle. Pipe the cream over the top of the cooled cakes.

Chocolate cream muffins
Add 55 g / 2 oz / ½ cup cocoa powder to the cupcake mixture to give these cupcakes a chocolatey flavour.

Blackberry and cream cheese muffins

PREPARATION TIME: **15 minutes**
COOKING TIME: **20-25 minutes**
MAKES: **12**

1 large egg
120 ml / 4 fl. oz / ½ cup sunflower oil
120 ml / 4 fl. oz / ½ cup milk
375 g / 12 ½ oz / 2 ½ cups self-raising flour, sifted
1 tsp baking powder
200 g / 7 oz / ¾ cup caster (superfine) sugar
200 g / 7 oz / ⅔ cup blackberry jam (jelly)

FOR THE FROSTING
225 g / 8 oz / 1 cup cream cheese
110 g / 4 oz / ½ cup butter, softened
225 g / 8 oz / 2 ¼ cups icing (confectioners') sugar
1 tsp blackberry jam
1 tbsp desiccated coconut to finish

- Preheat the oven to 180°C (160°C fan) / 350F / gas 4, then line a 12-hole muffin tray with paper cases.
- Beat the egg in a jug with the oil and milk.
- In a large mixing bowl, mix together the flour, baking powder and sugar. Pour in the egg mixture and stir just enough to combine.
- Divide half the mixture between the cases and top each one with a big spoonful of blackberry jam. Spoon the rest of the muffin mixture on top.
- Transfer the muffins to the oven and bake for 20–25 minutes. Test with a wooden toothpick; if it comes out clean, the cakes are done.
- Transfer the muffins to a wire rack and leave to cool completely.
- To make the frosting, beat the cream cheese and butter together with a wooden spoon until light and fluffy, then beat in the icing sugar a bit at a time.
- Stir in the blackberry jam, then spoon on top of the muffins and sprinkle over the desiccated coconut to finish.

Raspberry and cream cheese muffins
Replace the blackberry jam with the same quantity of raspberry jam, for centre of the cupcakes and the cream cheese topping.

Raspberry Swiss roll

PREPARATION TIME: **30 minutes**
COOKING TIME: **15-20 minutes**
SERVES: **8**

100 g / 3 ½ oz / ⅔ cup self-raising flour
1 tsp baking powder
100 g / 3 ½ oz / ½ cup caster (superfine) sugar
100 g / 3 ½ oz / ½ cup butter
2 large eggs
1 tsp vanilla extract
200 g / 7 oz / ⅔ cup raspberry jam (jelly)

- Preheat the oven to 180°C (160°C fan) / 350F
  / gas 4, then grease and line a Swiss roll tin.
- In a large mixing bowl, combine the flour,
  baking powder, sugar, butter, eggs and vanilla
  extract, then whisk until pale and well-
  whipped.
- Spoon the mixture into the prepared tin and
  spread into an even layer with a palette knife.
  Bake for 15–20 minutes or until the cake is
  springy to the touch.
- Turn the cake out onto a sheet of greaseproof
  paper. Spread the cake with raspberry
  jam, then roll up whilst warm, using the
  greaseproof paper to help you.
- Leave the cake to cool before serving.

Mixed berry Swiss roll
Sprinkle 150 g / 5 ½ oz / 1 cup fresh mixed
berries (such as chopped strawberries,
blueberries and blackberries) over the jam, then
roll the cake up tightly.

Almond and oat flour cake

PREPARATION TIME: **25 minutes**
COOKING TIME: **30-35 minutes**
SERVES: **8**

55 g / 2 oz / ⅓ cup oat flour, sifted
55 g / 2 oz / ½ cup ground almonds
55 g / 2 oz / ½ cup caster (superfine) sugar
110 g / 4 oz / ⅓ cup honey
110 g / 4 oz / ½ cup butter, softened
2 large eggs
1 tsp almond essence
icing (confectioners') sugar to dust

- Preheat the oven to 190°C (170°C fan) / 375F / gas 5, then grease and line a 23 cm (9 in) round cake tin.
- In a large mixing bowl, combine the flour, ground almonds, sugar, honey, butter, eggs and almond essence and whisk together for 2 minutes or until smooth.
- Transfer the mixture to the prepared tin and bake for 30–35 minutes.
- Test with a wooden toothpick; if it comes out clean, the cake is done.
- Transfer the cake to a wire rack to cool, then sprinkle with icing sugar to finish.

Lemon and almond cake
Add the zest and juice of 1 lemon to the mixture, stirring to combine, then bake as normal for a zesty kick.

Chocolate spice cookies

PREPARATION TIME: **10 minutes**
COOKING TIME: **24-30 minutes**
MAKES: **36**

225 g / 8 oz / 1 ⅓ cup dark brown sugar
100 g / 3 ½ oz / ½ cup caster (superfine) sugar
175 g / 6 oz / ¾ cup butter, melted
2 tsp vanilla extract
1 egg, plus 1 egg yolk
250 g / 9 oz / 1 ⅔ cup self-raising flour
3 tbsp unsweetened cocoa powder
1 tbsp ground cinnamon
½ tsp chilli (chili) powder
½ tsp bicarbonate of (baking) soda
¼ tsp Cayenne pepper
175 g / 6 oz / 1 ¼ cups chocolate chips

- Preheat the oven to 170°C (150°C fan) / 340F / gas 3, then line two baking trays with greaseproof paper. In a large mixing bowl, cream together the two sugars, butter and vanilla extract until pale and well-whipped. Beat in the egg and yolk, then beat in the flour and cocoa powder. Stir in the rest of the ingredients until the mixture is fully combined.
- Dollop tablespoons of the mixture onto the prepared baking trays, leaving plenty of room to spread. Bake in batches for 12–15 minutes. Transfer to a wire rack and leave to cool.

Chocolate and pink peppercorn cookies
Replace the spices, bicarbonate of soda and sea salt with 2 tsp crushed pink peppercorns for a different level of spice.

THE COOKERY COLLECTION

Carrot and rye cake

PREPARATION TIME: 25 minutes
COOKING TIME: 30-35 minutes
SERVES: 8-10

175 g / 6 oz / 1 cup soft light brown sugar

2 large eggs

150 ml / 5 fl. oz / ⅔ cup sunflower oil

100 g / 3 ½ oz / ⅔ cup stoneground wholemeal flour

75 g / 2 ½ oz / ½ cup rye flour

3 tsp baking powder

2 tsp ground cinnamon

200 g / 7 oz / 1 ⅔ cups carrots, washed and coarsely grated

FOR THE FROSTING

225 g / 8 oz / 1 cup cream cheese

110 g / 4 oz / ½ cup butter, softened

225 g / 8 oz / 2 ¼ cup icing (confectioners') sugar

1 tsp vanilla extract

zest of 1 lime

zest of 1 lemon

- Preheat the oven to 190°C (170°C fan) / 375F / gas 5, then line a cake tin with greaseproof paper.
- In a large mixing bowl, whisk together the sugar, eggs and oil.
- Fold in the flour, baking powder and cinnamon, followed by the carrots.
- Spoon the mixture into the prepared tin and bake for 30–35 minutes. Test the cake with a toothpick; if it comes out clean, the cake is done. Transfer to a wire rack and leave to cool completely.
- To make the icing, beat the cream cheese and butter together with a wooden spoon until light and fluffy, then beat in the icing sugar a bit at a time.
- Add the vanilla extract, then whisk the mixture until smooth.
- Spread the frosting over the cooled cake and sprinkle with lemon and lime zest to finish.

Banana and nut loaf cake

PREPARATION TIME: **10 minutes**
COOKING TIME: **55 minutes**
MAKES: **1 loaf**

3 very ripe bananas
110 g / 4 oz / ½ cup soft light brown sugar
2 large eggs
120 ml / 4 fl. oz / ½ cup sunflower oil
125 g / 4 ½ oz / ¾ cup plain (all-purpose) flour
2 tsp baking powder
100 g / 3 ½ oz / 1 cup ground hazelnuts (cobnuts)
100 g / 3 ½ oz / ⅔ cup walnuts, finely chopped
50 g / 1 ¾ oz / ⅓ cup chocolate chunks
1 tsp ground cinnamon
1 tbsp flaked (slivered) almonds

- Preheat the oven to 170°C (150°C fan) 340F / gas 3. Line a large loaf tin with greaseproof paper.
- In a large mixing bowl, mash the bananas roughly with a fork, then whisk in the sugar, eggs and oil.
- Sieve the flour and baking powder into the bowl, then add the ground hazelnuts, walnuts, chocolate chunks and ground cinnamon. Stir just enough to evenly mix all the ingredients together.
- Scrape the mixture into the loaf tin and sprinkle with flaked almonds.
- Bake for 55 minutes. Test the cake with a toothpick: if it is clean, the cake is done.
- Transfer the cake to a wire rack and leave to cool completely.

Wholemeal pear and caramel cake

PREPARATION TIME: **15 minutes**
COOKING TIME: **55 minutes**
SERVES: **8**

225 g / 8 oz / 1 ½ cups stoneground wholemeal flour
2 tsp baking powder
100 g / 3 ½ oz / ½ cup butter, cubed
100 g / 3 ½ oz / ½ cup light brown sugar
2 pears, peeled, cored and roughly chopped
1 tsp ground ginger
1 large egg
75 ml / 2 ½ fl. oz / ⅓ cup whole milk
300 ml / 10 fl. oz / 1 ¼ cups double (heavy) cream
150 g / 5 ½ oz / ⅔ cup caster (superfine) sugar
1 tbsp golden syrup
1 tsp vanilla extract

- Preheat the oven to 180°C (160°C fan) / 350F / gas 4, then line a 23 cm (9 in) round cake tin with greaseproof paper. Sieve the baking powder into a mixing bowl, then rub in the butter using your fingertips. Stir in the chopped pears and ginger.
- Lightly beat the egg with the milk, then stir it into the dry ingredients until just combined. Bake in a tin for 55 minutes. Test with a wooden toothpick. Transfer to a wire rack to cool.
- Heat the cream, sugar and golden syrup in a saucepan set over a medium heat until the sugar has dissolved. Stir in the vanilla and salt. Pour over the cake and allow to drip down the sides.

Wholemeal apple and caramel cake
Replace the pears with 2 eating apples, peeled, cored and chopped, then stir into the mixture.

Wholemeal chocolate chip cookies

PREPARATION TIME: **10 minutes**
COOKING TIME: **12-15 minutes**
MAKES: **36**

225 g / 8 oz / 1 ⅓ cup soft brown sugar, plus extra for sprinkling
100 g / 3 ½ oz / ½ cup caster (superfine) sugar
175 g / 6 oz / ¾ cup butter, melted
2 tsp vanilla extract
1 egg, plus 1 egg yolk
125 g / 4 ½ oz / ¾ cup self-raising flour
125 g / 4 ½ oz / ¾ cup stoneground wholemeal flour
125 g / 4 ½ oz / 1 cup chocolate chips

- Preheat the oven to 170°C (150°C fan) / 340F / gas 3, then line two baking trays with greaseproof paper. In a large mixing bowl, cream together the two sugars, butter and vanilla extract until pale and well-whipped. Beat in the egg and the yolk, then beat in the flours and chocolate chips.
- Dollop tablespoons of the mixture onto the prepared baking trays, leaving room for the cookies to spread.
- Bake the cookies in batches for 12–15 minutes or until the edges start to crisp, but the centres are still chewy. Transfer to a wire rack to cool, then sprinkle with the remaining brown sugar.

Wholemeal chocolate and nut cookies
Add 2 tbsp unsweetened cocoa powder and 125 g / 4 ½ oz / 1 cup mixed nuts to the mixture along with the chocolate chips, to make these cookies more indulgent.

Black Forest gateau

PREPARATION TIME: **10 minutes**
COOKING TIME: **30-35 minutes**
SERVES: **10-12**

225 g / 8 oz / 1 ½ cups self-raising flour
55 g / 2 oz / ½ cup unsweetened cocoa powder
3 tsp baking powder
225 g / 8 oz / 1 cup caster (superfine) sugar
225 g / 8 oz / 1 cup butter
4 large eggs

FOR THE FILLING

500 ml / 17 fl. oz / 2 cups double (heavy) cream
300 g / 10 ½ oz / 1 ⅓ cups cherries, pitted
3 tbsp cherry jam
chocolate flakes to decorate

- Preheat the oven to 180°C (160°C fan) / 350F / gas 4, then grease and line three 20 cm (8 in) round cake tins.

- In a large mixing bowl, whisk together the cake ingredients until well-whipped.
- Divide the mixture between the tins and bake for 30–35 minutes. Test with a wooden toothpick; if it comes out clean, the cakes are done.
- Transfer the cakes to a wire rack to cool completely.
- In a clean bowl, whip the cream until it thickens and has a smooth texture, then halve most of the cherries, reserving some to decorate.
- Place one of the cakes on a serving plate, spread a layer of cherry jam over the top, followed by a layer of whipped cream. Sprinkle over half of the chopped cherries.
- Place the second cake on top, pressing down slightly, then spread with jam and cream, followed by the remaining chopped cherries.
- Place the final cake layer on top, then use a palette knife to spread the remaining cream around the top and sides.
- Decorate with the reserved cherries and chocolate flakes to finish.

Chocolate and pecan bundt cake

PREPARATION TIME: 5 minutes
COOKING TIME: 45 minutes
SERVES: 8-10

225 g / 8 oz / 1 cup butter, softened
225 g / 8 oz / 1 cup dark brown sugar
4 large eggs, beaten
125 g / 4 ½ oz / ¾ cup self-raising flour
100 g / 3 ½ oz / 1 cup ground pecan nuts
100 g / 3 ½ oz dark chocolate (minimum 60 % cocoa solids), chopped

FOR THE GLAZE
100 g / 3 ½ oz / ⅔ cup dark chocolate (minimum 60 % cocoa solids), chopped
2 tbsp butter
2 tbsp golden syrup
55 g / 2 oz / ½ cup pecan nuts, chopped

- Preheat the oven to 180°C (160°C fan) / 350F / gas 4, then grease a bundt tin.
- In a large mixing bowl, cream together the butter and sugar until well-whipped, then gradually whisk in the eggs, beating well after each addition.
- Fold in the flour, ground pecans and chocolate chunks, then scrape the mixture into the prepared tin.
- Bake the cake for 45 minutes. Test the cake with a toothpick; if it comes out clean, the cake is done.
- Turn the cake out onto a wire rack and leave to cool.
- Melt the chocolate, butter and syrup together over a low heat, stirring regularly, then spoon it over the cake. Sprinkle with chopped pecan nuts.

White chocolate and pecan bundt cake
Replace the dark chocolate with white chocolate for both the cake mixture and glaze, omitting the golden syrup for the glaze.

Marmalade biscuits

PREPARATION TIME: **1 hour, 15 minutes**
COOKING TIME: **25-30 minutes**
MAKES: **36**

150 g / 5 ½ oz / ⅔ cup caster (superfine) sugar
350 g / 12 oz / 1 ½ cup butter, softened
1 tsp vanilla extract
300 g / 10 ½ oz / 2 cup plain (all-purpose) flour
150 g / 5 ½ oz / 1 ½ cup ground almonds
200 g / 7 oz / ⅔ cup marmalade
icing (confectioners') sugar to dust

- In a large mixing bowl, cream together the sugar, butter and vanilla extract until pale, then stir in the flour and ground almonds.
- Bring the mixture together into a ball, then wrap in cling film and chill for 45 minutes.
- Preheat the oven to 140°C (120°C fan) / 280F / gas 1, then line two baking trays with greaseproof paper.
- Roll out the dough on a lightly floured surface to 5 mm thick.
- Use different shaped cutters (such as heart-shaped and fluted cutters) to cut out 72 biscuits.
- Use a small, circular cutter to cut a hole out of 36 of the biscuits.
- Transfer the biscuits to the prepared trays and bake in batches for 25–30 minutes, or until cooked through and starting to turn golden.
- Transfer the biscuits to a wire rack and leave to cool.
- Spoon teaspoons of marmalade on the plain biscuits and top with the biscuits with the hole cut out. Dust liberally with icing sugar.

Almond and lemon pie

PREPARATION TIME: **25 minutes**
COOKING TIME: **35-40 minutes**
SERVES: **8**

450 g / 1 lb filo pastry
200 g / 7 oz / ¾ cup butter, melted
450 g / 1 lb / 3 cups blanched almonds
100 g / 3 ½ oz / ½ cup caster (superfine) sugar
1 lemon, zest finely grated
1 egg, beaten
2 tbsp flaked (slivered) almonds

- Preheat the oven to 180°C (160°C fan) / 350F / gas 4, then grease a 23cm (9in) round baking tray. Brush 10 sheets of filo pastry with melted butter and use to line the baking tray.
- Place the almonds, sugar and lemon zest in a food processor and pulse until finely chopped. Add half of the remaining butter and pulse again. Spread a third of the almond mixture across the bottom of the tray on top of the pastry.
- Top with a third of the remaining pastry sheets, making sure each one is well buttered.
- Continue to layer the pastry and almond mixture, finishing with a layer of buttered filo pastry, then fold in the edges to neaten.
- Brush the top of the pie with beaten egg, then sprinkle over the flaked almonds. Bake the pie in the oven for 35–45 minutes or until the pastry is golden and cooked through in the centre. Transfer to a wire rack to cool.

Almond and rose water pie
Add 1 tbsp of rose water to the almond mixture before adding to the food processor, to give this pie an extra hint of flavour.

Cottage cheese and walnut loaf

PREPARATION TIME: 15 minutes
COOKING TIME: 30-35 minutes
MAKES: 1 loaf

2 large eggs
120 ml / 4 fl. oz / ½ cup sunflower oil
180 ml / 6 fl. oz / ¾ cup Greek yoghurt
225 g / 8 oz cottage cheese, crumbled
110 g / 3 ½ oz / ¾ cup walnuts, chopped
225 g / 8 oz / 1 ½ cup plain (all-purpose) flour
2 tsp baking powder
½ tsp bicarbonate of soda
½ tsp salt

- Preheat the oven to 180°C (160°C fan) / 350F / gas 4, then line a large loaf tin with greaseproof paper.
- Beat the eggs in a jug with the oil and yoghurt until well mixed.
- In a large mixing bowl, mix together the cottage cheese, walnuts, flour, baking powder, bicarbonate of soda and salt, then pour in the egg mixture and stir everything just enough to combine.
- Scrape the mixture into the tin and bake for 30-35 minutes. Test with a wooden toothpick; if it comes out clean, the cake is done.
- Transfer the loaf to a wire rack and leave to cool completely.

Chocolate and strawberry gateau

PREPARATION TIME: 10 minutes
COOKING TIME: 30-35 minutes
SERVES: 10-12

150 g / 6 oz / 1 cup self-raising flour
3 tbsp cocoa powder
2 tsp baking powder
175 g / 6 oz / ¾ cup caster (superfine) sugar
175 g / 6 oz / ¾ cup butter
3 eggs

FOR THE GANACHE
100 ml / 3 ½ fl. oz / ⅔ cup double (heavy) cream
100 g / 3 ½ oz / ⅔ cup milk chocolate, chopped
300 g / 10 ½ oz / 2 cup strawberries, sliced

- Preheat the oven to 180°C (160°C fan) / 350F / gas 4, then grease and line a 23cm (9in) round cake tin.
- In a large mixing bowl, whisk together all the cake ingredients until fully combined.
- Scrape the mixture into the prepared cake tin and bake for 30–35 minutes.
- Test the cake with a toothpick; if it comes out clean, the cake is done.
- Transfer the cake to a wire rack to cool.
- Heat the cream in a small saucepan set over a medium heat and bring to a simmer. Pour it over the chopped chocolate and stir until smooth.
- Pour the slightly cooled chocolate glaze over the cakes, allowing it to drip down the sides.
- Put the cake in the fridge for 1 hour to set, then pile the strawberries on top to finish.

Daisy cupcakes

PREPARATION TIME: 20 minutes
COOKING TIME: 15-20 minutes
MAKES: 12

110 g / 4 oz / ⅔ cup self-raising flour, sifted
110 g / 4 oz / ½ cup caster (superfine) sugar
220 g / 8 oz / 1 cup butter, softened
2 large eggs
1 tsp vanilla extract
110 g / 4 oz / ½ butter, softened
225 g / 8 oz / 2 ¼ cups icing (confectioner's) sugar
2 tbsp milk
a few drops of yellow food dye
sugar daisies to decorate

- Preheat the oven to 190°C (170°C fan) / 375F / gas 5, then line a 12-hole cupcake tin with paper cases. In a large mixing bowl, combine the flour, sugar, half the butter, eggs and vanilla extract and whisk together until smooth.
- Divide the mixture between the paper cases, then bake for 15–20 minutes. Test the cakes with a wooden toothpick; if it comes out clean, the cakes are done. Transfer to a wire rack to cool.
- Beat the remaining butter with a wooden spoon until light and fluffy, then beat in the icing sugar a bit at a time. Use a whisk to incorporate the milk, then whisk until smooth. Add a few drops of yellow food dye to the buttercream and spoon into a piping bag fitted with a round nozzle. Pipe a rosette onto each cupcake and press a sugar daisy into the top.

Rose water daisy cupcakes
Add 1 tbsp rose water to the cake mixture along with the vanilla extract, then a further teaspoon to the buttercream.

Sesame seed and cinnamon cookies

PREPARATION TIME: 10 minutes
COOKING TIME: 12-15 minutes
MAKES: 36

225 g / 8 oz / 1 ⅓ cup light brown sugar
100 g / 3 ½ oz / ½ cup caster (superfine) sugar
175 g / 6 oz / ¾ cup butter, melted
2 tsp ground cinnamon
1 egg, plus 1 egg yolk
250 g / 9 oz / 1 ½ cups self-raising flour
100 g / 3 ½ oz / ⅔ cup sesame seeds

- Preheat the oven to 170°C (150°C fan) / 340F / gas 3, then line two baking trays with greaseproof paper.
- In a large mixing bowl, cream together the sugars, butter and ground cinnamon until pale and well-whipped.
- Beat in the egg and the yolk, followed by the flour and most of the sesame seeds.
- Dollop tablespoons of the mixture onto the prepared baking trays, leaving room for the cookies to spread, and sprinkle over the sesame seeds.
- Bake the cookies in batches for 12–15 minutes or until the edges start to brown, but the centres are still chewy. Transfer to a wire rack and leave to cool completely.

Sunflower seed chocolate cookies
Replace the ground cinnamon with 100 g / 3 ½ oz / ⅔ cup milk chocolate chips, then top the cookies with sunflower seeds and bake as normal.

Toffee drizzle cake

PREPARATION TIME: 20 minutes
COOKING TIME: 45-50 minutes
SERVES: 12

150 g / 5 ½ oz / 1 cup self-raising flour
150 g / 5 ½ oz / ¾ cup muscovado sugar
150 g / 5 ½ oz / ⅔ cup butter
3 large eggs
1 tsp baking powder
1 tsp vanilla extract

FOR THE TOFFEE SAUCE
100 g / 3 ½ oz / ½ cup butter
100 g / 3 ½ oz / ½ cup muscovado sugar
100 g / 3 ½ oz / ⅓ cup golden syrup

- Preheat the oven to 180°C (160°C fan) / 350F / gas 4, then grease and line a 23 cm (9 in) round cake tin.
- Put all the cake ingredients in a large mixing bowl and whisk until pale and well-whipped. Scrape the mixture into the prepared tin and level the top with a spatula.
- Bake for 45–50 minutes. Test the cake with a wooden toothpick; if it comes out clean, the cake is done.
- Meanwhile, put the toffee sauce ingredients in a small saucepan and stir over a low heat until the butter melts and the sugar dissolves. When it reaches boiling stage, take the pan off the heat.
- When the cake is done, prick the top with a skewer and spoon over half of the sauce.
- Allow the cake to cool for at least 15 minutes, then pour over the remaining sauce to finish.

Toffee and chocolate drizzle cake
Add 100 g / 3 ½ oz / ⅔ cup milk chocolate chips to the cake mixture, stirring until evenly distributed, then bake as normal.

Strawberry and mascarpone tart

PREPARATION TIME: 20 minutes
COOKING TIME: 10-18 minutes
SERVES: 8

450 g / 1 lb / 2 cups mascarpone
100 g / 3 ½ oz / 1 cup icing (confectioners') sugar
1 tsp vanilla extract
200 g / 7 oz / 1 ⅓ cups fresh strawberries, halved
1 tbsp runny honey
fresh mint leaves to garnish

FOR THE PASTRY
100 g / 3 ½ oz / ½ cup butter, cubed
200 g / 7 oz / 1 ⅓ cups plain (all-purpose) flour
1 egg, beaten

> **Plum and mascarpone tart**
> Replace the strawberries with the same
> quantity of ripe plums, halved and stoned.
> Coat the plums in sugar, then roast in the
> oven at 180°C (160°C fan) / 350F / gas 4 for
> 10–15 minutes until soft. Arrange on top of the
> mascarpone and brush with honey to finish.

- Preheat the oven to 200°C (180°C fan) / 400F / gas 6.
- Make the pastry first. Using your fingertips, rub the butter into the flour in a large mixing bowl until the mixture resembles fine breadcrumbs. Add enough cold water to bind.
- Chill the dough for 30 minutes, then roll out on a lightly floured surface and use to line a fluted baking tin.
- Prick the case with a fork, line with greaseproof paper and fill with baking beans or rice.
- Bake for 10 minutes, then remove the greaseproof paper and baking beans.
- Brush the inside of the pastry case with beaten egg and cook for another 8 minutes to crisp.
- In a clean bowl, whisk the mascarpone with the icing sugar and vanilla extract until smooth.
- When the pastry case has cooled to room temperature, spoon in the filling and level the top with a palette knife.
- Arrange the strawberries on top, brush with the honey and garnish with fresh mint leaves to finish.

Apple crumble tart

PREPARATION TIME: **50 minutes**
COOKING TIME: **35-40 minutes**
SERVES: **8**

450 g / 1 lb Bramley apples, peeled and chopped
50 g / 1 ¾ oz / ¼ cup caster (superfine) sugar
1 tbsp cornflour (cornstarch)
1 tsp ground cinnamon
200 g / 7 oz / 1 ⅓ cups plain (all-purpose) flour
100 g / 3 ½ oz / ½ cup butter, cubed and chilled

FOR THE PASTRY
150 g / 5 oz / ⅔ cup butter
100 g / 3 ½ oz / ⅔ cup plain (all-purpose) flour
50 g / 1 ¾ oz / ¼ cup ground almonds
75 g / 2 ½ oz / ½ cup light brown sugar

- Preheat the oven to 200°C (180°C fan) / 400F
  / gas 6. Make the pastry first. Sieve the flour into a
  mixing bowl. Rub in the butter using your fingers
  until the mixture resembles breadcrumbs.
- Stir in just enough cold water to bring the pastry
  together into a pliable dough, then chill for 30
  minutes. In a separate bowl, mix together the
  chopped apple, sugar, cornflour and cinnamon.
- Roll out the pastry on a lightly floured surface into
  a large circle. Transfer the pastry to a fluted baking
  tray, pressing it into the sides, then prick the base
  with a fork. Spoon the apples over the pastry.
- Sieve the flour into a large mixing bowl, then rub
  in the butter. Stir in the almonds and brown sugar.
  Take handfuls of the topping and squeeze it into a
  clump, then crumble it over the apples. Fold up the
  pastry edges and pinch to secure. Bake the tart for
  35–40 minutes until golden brown.

Apple and oat crumble
Replace the ground almonds with the same
quantity of rolled porridge oats.

Almond, lemon and treacle tart

PREPARATION TIME: **50 minutes**
COOKING TIME: **25-30 minutes**
SERVES: **8**

350 g / 12 ½ oz / 1 cup golden syrup
2 lemons, zest and juice
100 g / 3 ½ oz / 1 ⅓ cups white breadcrumbs
75 g / 2 ½ oz / ¾ cups ground almonds
icing (confectioners') sugar to dust
200 g / 7 oz / 1 ⅓ cups plain (all-purpose) flour
100 g / 3 ½ oz / ½ cup butter, cubed and chilled

- Preheat the oven to 200°C (180°C fan) / 400F
  / gas 6. Make the pastry first. Sieve the flour into
  a large mixing bowl, then rub in the butter using
  your fingertips until the mixture resembles fine
  breadcrumbs. Stir in just enough cold water to
  bring the pastry together into a pliable dough,
  then chill for 30 minutes.
- Heat the golden syrup, lemon juice and zest in a
  small saucepan set over a medium heat, then stir
  in the breadcrumbs and almonds.
- Roll out the pastry on a lightly floured surface
  and use it to line a 23 cm (9 in) round pie dish.
- Spoon the filling into the pastry case and level
  the top. Bake for 25–30 minutes or until the
  pastry is cooked through underneath. Dust with
  icing sugar to finish.

Orange and treacle tart
Substitute the lemon with the zest and juice of 1
large orange and bake as normal for a different
citrus flavour.

Gluten-free coconut loaf

PREPARATION TIME: 5 minutes
COOKING TIME: 45-55 minutes
SERVES: 8-10

225 g / 8 oz / 1 cup butter, softened
225 g / 8 oz / 1 cup caster (superfine) sugar
1 vanilla pod, seeds only
4 large eggs, beaten
225 g / 4 ½ oz / 1 ½ cups rice flour
1 tsp baking powder
100 g / 3 ½ oz / 1 cup desiccated coconut

- Preheat the oven to 180°C (160°C fan) / 350F / gas 4, then grease and line a large loaf tin with greaseproof paper.
- In a large mixing bowl, cream the butter, sugar and vanilla seeds until well-whipped.
- Gradually whisk in the eggs, beating well each time.
- Fold in the flour and coconut, then scrape the mixture into the tin.
- Bake the cake for 45–55 minutes. Test the cake with a wooden toothpick; if it comes out clean, the cake is done.

Classic carrot cake

PREPARATION TIME: 25 minutes
COOKING TIME: 30-35 minutes
SERVES: 8-10

75 g / 6 oz / 1 cup light brown sugar
2 large eggs
150 ml / 5 fl. oz / ⅔ cup sunflower oil
175 g / 6 oz / 1 ¼ cup stoneground wholemeal flour
3 tsp baking powder
2 tsp ground cinnamon
½ tsp nutmeg freshly grated
1 orange, zest finely grated
200 g / 7 oz / 1 ⅔ cup carrots, washed and coarsely grated

FOR THE FROSTING
225g / 8 oz / 1 cup cream cheese
110 g / 4 oz / ½ cup butter, softened
225 g / 8 oz / 2 ¼ cups icing (confectioners') sugar
1 tsp vanilla extract
75 g / 2 2/3 oz / ⅔ cup walnuts, chopped

- Preheat the oven to 190°C (170°C fan) / 375F / gas 5, then line two 23 cm (9 in) round baking tins with greaseproof paper.
- In a large mixing bowl, whisk together the sugar, eggs and oil together until thick. Fold in the flour, baking powder, cinnamon and nutmeg then the orange zest and carrots.
- Divide the mixture between the tins and bake for 30–35 minutes. Test with a wooden toothpick; if it comes out clean, the cakes are done. Transfer the cakes to a wire rack and leave to cool completely.
- To make the icing, beat the cream cheese and butter together with a wooden spoon until light and fluffy, then beat in the icing sugar a bit at a time.
- Add the vanilla extract, then whisk the mixture until smooth and light.
- Use a third of the icing to sandwich the cakes together and spread the rest over the top and sides of the cake with a palette knife. Sprinkle over the chopped walnuts to finish.

Basil and Parmesan biscuits

PREPARATION TIME: **5 minutes**
COOKING TIME: **5-10 minutes**
MAKES: **15**

300 g / 10 oz / 2 cups plain (all-purpose) flour
200 g / 7 oz / 2 cup Parmesan, grated
2 tbsp basil leaves, finely chopped
2 tsp baking powder
¼ tsp bicarbonate of (baking) soda
½ tsp sea salt
3 tbsp butter, chilled
100 ml / 3 ½ fl. oz / ½ cup milk
3 tbsp olive oil

- Preheat the oven to 200°C (180°C fan) / 400F / gas 6, the line a baking tray with greaseproof paper.
- Combine the flour, Parmesan, basil, baking powder, bicarbonate of soda and salt in a large bowl.
- Add the butter, then stir in the milk and oil until moistened.
- Spoon mounds onto the prepared baking tray, to make 15 biscuits.
- Bake them in the oven for 5–10 minutes or until golden brown.
- Transfer to a wire rack to cool.

Basil and sun-dried tomato biscuits
Add 100 g / 3 ½ oz / 1 cup chopped sun-dried tomatoes with the Parmesan to add an extra flavour.

Walnut choc-chip cookies

PREPARATION TIME: **10 minutes**
COOKING TIME: **12-15 minutes**
MAKES: **36**

225 g / 8 oz / 1 ⅓ cup light brown sugar
100 g / 3 ½ oz / ½ cup caster (superfine) sugar
175 g / 6 oz / ¾ cup butter, melted
2 tsp almond extract
1 egg, plus 1 egg yolk
250 g / 9 oz / 1 ⅔ cups self-raising flour
100 g / 3 ½ oz / ¾ cup walnuts, chopped
100 g / 3 ½ oz / ¾ cup chocolate chips

- Preheat the oven to 170°C (150°C fan) / 340F / gas 3, then line two baking trays with greaseproof paper.
- In a large mixing bowl, cream together the two sugars, butter and almond extract until pale and well-whipped.
- Beat in the egg and the yolk, then beat in the flour, walnuts and chocolate chips.
- Dollop tablespoons of the mixture onto the prepared baking trays, leaving room for the cookies to spread.
- Bake the cookies in batches for 12–15 minutes or until the edges are starting to brown, but the centres are still chewy. Transfer to a wire rack and leave to cool.

Chilli chocolate and walnut cookies
Add 1 tsp cayenne pepper into the mixture along with the walnuts and chocolate chips – you can double the quantity if you want your cookies even spicier. Bake as normal.

EVERYDAY COOKING | **BAKING**

White chocolate and raspberry banana loaf

PREPARATION TIME: 15 minutes
COOKING TIME: 55 minutes
MAKES: 1 loaf

3 very ripe bananas
110 g / 4 oz / ½ cup soft light brown sugar
2 large eggs
120 ml / 4 fl. oz / ½ cup sunflower oil
125 g / 4 ½ oz / ¾ cup plain (all-purpose) flour
2 tsp baking powder
100 g / 3 ½ oz / 1 cup white chocolate chunks
100 g / 3 ½ oz / ⅔ cup fresh raspberries
icing (confectioners') sugar to dust

- Preheat the oven to 170°C (150°C fan) 340F / gas 3. Line a large loaf tin with greaseproof paper.
- In a large mixing bowl, mash the bananas roughly with a fork, then whisk in the sugar, eggs and oil.
- Sieve the flour and baking powder into the bowl, then add the white chocolate and raspberries. Stir just enough to evenly mix all the ingredients together.
- Scrape the mixture into the prepared loaf tin.
- Bake for 55 minutes. Test the cake with a toothpick; if it is clean, the cake is done.
- Transfer the cake to a wire rack and leave to cool completely, then dust with icing sugar to finish.

Double chocolate raspberry and banana loaf
Add 55 g / 2 oz / ½ cup cocoa powder to the cake mixture and use either white, milk or dark chocolate chips (or a mixture) to give this cake a more indulgent chocolate flavour.

Lemon drizzle muffins

PREPARATION TIME: **10 minutes**
COOKING TIME: **15-20 minutes**
MAKES: **12**

110 g / 4 oz / ⅔ cup self-raising flour, sifted
110 g / 4 oz / ½ cup caster (superfine) sugar
110 g / 4 oz / ½ cup butter, softened
2 large eggs
1 lemon, zest finely grated

FOR THE DRIZZLE
2 lemons, juice and zest finely grated
4 tbsp caster (superfine) sugar
2 tbsp lemon curd
candied lemon peel

- Preheat the oven to 190°C (170°C fan) / 375F / gas 5, then grease a 12-hole muffin tin.
- In a large mixing bowl, combine the flour, sugar, butter, eggs and lemon zest and whisk together for 2 minutes or until smooth.
- Divide the mixture between the paper cases, then transfer the tin to the oven and bake for 15–20 minutes.
- Meanwhile, put the lemon juice, zest and sugar in a small saucepan and heat over a medium heat until the sugar dissolves. Stir in the lemon curd.
- When the cakes come out of the oven, spoon the syrup over the top and allow it to soak in as the cakes cool. Top with candied lemon peel to finish.

Pumpkin spice cupcakes

PREPARATION TIME: **10 minutes**
COOKING TIME: **15-20 minutes**
MAKES: **12**

100 g / 3 ½ oz / ⅔ cup self-raising flour, sifted
100 g / 3 ½ oz / ½ cup caster (superfine) sugar
100 g / 3 ½ oz / ½ cup butter, softened
3 large eggs
100 g / 3 ½ oz / ¾ cup pumpkin, finely grated
½ tsp nutmeg, freshly grated
½ tsp ground cinnamon
light brown sugar for dusting

* Preheat the oven to 190°C (170°C fan) / 375F / gas 5, then line a 12-hole cupcake tin with paper cases.
* In a large mixing bowl, combine the flour, sugar, butter and eggs, then whisk together until smooth. Fold in the grated pumpkin, nutmeg and cinnamon until just combined.
* Divide the mixture between the cupcake cases and sprinkle with light brown sugar, then bake for 15-20 minutes.
* Test with a wooden toothpick; if it comes out clean, the cakes are done. Transfer the cakes to a wire rack and leave to cool completely.

Pumpkin and raisin cupcakes
Add 100 g / 3 ½ oz / ⅔ cup raisins to the cupcake mixture along with the grated pumpkin, to give these cupcakes an extra fruity flavour.

Raspberry and chocolate sandwich

PREPARATION TIME: **10 minutes**
COOKING TIME: **45-50 minutes**
SERVES: **10-12**

225 g / 8 oz / 1 ½ cups self-raising flour
55 g / 2 oz / ½ cup unsweetened cocoa powder
3 tsp baking powder
275 g / 10 oz / 1½ cup caster (superfine) sugar, plus extra for dusting
225 g / 8 oz / 1 cup butter
4 large eggs
300 ml / 10 ½ fl. oz / 1 ¼ cup double (heavy) cream
200 g / 7 oz / ⅔ cup seedless raspberry jam (jelly)

* Preheat the oven to 180°C (160°C fan) / 350F / gas 4, then grease and line a 23 cm (9 in) round cake tin.
* In a large mixing bowl, whisk together the flour, cocoa, baking powder, 225g of the sugar, butter and eggs until well-whipped. Scrape the mixture into the prepared tin and bake for 45-50 minutes. Test the cake with a wooden toothpick.
* Transfer to a wire rack to cool, then use a serrated knife to slice the cake in half horizontally. Whisk the cream with the remaining sugar until it thickens and has a smooth texture, then use a palette knife to spread over the base of the cake. Spread the raspberry jam on the cut-side of the top half of the cake, then sandwich the cakes together. Sprinkle with sugar to finish.

Chocolate and blackberry sandwich
Replace the raspberry jam with the same quantity of blackberry jam, then sprinkle 100 g / 3 ½ oz / ⅔ cup blackberries over the filling.

THE COOKERY COLLECTION

Raisin and poppy seed loaf cake

PREPARATION TIME: 10 minutes
COOKING TIME: 35-40 minutes
MAKES: 1 loaf

150 g / 5 ½ oz / 1 cup self-raising flour
150 g / 5 ½ oz / ⅔ cup caster (superfine) sugar
150 g / 5 ½ oz / ⅔ cup butter
3 eggs
1 tsp baking powder
100 g / 3 ½ oz / ⅔ cup raisins
1 tbsp lemon juice
2 tbsp poppy seeds
icing (confectioners') sugar, to dust

- Preheat the oven to 180°C (160°C fan) / 350F / gas 4, then grease and line a large loaf tin with greaseproof paper.
- Put all the ingredients in a mixing bowl and whisk them together until pale and whipped.
- Scrape the mixture into the tin and level the top with a palette knife.
- Bake for 35–40 minutes. Test the cake with a wooden toothpick; if it comes out clean, the cake is done.
- Transfer the cake to a wire rack to cool completely, then dust liberally with the icing sugar.

Ginger snap biscuits

PREPARATION TIME: **10 minutes**
COOKING TIME: **12-15 minutes**
MAKES: **36**

75 g / 2 ½ oz / ⅓ cup butter, softened
100 g / 3 ½ oz / ⅓ cup golden syrup
225 g / 8 oz / 1 ½ cups self-raising flour
100 g / 3 ½ oz / ½ cup caster (superfine) sugar
1 tsp ground ginger
1 large egg, beaten

- Preheat the oven to 180°C (160°C fan) / 35oF / gas 4, then line two baking trays with greaseproof paper.
- Over a low heat, melt the butter and golden syrup together in a small saucepan.
- In a large mixing bowl, mix together the flour, sugar and ginger.
- Stir in the melted butter mixture and the egg.
- Dollop teaspoons of the mixture onto the prepared baking trays, leaving plenty of room for the biscuits to spread. Use the back of the teaspoon to flatten the tops slightly.
- Bake in batches for 12–15 minutes or until golden.
- Transfer the biscuits to a wire rack and leave to cool completely.

Ginger and raisin snaps
Add 100 g / 3 ½ oz / ½ cup raisins to the mixture just before baking, to give these biscuits a chewy texture.

Almond torte

PREPARATION TIME: 15 minutes
COOKING TIME: 25-30 minutes
SERVES: 8

2 large eggs, separated
150 g / 5 ½ oz / ⅔ cup caster (superfine) sugar
150 g / 5 ½ oz / ⅔ cup butter, melted
200 g / 7 oz / 2 cups ground almonds
2 tbsp flaked (slivered) almonds
icing (confectioners') sugar to dust

- Preheat the oven to 180°C (160°C fan) / 350F
  / gas 4 and line a loose-bottomed round cake
  tin.
- In a large mixing bowl, whisk together the
  egg yolks, sugar and butter for 4 minutes or
  until pale and thick, then fold in the ground
  almonds.
- In a separate bowl, whip the egg whites to
  stiff peaks, then fold it into the cake mixture.
- Scrape the mixture into the tin, being careful
  to retain the air, then sprinkle with flaked
  almonds.
- Bake for 25–30 minutes. Test the cake with a
  toothpick; if it comes out clean, the cake
  is done.
- Leave to cool in the tin for 10 minutes before
  transferring to a wire rack to cool completely.
- Dust with icing sugar before serving.

Almond and lemon torte
Add the zest and juice of 1 lemon to the mixture
along with the ground almonds to give this cake
a zesty kick.

Iced lemon loaf cake

PREPARATION TIME: **20 minutes**
COOKING TIME: **35-40 minutes**
MAKES: **1 loaf**

150 g / 5 ½ oz / 1 cup self-raising flour
150 g / 5 ½ oz / ⅔ cup caster (superfine) sugar
150 g / 5 ½ oz / ⅔ cup butter
3 eggs
1 tsp baking powder
1 tbsp lemon zest
2 tbsp lemon juice

FOR THE ICING
200 g / 7 oz / 2 cups icing (confectioners') sugar
1–2 tbsp lemon juice

- Preheat the oven to 180°C (160°C fan) / 350F / gas 4, then grease and line a large loaf tin with greaseproof paper.
- Put all the cake ingredients in a large mixing bowl and whisk them together until pale and well whipped.
- Scrape the mixture into the tin and level the top with a spatula.
- Bake for 35–40 minutes. Test the cake with a wooden toothpick; if it comes out clean, the cake is done.
- Transfer the cake to a wire rack to cool.
- Sieve the icing sugar into a bowl and stir in just enough lemon juice to produce a pourable icing.
- Pour the icing all over the cake, allowing it to drop down the sides.

Iced lemon and blueberry loaf
Add 100 g / 3 ½ oz / 1 cup fresh blueberries to the cake mixture, stirring to combine, then sprinkle a few blueberries over the icing to decorate.

Strawberry custard tarts

PREPARATION TIME: **45 minutes**
COOKING TIME: **15-20 minutes**
MAKES: **4**

FOR THE PASTRY
200 g / 7 oz / 1 ⅓ cups plain (all-purpose) flour
100 g / 3 ½ oz / ½ cup butter, cubed

FOR THE CUSTARD
2 large egg yolks
55 g / 2 oz / ¼ cup caster (superfine) sugar
1 tsp vanilla extract
2 tsp cornflour (cornstarch)
225 ml / 8 fl. oz / ¾ cup whole milk
200 g / 7 oz / 1 ⅓ cups strawberries, sliced
mint leaves to garnish

- Make the pastry first. Using your fingertips, rub the butter into the flour and add just enough cold water to bind. Chill the dough for 30 minutes.
- Preheat the oven to 200°C (180°C fan) / 400F / gas 6.
- Roll out the pastry on a lightly floured surface and use it to line four tartlet cases, rerolling the trimmings as necessary.
- Whisk the custard ingredients together in a jug and pour into the pastry cases.
- Arrange the strawberries around the top of the custard, cut side up.
- Bake the tarts for 15–20 minutes or until the custard has set and the pastry is crisp. Garnish with mint leaves to finish.

Blackberry custard tarts
Replace the strawberries with the same quantity of blackberries, pressing them into the top of the custard before baking.

Chocolate chunk cookies

PREPARATION TIME: **10 minutes**
COOKING TIME: **12-15 minutes**
MAKES: **36**

300 g / 12 oz / 1 ¾ cups caster (superfine) sugar
175 g / 6 oz / ¾ cup butter, melted
2 tsp vanilla extract
1 egg, plus 1 egg yolk
250 g / 9 oz / 1 ⅔ cups self-raising flour
100 g / 3 ½ oz / ⅔ cup chocolate chunks

- Preheat the oven to 170°C (150°C fan) / 340F / gas 3, then line two baking trays with greaseproof paper.
- In a large mixing bowl, cream together the sugar, butter and vanilla extract until pale and whipped.
- Beat in the egg and yolk, then beat in the flour and chocolate chunks.
- Dollop tablespoons of the mixture onto the prepared baking trays, leaving room for the cookies to spread.
- Bake the cookies in batches for 12–15 minutes or until the edges start to brown, but the centres are still chewy. Transfer to a wire rack and leave to cool.

White chocolate chunk cookies
Replace the chocolate chunks with white chocolate; use a rolling pin to break 100 g of white chocolate into chunks, then stir into the mixture with the flour.

Cranberry muffins

PREPARATION TIME: **10 minutes**
COOKING TIME: **20-25 minutes**
MAKES: **12**

175 g / 6 oz / 1 ¼ cups self-raising flour
2 tsp baking powder
175 g / 6 oz / ¾ cup caster (superfine) sugar
175 g / 6 oz / ¾ cup butter
3 eggs
200 g / 7 oz / 1 ⅓ cups cranberries
icing (confectioners') sugar to dust

- Preheat the oven to 180°C (160°C fan) / 350F / gas 4, then line a 12-hole cupcake tray with paper cases.
- In a large mixing bowl, whisk together the flour, baking powder, sugar, butter and eggs until pale and well-whipped.
- Fold in the cranberries, reserving a few to garnish, then divide the mixture between the paper cases.
- Bake for 20–25 minutes. Test the cupcakes with a toothpick; if it comes out clean, the cakes are done. Transfer the cupcakes to a wire rack to cool, the dust with icing sugar and top the cakes with a few cranberries.

Cranberry and almond muffins
Halve the quantity of cranberries for the cake mixture, then stir in 100 g / 3 ½ oz / ⅔ cup chopped, blanched almonds and bake as normal. Top with cranberries and flaked (slivered) almonds.

THE COOKERY COLLECTION

Wholemeal banana loaf cake

PREPARATION TIME: 10 minutes
COOKING TIME: 55 minutes
MAKES: 1 loaf

3 very ripe bananas

110 g / 4 oz / ½ cup soft light brown sugar

2 large eggs

120 ml / 4 fl. oz / ½ cup sunflower oil

225 g / 8 oz / 1 ½ cups stoneground wholemeal flour

2 tsp baking powder

100 g / 3 ½ oz / ⅔ cup walnuts, chopped

- Preheat the oven to 170°C (150°C fan) / 340F / gas 3, then line a large loaf tin with greaseproof paper.
- In a large mixing bowl, mash the bananas roughly with a fork, then whisk in the sugar, eggs and oil.
- Sieve the flour and baking powder into the bowl and stir just enough to evenly mix all the ingredients together.
- Scrape the mixture into the loaf tin and sprinkle over the chopped walnuts, then bake for 55 minutes.
- Test the cake with a wooden toothpick; if it comes out clean, the cake is done.
- Transfer the cake to a wire rack and leave to cool completely.

Breads and other loaves

Milk bread rolls

PREPARATION TIME: 2 hours, 30 minutes
COOKING TIME: 15-20 minutes
MAKES: 16

400 g / 7 oz / 2 ⅔ cup strong white bread flour,
plus extra for dusting
½ tsp easy-blend dried yeast
1 tbsp caster (superfine) sugar
1 tsp fine sea salt
280 ml / 10 fl. oz / 1 ¼ cups whole milk, warmed

- In a large mixing bowl, combine the flour, yeast,
  sugar and salt, then stir in the warm milk.
- Knead the mixture on a lightly oiled surface for
  10 minutes or until smooth and elastic.
- Transfer the dough to a lightly oiled bowl, cover with
  cling film and leave to rest for 1–2 hours.

- Knead the dough for 2 minutes, then divide it into 16 even
  pieces and shape into small rolls.
- Transfer the rolls to a greased baking tray and cover with
  oiled cling film. Leave to prove for 1 hour or until doubled
  in size.
- Preheat the oven to 220°C (200°C fan) / 425F / gas 7.
- Transfer the rolls to the top shelf of the oven and pour
  a small cupful of water into the base of the oven.
- Bake for 15–20 minutes or until the rolls sound hollow
  underneath.
- Transfer to a wire rack and leave to cool.

Treacle bread

PREPARATION TIME: **2 hours, 30 minutes**
COOKING TIME: **35-40 minutes**
MAKES: **1 loaf**

400 g / 14 oz / 2 ⅔ cups strong white bread flour,
plus extra for dusting
¼ tsp easy-blend dried yeast
3 tbsp treacle
1 tsp fine sea salt
1 tbsp olive oil

- In a large mixing bowl, mix together the flour,
  yeast, treacle and salt.
- Stir the oil into 280 ml of warm water, then
  stir into the dry ingredients.
- Knead the dough on a lightly oiled surface
  for 10 minutes.
- Cover the dough with oiled cling film and
  leave to rest for 1–2 hours, or until doubled
  in size.
- Knead the dough for 2 minutes, then shape
  it into a round loaf.
- Transfer the loaf to a greased baking tray and
  cover again with oiled cling film. Leave to
  prove for 1 hour or until doubled in size.
- Preheat the oven to 220°C (200°C fan) / 430F
  / gas 7.
- When the dough has risen, score the top with
  a knife and dust with flour.
- Bake for 35–40 minutes or until the loaf
  sounds hollow underneath. Transfer the
  bread to a wire rack and leave to cool.

Beer bread

PREPARATION TIME: 2 hours, 30 minutes
COOKING TIME: 35-40 minutes
MAKES: 1 loaf

200 g / 7 oz / 1⅓ cup strong white bread flour,
plus extra for dusting

200 g / 7 oz / 1⅓ cup stone-ground wholemeal flour

½ tsp easy-blend dried yeast

1 tbsp caster (superfine) sugar

1 tsp fine sea salt

280 ml / 10 fl. oz / 1¼ cups real ale

1 tbsp mustard oil

Beer and mustard seed loaf
Add 1 tbsp of mustard seeds with the flour for an
extra burst of mustard flavour and a seeded texture.

- Mix together the flour, yeast, sugar and salt, then stir in
  the beer and oil.
- Knead the mixture on a lightly-oiled surface, then leave
  to rest in an oiled bowl for 2 hours.
- When the dough is ready, roll it into a large sausage
  shape, then turn it around and roll it the other way.
  Tuck the ends under and transfer the dough to a loaf tin,
  making sure the seam is underneath.
- Cover the tin loosely with oiled cling film and leave to
  prove for 45 minutes.
- Preheat the oven to 220°C (200°C fan) / 425F / gas 7.
- Transfer the tin to top shelf of the oven, then pour a small
  cup of water onto the over floor and close the door.
- Bake for 35–40 minutes or until the loaf sounds hollow
  when you tap it underneath. Transfer the bread to a wire
  rack and leave to cool completely before slicing.

Cheese-stuffed bread rolls

PREPARATION TIME: **2 hours, 30 minutes**
COOKING TIME: **15-20 minutes**
MAKES: **12**

350 g / 12 ½ oz / 2 ⅓ cups strong white bread flour,
plus extra for dusting
50 g / 1 ¾ oz / ⅓ cup stoneground wholemeal flour
½ tsp easy-blend dried yeast
1 tbsp caster (superfine) sugar
1 tsp fine sea salt
100 g / 3 ½ oz / ⅔ cup cottage cheese
1 tbsp dried parsley

- In a large mixing bowl, mix together the flours, yeast, sugar and salt, then stir in 280 ml of warm water.
- Knead the mixture on a lightly oiled surface until smooth and elastic. Transfer to a lightly oiled bowl, cover with cling film and leave to rest for 1–2 hours.
- Knead the dough for 2 more minutes, then divide it into 12 even pieces and shape into rolls.
- Transfer the rolls to a greased baking tray and cover with oiled cling film. Leave to prove for 1 hour.
- Preheat the oven to 220°C (200°C fan) / 425F / gas 7. Slash the tops of the rolls with a sharp knife and press a teaspoon of cheese on top and sprinkle with parsley.
- Bake for 15–20 minutes or until the rolls sound hollow underneath. Transfer to a rack and serve warm or cooled.

Stilton-stuffed bread rolls
Substitute the cottage cheese for the same quantity of
Stilton to give these bread rolls a stronger flavour.

Poppy seed twist bread

PREPARATION TIME: **2 hours, 30 minutes**
COOKING TIME: **25-30 minutes**
MAKES: **1 loaf**

400 g / 14 oz / 2 ⅔ cups strong white bread flour, plus extra for dusting

½ tsp easy-blend dried yeast

1 tbsp caster (superfine) sugar

1 tsp fine sea salt

4 tbsp poppy seeds

1 tbsp olive oil

1 egg, beaten

- In a large mixing bowl, mix together the flour, yeast, sugar, salt and poppy seeds, reserving some to decorate.
- Stir in the oil and add 280 ml of warm water.
- Knead the mixture on a lightly oiled surface for 10 minutes or until smooth and elastic.
- Cover the dough with cling film and leave to rest for 1-2 hours, or until doubled in size.
- Knead the dough again, then divide in two and shape into long batons.
- Twist the batons together and transfer to a greased baking tray. Cover with oiled cling film and leave to prove for 1 hour or until doubled in size.
- Preheat the oven to 220°C (200°C fan) / 425F / gas 7.
- Brush the dough with egg and sprinkle with the remaining poppy seeds.
- Bake for 25-30 minutes or until the loaf sounds hollow underneath.
- Transfer to a wire rack and leave to cool.

Wholemeal twist bread
Replace half of the bread flour with stoneground wholemeal flour, then bake as normal.

Round spelt loaf

PREPARATION TIME: **2 hours, 30 minutes**
COOKING TIME: **35-40 minutes**
MAKES: **1 loaf**

400 g / 14 oz / 2 ⅔ cup spelt flour
½ tsp easy-blend dried yeast
1 tbsp caster (superfine) sugar
1 tsp fine sea salt
1 tbsp olive oil

- In large mixing bowl, mix together the flour, yeast, sugar and salt.
- Stir in the oil and add 280 ml of warm water.
- Knead on a lightly oiled surface for 10 minutes or until the dough is elastic.
- Cover the dough with oiled cling film and leave to rest for 1-2 hours, or until the dough has doubled in size.
- Knead the dough for 2 minutes, then shape it into a round loaf.
- Transfer the loaf to a greased baking tray and cover with oiled cling film. Leave to prove for 1 hour or until doubled in size.
- Preheat the oven to 220°C (200°C fan) / 425F / gas 7.
- When the dough has risen, score the top with a knife and dust with flour.
- Bake for 35-40 minutes. Transfer the bread to a wire rack and leave to cool.

Nutty granary bread

PREPARATION TIME: 2 hours, 30 minutes
COOKING TIME: 35-40 minutes
MAKES: 1 loaf

300 g / 10 ½ oz / 2 cups malted granary flour
100 g / 3 ½ oz / ⅔ cup strong white bread flour,
plus extra for dusting
75 g / 2 ½ oz / ⅔ cup hazelnuts (cobnuts), chopped
75 g / 2 ½ oz / ⅔ cup walnuts, chopped
75 g / 2 ½ oz / ⅔ cup pistachios, chopped
½ tsp easy-blend dried yeast
2 tbsp caster (superfine) sugar
1 tsp fine sea salt
1 tbsp olive oil

- In a large mixing bowl, mix together the flours, nuts, yeast, sugar and salt.
- Stir in the oil and add 280 ml of warm water.
- Knead the mixture on a lightly oiled surface for 10 minutes or until smooth and elastic.
- Cover the dough with oiled cling film and leave to rest for 1–2 hours or until doubled in size.
- Knead for 2 minutes, then shape the dough into a round, dome-shaped loaf.
- Transfer the loaf to an oiled baking tray, cover with oiled cling film and leave to prove for 1 hour or until it has doubled in size.
- Preheat the oven to 220°C (200°C fan) / 430F / gas 7.
- When the dough is ready, dust the loaf with flour and slash the top with a knife.
- Bake for 35–40 minutes or until the loaf sounds hollow underneath when tapped.
- Transfer to a wire rack and leave to cool.

Sun-dried tomato and feta bread

PREPARATION TIME: 2 hours, 30 minutes
COOKING TIME: 35-40 minutes
MAKES: 1 loaf

400 g / 14 oz / 2 ⅔ cups strong white bread flour
½ tsp easy-blend dried yeast
1 tbsp caster (superfine) sugar
1 tsp fine sea salt
100 g / 3 ½ oz / ½ cup sun-dried tomatoes in oil, drained
1 tbsp oil from the sun-dried tomatoes
100 g / 3 ½ oz / ½ cup feta, chopped

Wholemeal sun-dried tomato and feta bread
Replace the bread flour with the same quantity of
stoneground wholemeal flour, then bake as normal.

- In a large mixing bowl, mix together the flours, yeast, sugar and salt. Stir in the sun-dried tomatoes, the oil, feta and 280 ml of warm water.
- Knead on a lightly oiled surface for 10 minutes. Cover with oiled cling film and leave the dough to rest for 1–2 hours, or until doubled in size.
- Knead again, then shape the dough into a round loaf. Transfer the loaf to a greased baking tray and cover again with oiled cling film. Leave to prove for 1 hour.
- Preheat the oven to 220°C (200°C fan) / 425F / gas 7.
- When the dough has risen, transfer to the top shelf of the oven, then pour a small cupful of water onto the base of the oven and close the door.
- Bake for 35–40 minutes or until the loaf sounds hollow underneath. Transfer the bread to a wire rack and leave to cool.

Walnut bread

PREPARATION TIME: 2 hours, 30 minutes
COOKING TIME: 35-40 minutes
MAKES: 1 loaf

200 g / 7 oz / 1 ⅓ cups strong white bread flour, plus extra for dusting
200 g / 7 oz / 1 ⅓ cups stoneground wholemeal flour
½ tsp easy-blend dried yeast
1 tbsp caster (superfine) sugar
1 tsp fine sea salt
100 g / 3 ½ oz / ¾ cup walnuts, chopped
1 tbsp walnut oil

- In a large mixing bowl, mix together the flours, yeast, sugar, salt and walnuts.
- Stir the walnut oil into 280 ml of warm water, then stir into the dry ingredients.
- Knead the dough on a lightly oiled surface for 10 minutes, or until the dough is smooth and elastic in consistency.
- Cover the dough with oiled cling film and leave to rest for 1–2 hours, or until doubled in size.
- Knead the dough for 2 minutes, then shape it into a long loaf.
- Transfer the loaf to a greased baking tray and cover again with oiled cling film. Leave to prove for 1 hour or until doubled in size.
- Preheat the oven to 220°C (200°C fan) / 430F / gas 7.
- When the dough has risen, slash the top with a knife.
- Transfer the tray to the top shelf of the oven, then pour a small cupful of water into the base of the oven.
- Bake for 35–40 minutes or until the loaf sounds hollow underneath. Transfer the bread to a wire rack and leave to cool.

White walnut bread
Remove the stoneground wholemeal flour and double the quantity of strong white bread flour if you prefer a white loaf.

Carrot and walnut loaf

PREPARATION TIME: **10 minutes**
COOKING TIME: **55 minutes**
MAKES: **1 Loaf**

300 g / 10 ½ oz / 2 cups self-raising flour
2 tsp baking powder
250 g / 9 oz / 1 ¼ cup butter, softened
5 large eggs
2 carrots, peeled and grated
150 g / 5 ½ oz / 1 cup walnuts, chopped

- Preheat the oven to 170°C (150°C fan) / 340F / gas 3. Line a loaf tin with greaseproof paper.
- Sieve the flour and baking powder into a large mixing bowl, then add the butter and eggs. Beat the mixture until smooth.
- Fold in the carrots and walnuts, then scrape the mixture into the loaf tin.
- Bake for 55 minutes. Test with a wooden toothpick; if it comes out clean, it is done.
- Transfer the loaf to a wire rack and leave to cool completely before serving.

Carrot and Roquefort loaf
For a more savoury flavour, replace the walnuts with 150 g / 5 ½ oz / 1 cup cubed Roquefort and 75 g / 2 ½ oz / ¾ cup grated Parmesan, folded into the mixture with the carrots. Bake in the same way as the above recipe.

Cheese and onion loaf

PREPARATION TIME: 10 minutes
COOKING TIME: 20-25 minutes
SERVES: 8

2 large eggs
120 ml / 4 fl. oz / ½ cup sunflower oil
180 ml / 6 fl. oz / ⅔ cup Greek yogurt
110 g / 4 oz / 1 cup Cheddar, grated
110 g / 4 oz / 1 cup goat's cheese, cubed
110 g / 4 oz / 1 cup Roquefort, cubed
2 spring onions (scallions), trimmed and finely sliced
225 g / 8 oz / 1 ½ cups plain (all-purpose) flour
2 tsp baking powder
½ tsp bicarbonate of (baking) soda
½ tsp salt

- Preheat the oven to 180°C (160°C fan) / 350F / gas 4. Line a large loaf tin with greaseproof paper.
- Beat the eggs in a jug with the oil, yogurt and cheeses until well mixed.
- Mix the spring onions, flour, baking powder, bicarbonate of soda and salt in a bowl, then pour in the egg mixture and stir just enough to combine.
- Scrape the mixture into the tin, then bake in the oven for 20–25 minutes.
- Test with a wooden toothpick; if it comes out clean, the cake is done.
- Transfer the loaf to a wire rack and leave to cool completely.

Kamut loaf

PREPARATION TIME: 2 hours, 30 minutes
COOKING TIME: 35-40 minutes
MAKES: 1 loaf

200 g / 7 oz / 1 ⅓ cups strong white bread flour, plus extra for dusting

200 g / 7 oz / 1 ⅓ cups kamut flour

½ tsp easy-blend dried yeast

1 tbsp caster (superfine) sugar

1 tsp fine sea salt

1 tbsp olive oil

- In a large mixing bowl, mix together the flours, yeast, sugar and salt.
- Stir in the oil and add 280 ml of warm water.
- Knead the dough on a lightly oiled surface for 10 minutes, or until smooth and elastic.
- Cover the dough with oiled cling film and leave to rest for 1–2 hours, or until doubled in size.
- Knead the dough for 2 minutes, then shape it into a round loaf.
- Transfer the loaf to a greased baking tray and cover with oiled cling film. Leave to prove for 1 hour or until doubled in size.
- Preheat the oven to 220°C (200°C fan) / 425F / gas 7.
- When the dough has risen, score the top with a knife and dust with flour.
- Bake for 35–40 minutes or until the loaf sounds hollow underneath. Transfer the bread to a wire rack and leave to cool.

Olive and sun-dried tomato loaf

PREPARATION TIME: **25 minutes**
COOKING TIME: **20-25 minutes**
MAKES: **1 loaf**

2 large eggs
120 ml / 4 fl. oz / ½ cup sunflower oil
180 ml / 6 fl. oz / ⅔ cup Greek yogurt
110 g / 4 oz / ⅔ cup sun-dried tomatoes, chopped
110 g / 4 oz / ⅔ cup black olives, pitted and sliced
225 g / 8 oz / 1 ½ cups plain (all-purpose) flour
2 tsp baking powder
½ tsp bicarbonate of (baking) soda
½ tsp salt

- Preheat the oven to 180°C (160°C fan) / 350F / gas 4. Line a large loaf tin with greaseproof paper.
- Beat the eggs in a jug with the oil, yogurt, sun-dried tomatoes and olives until mixed.
- In a large mixing bowl, mix together the flour, baking powder, bicarbonate of soda and salt, then pour in the egg mixture and stir just enough to combine.
- Scrape the mixture into the tin, then bake in the oven for 20–25 minutes. Test with a wooden toothpick; if it comes out clean, the loaf is done.
- Transfer the loaf to a wire rack and leave to cool completely.

Chorizo and olive loaf cake
Add 110 g / 4 oz / ⅔ cup cubed chorizo to the mixture along with the tomatoes and olives, to give this loaf a spicy flavour.

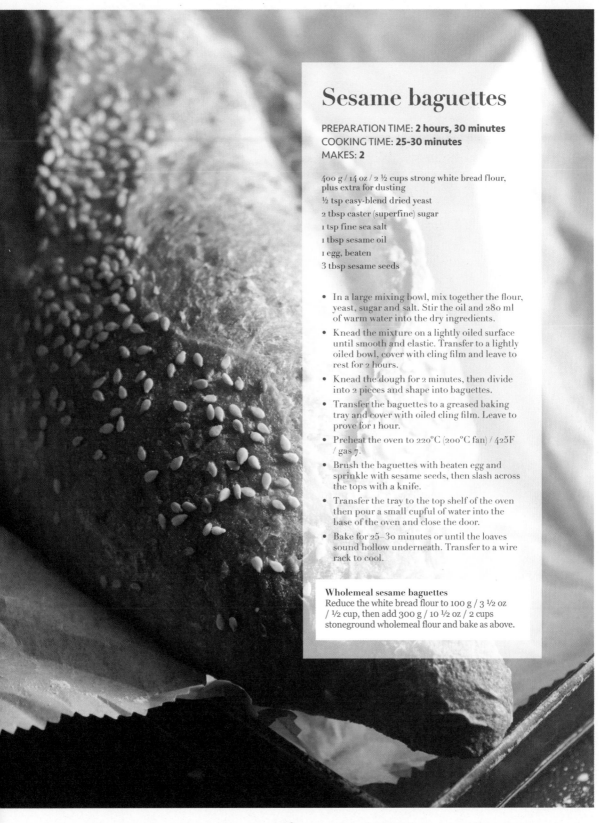

Sesame baguettes

PREPARATION TIME: **2 hours, 30 minutes**
COOKING TIME: **25-30 minutes**
MAKES: **2**

400 g / 14 oz / 2 ½ cups strong white bread flour, plus extra for dusting
½ tsp easy-blend dried yeast
2 tbsp caster (superfine) sugar
1 tsp fine sea salt
1 tbsp sesame oil
1 egg, beaten
3 tbsp sesame seeds

- In a large mixing bowl, mix together the flour, yeast, sugar and salt. Stir the oil and 280 ml of warm water into the dry ingredients.
- Knead the mixture on a lightly oiled surface until smooth and elastic. Transfer to a lightly oiled bowl, cover with cling film and leave to rest for 2 hours.
- Knead the dough for 2 minutes, then divide into 2 pieces and shape into baguettes.
- Transfer the baguettes to a greased baking tray and cover with oiled cling film. Leave to prove for 1 hour.
- Preheat the oven to 220°C (200°C fan) / 425F / gas 7.
- Brush the baguettes with beaten egg and sprinkle with sesame seeds, then slash across the tops with a knife.
- Transfer the tray to the top shelf of the oven then pour a small cupful of water into the base of the oven and close the door.
- Bake for 25–30 minutes or until the loaves sound hollow underneath. Transfer to a wire rack to cool.

Wholemeal sesame baguettes
Reduce the white bread flour to 100 g / 3 ½ oz / ½ cup, then add 300 g / 10 ½ oz / 2 cups stoneground wholemeal flour and bake as above.

Cinnamon and raisin bagels

PREPARATION TIME: 2 hours, 30 minutes
COOKING TIME: 20-25 minutes
MAKES: 10

500 g / 17 oz / 3 ⅓ cups strong white bread flour
½ tsp easy-blend dried yeast
4 tbsp caster (superfine) sugar
3 tsp ground cinnamon
100 g / 3 ½ oz / ⅔ cup raisins
1 tbsp sunflower oil
1 egg, beaten

- In a large mixing bowl, mix together the flour, yeast, sugar, cinnamon and raisins.
- Stir the oil into 280 ml of warm water, then add to the dry ingredients.
- Knead on a lightly oiled surface for 10 minutes or until the dough is smooth and elastic. Cover the dough with cling film, then leave to rest for 1–2 hours or until doubled in size.
- Divide the dough into 10 equal portions, shape into balls, then cover with cling film and leave to prove for 30 minutes.
- Preheat the oven to 180°C (160°C fan) / 350F / gas 4, then grease two baking trays.
- When the dough has risen, use your finger to make a hole in the centre of each ball, swirling to stretch the dough a little. Be careful not to knock all the air out of the dough.
- Fill a large saucepan with water until boiling. Place 1–2 bagels in the water at a time and boil for 1 minute, turning over halfway. Drain well and arrange the bagels on the prepared baking tray.
- Brush the bagels with beaten egg and bake for 20–25 minutes or until cooked. Transfer to a wire rack to cool.

Spiced cranberry bagels
Replace the raisins with the same quantity of dried cranberries and the cinnamon with 3 tsp allspice, to give these bagels a festive twist.

Rustic wholemeal olive loaf

PREPARATION TIME: 2 hours, 30 minutes
COOKING TIME: 35-40 minutes
MAKES: 1 loaf

200 g / 7 oz / ⅓ cup strong white bread flour,
plus extra for dusting

200 g / 7 oz / 1 ⅓ cups stoneground wholemeal flour

½ tsp easy-blend dried yeast

1 tbsp caster (superfine) sugar

1 tsp fine sea salt

100 g / 3 ½ oz / ⅔ cup mixed olives, pitted and sliced

1 tbsp olive oil

- In a large mixing bowl, mix together the flours, yeast, sugar, salt and olives.
- Stir in the oil and add 280 ml warm water.

- Knead the mixture on a lightly oiled surface for 10 minutes or until smooth.
- Transfer the dough to a lightly oiled bowl and leave to rest for 1–2 hours.
- Knead for 2 minutes, then shape into an oval loaf and transfer to a greased loaf tin.
- Cover the tin loosely with oiled cling film and leave to prove for 45 minutes.
- Preheat the oven to 220°C (200°C fan) / 425F / gas 7.
- Transfer the tin to the top shelf of the oven, then pour a small cupful of water into the base of the oven.
- Bake for 35–40 minutes or until the loaf sounds hollow underneath. Transfer the bread to a wire rack and leave to cool completely before slicing.

Wholemeal sun-dried tomato bread

PREPARATION TIME: **2 hours, 30 minutes**
COOKING TIME: **35-40 minutes**
MAKES: **1 loaf**

200 g / 7 oz / 1 ⅓ cup strong white bread flour,
plus extra for dusting

200 g / 7 oz / 1 ⅓ cup stoneground wholemeal flour

½ tsp easy-blend dried yeast

1 tbsp caster (superfine) sugar

1 tsp fine sea salt

150 g / 5 ½ oz / ¾ cup sun-dried tomatoes in oil, drained

1 tbsp olive oil

1 tbsp mixed dried herbs

- In a large mixing bowl, mix together the flours, yeast, sugar, salt and tomatoes.

- Stir in the oil and add 280 ml warm water. Knead the mixture on a lightly oiled surface for 10 minutes or until smooth and elastic.

- Transfer the dough to a lightly oiled bowl and leave to rest for 1–2 hours.

- Roll the dough with your hands into a fat sausage, then turn it around and roll it tightly the other way. Tuck the ends under and transfer the dough to a greased loaf tin, keeping the seam underneath.

- Cover the tin loosely with oiled cling film and leave to prove somewhere warm for 45 minutes.

- Preheat the oven to 220°C (200°C fan) / 425F / gas 7.

- Sprinkle the mixed herbs over the top, then transfer the tin to the top shelf of the oven. Pour a small cupful of water onto the base of the oven and close the door.

- Bake for 35–40 minutes or until the loaf sounds hollow when you tap it underneath.

Corn bread

PREPARATION TIME: **2 hours, 30 minutes**
COOKING TIME: **35-40 minutes**
MAKES: **1 loaf**

200 g / 7 oz / 1 ⅓ cup strong white bread flour
200 g / 7 oz / 1 ⅓ cup fine corn meal
1 tsp easy-blend dried yeast
2 tbsp caster (superfine) sugar
1 tsp fine sea salt
1 tbsp olive oil

- In a mixing bowl, mix together the flour, corn meal, yeast, sugar and salt. Stir in the oil and 280 ml of warm water.
- Knead the mixture on a lightly oiled surface for 10 minutes or until smooth and elastic.
- Cover the dough with cling film and leave to rest for 1–2 hours, or until doubled in size.
- Knead for 2 minutes, then roll the dough into a fat sausage. Roll it up the other way, then place into a greased loaf tin with the seam underneath. Cover the tin with oiled cling film and leave for 1 hour.
- Preheat the oven to 220°C (200°C fan) / 425F / gas 7.
- Bake for 35–40 minutes or until the loaf sounds hollow underneath. Transfer to a wire rack and leave to cool.

Granary corn bread
Replace the bread flour with the same quantity of granary flour, then bake as normal.

Onion bread

PREPARATION TIME: 2 hours, 30 minutes
COOKING TIME: 35-40 minutes
MAKES: 1 loaf

2 large onions, thinly sliced

3 tbsp olive oil

300 g / 10 ½ oz / 2 cups strong white bread flour, plus extra for dusting

100 g / 3 ½ oz / ⅔ cup stoneground wholemeal flour

½ tsp easy-blend dried yeast

1 tbsp caster (superfine) sugar

1 tsp fine sea salt

- Fry the onions in the oil over a low heat for 15 minutes or until starting to caramelise. Leave to cool.
- In a large mixing bowl, mix together the flours, yeast, sugar and salt. Add the onions, then stir in 280 ml of warm water.

- Knead the mixture on a lightly oiled surface for 10 minutes or until the dough is smooth and elastic.
- Transfer the dough to a lightly oiled bowl, cover with cling film and leave to rest for 1–2 hours.
- Roll the dough into a loaf shape, transfer to a lined baking tray and cover with cling film. Leave to prove for 1 hour.
- Preheat the oven to 220°C (200°C fan) / 425F / gas 7.
- Bake the loaf for 35–40 minutes or until it sounds hollow when tapped underneath.

Cheese and onion bread
Add 100 g / 3 ½ oz / ⅔ cup grated cheese, such as Cheddar, to the mixture along with the onions, stirring to incorporate. Bake as normal.

Herby cheese loaf

PREPARATION TIME: 10 minutes
COOKING TIME: 55 minutes
MAKES: 1 loaf

300 g / 10 ½ oz / 2 cups self-raising flour
2 tsp baking powder
250 g / 9 oz / 1 ¼ cups butter, softened
5 large eggs
100 g / 3 ½ oz / 1 cup Cheddar, grated
2 tbsp flat-leaf parsley, chopped
2 tbsp chives, chopped

- Preheat the oven to 170°C (150°C fan) / 340F / gas 3, then line a large loaf tin with greaseproof paper.
- Sieve the flour and baking powder into a large mixing bowl, then add the butter and eggs. Beat the mixture until smooth and well-whipped.
- Fold in the cheese and herbs, then scrape the mixture into the prepared loaf tin.
- Bake for 55 minutes. Test the loaf with a toothpick; if it comes out clean, the cake is done.
- Transfer the loaf to a wire rack and leave to cool completely before serving.

Herby cheese and tomato loaf
Add 100 g / 3 ½ oz / 2/3 cup sun-dried tomatoes (oil drained) to the mixture along with the cheese and herbs.

Wholemeal poppy seed loaf

PREPARATION TIME: 2 hours, 30 minutes
COOKING TIME: 35-40 minutes
MAKES: 1 loaf

300 g / 10 ½ oz / 2 cups stoneground wholemeal flour
100 g / 3 ½ oz / ⅔ cup strong white bread flour, plus extra for dusting
½ tsp easy-blend dried yeast
2 tbsp caster (superfine) sugar
1 tsp fine sea salt
1 tbsp olive oil
3 tbsp poppy seeds

- In a large mixing bowl, mix together the flours, yeast, sugar and salt.
- Stir in the oil and add 280 ml of warm water.
- Knead the mixture on a lightly oiled surface for 10 minutes or until smooth and elastic.
- Transfer the dough to a lightly oiled bowl, cover with cling film and leave to rest for 1–2 hours.
- Knead the dough for 2 minutes, then shape into an oval loaf and transfer to a greased baking tray.
- Cover with oiled cling film and leave to prove for 1 hour or until doubled in size.
- Preheat the oven to 220°C (200°C fan) / 425F / gas 7.
- When the dough is ready, sprinkle the top with poppy seeds.
- Transfer the tray to the top shelf of the oven, then pour a small cupful of water into the base of the oven.
- Bake for 35–40 minutes or until the loaf sounds hollow underneath. Transfer to a wire rack to cool.

Crusty bread rolls

PREPARATION TIME: 2 hours, 30 minutes
COOKING TIME: 15-20 minutes
MAKES: 12 rolls

350 g / 12 ½ oz / 2 ⅓ cups strong white bread flour,
plus extra for dusting
50 g / 1 ¾ oz / ⅓ cup stoneground wholemeal flour
½ tsp easy-blend dried yeast
1 tbsp caster (superfine) sugar
1 tsp fine sea salt
1 tbsp olive oil

- In a large mixing bowl, mix together the flours, yeast, sugar and salt. Stir in the oil and add 280 ml of warm water.

- Knead the mixture on a lightly oiled surface for 10 minutes or until smooth and elastic.
- Transfer the dough to a lightly oiled bowl and cover with cling film. Leave to rest for 2 hours.
- Knead the dough for 2 minutes, then portion into 12 pieces and shape into rolls.
- Transfer the rolls to a greased baking tray and cover with oiled cling film. Leave to prove for 1 hour.
- Preheat the oven to 220 C (200 C fan) / 425F / gas 7.
- Remove the cling film and dust the rolls with flour. Transfer the tray to the top shelf of the oven, then pour a small cupful of water into the base of the oven.
- Bake for 15–20 minutes or until the rolls sound hollow underneath and are crusty on top. Transfer to a wire rack and leave to cool.

Focaccia with rosemary

PREPARATION TIME: 2 hours, 30 minutes
COOKING TIME: 25-35 minutes
SERVES: 6

300 g / 10 ½ oz / 2 cups strong white bread flour
½ tsp easy-blend dried yeast
2 tsp fine sea salt
2 tbsp olive oil
1 tbsp dried rosemary leaves

- In a large mixing bowl, mix together the flour, yeast and 1 tsp of the salt.
- Stir in the oil and add 280 ml of warm water.
- Knead the mixture on a lightly oiled surface for 10 minutes or until smooth and elastic.
- Cover the dough with oiled cling film and leave to rest for 1–2 hours or until doubled in size.
- Oil a large rectangular cake tin, then stretch out the dough to fill the base of the tin.
- Cover the focaccia with oiled cling film and prove for 1 hour or until doubled in size.
- Preheat the oven to 220°C (200°C fan) / 425F / gas 7.
- Bake the focaccia for 25–35 minutes or until the top is starting to turn golden and the base is cooked through.
- Leave to cool on a wire rack then sprinkle with the remaining sea salt and dried rosemary.

Rosemary and olive focaccia
Knead 100 g / 3 ½ oz / ⅔ cup of pitted and chopped black olives into the mixture to make this focaccia more indulgent. Bake as normal.

Dried fig bread loaf

PREPARATION TIME: **2 hours, 30 minutes**
COOKING TIME: **35-40 minutes**
MAKES: **1 loaf**

400 g / 14 oz / 2 ⅔ cups strong white bread flour, plus extra for dusting
½ tsp easy-blend dried yeast
3 tbsp runny honey
100 g / 3 ½ oz / ½ cup dried figs, quartered
1 tsp fine sea salt
1 tbsp olive oil

Date and fig bread
Add 100 g / 3 ½ oz / ½ cup of coarsely chopped dates to the mixture along with the figs, to add an extra fruity kick to this bread loaf.

- In a large mixing bowl, mix together the flours, yeast, honey, figs and salt.
- Stir in the oil and add 280 ml of warm water.
- Knead the dough on a lightly oiled surface for 10 minutes or until the dough is smooth and elastic.
- Transfer the dough to a bowl and cover with oiled cling film. Leave to rest for 1–2 hours or until doubled in size.
- Knead the dough for 2 more minutes, then shape into a round loaf.
- Transfer the loaf to a greased baking tray and cover with oiled cling film. Leave to prove for 1 hour.
- Preheat the oven to 220 C (200 C fan) / 425F / gas 7.
- Remove the cling film from the dough, then slash the top with a knife and dust with flour.
- Bake for 35–40 minutes. Transfer the bread to a wire rack and leave to cool.

Rustic rye bread

PREPARATION TIME: 2 hours, 30 minutes
COOKING TIME: 35-40 minutes
MAKES: 1 loaf

200 g / 7 oz / 1 ⅓ cup strong white bread flour,
plus extra for dusting
200 g / 7 oz / 1 ⅓ cup rye flour
½ tsp easy-blend dried yeast
1 tbsp caster (superfine) sugar
1 tsp fine sea salt
1 tbsp olive oil

- In a large mixing bowl, mix together the flour, yeast, sugar and salt.
- Stir the oil into 280 ml of warm water, then stir into the dry ingredients.

- Knead the dough on a lightly oiled surface for 10 minutes.
- Cover the dough with oiled cling film, then leave to rest for 1–2 hours or until doubled in size.
- Knead the dough for 2 more minutes, then shape it into an oval loaf.
- Transfer the loaf to a greased baking tray and cover with oiled cling film. Leave to prove for 1 hour or until doubled in size.
- Preheat the oven to 220°C (200°C fan) / 425F / gas 7.
- When the dough has risen, bake for 35–40 minutes.
- Transfer the bread to a wire rack and leave to cool, then dust with flour to serve.

Rye and ginger bread
To give this loaf a hit of spice, add 1 tsp ground ginger to the mixture along with the rest of the dry ingredients, then bake as normal.

White bloomer loaves

PREPARATION TIME: **2 hours, 30 minutes**
COOKING TIME: **35-40 minutes**
MAKES: **2 loaves**

400 g / 14 oz / 2 ⅔ cups strong white bread flour,
plus extra for dusting

½ tsp easy-blend dried yeast

1 tbsp caster (superfine) sugar

1 tsp fine sea salt

1 tbsp olive oil

- In a large mixing bowl, mix together the flour, yeast, sugar and salt.
- Stir the oil into 280 ml of warm water, then stir it into the dry ingredients.
- Knead the mixture on a lightly oiled surface for 10 minutes or until smooth and elastic.
- Transfer the dough to a lightly oiled bowl, cover with oiled cling film and leave to rest for 1–2 hours or until doubled in size.
- Knead the dough for 2 minutes, then divide it into two even pieces and shape into two round loaves.
- Transfer the loaves to a greased baking tray and cover with oiled cling film. Leave to prove for 1 hour or until doubled in size.
- Preheat the oven to 220°C (200°C fan) / 425F / gas 7. Dust the loaves with flour and use a knife to slash a star shape in the tops of the loaves.
- Transfer the tray to the top shelf of the oven, then pour a small cupful of water into the base of the oven.
- Bake for 35–40 minutes or until the loaves sound hollow underneath. Transfer to a wire rack and leave to cool.

Tuscan bloomer

PREPARATION TIME: 2 hours, 30 minutes
COOKING TIME: 35-40 minutes
MAKES: 1 loaf

300 g / 10 ½ oz / 2 cups strong white bread flour, plus extra for dusting

100 g / 3 ½ oz / ⅔ cup whole wheat flour

½ tsp easy-blend dried yeast

2 tbsp olive oil

- Add the flour and yeast to a large mixing bowl and combine.
- Stir the oil into 280 ml of warm water, then stir into the dry ingredients.
- Knead the mixture on a lightly oiled surface for 10 minutes or until smooth and elastic.

- Transfer the dough to a lightly oiled bowl, cover with oiled cling film and leave to rest for 1–2 hours or until doubled in size.
- Knead the dough for 2 minutes, then shape into a round loaf.
- Transfer the loaf to a greased baking tray and cover with oiled cling film. Leave to prove for 1 hour or until doubled in size.
- Preheat the oven to 220°C (200°C fan) / 430F / gas 7. Dust the loaf with flour and slash the top with a knife.
- Transfer the tray to the top shelf of the oven, then pour a small cupful of water into the base of the oven. Bake for 35–40 minutes or until the loaf sounds hollow underneath. Transfer to a wire rack and leave to cool.

Poppy seed rolls

PREPARATION TIME: 2 hours, 30 minutes
COOKING TIME: 15-20 minutes
MAKES: 12

350 g / 12 ½ oz / 2 ⅓ cups strong white bread flour, plus extra for dusting

50 g / 1 ¾ oz / ⅓ cup stoneground wholemeal flour

½ tsp easy blend dried yeast

1 tbsp caster (superfine) sugar

1 tsp fine sea salt

1 tbsp olive oil

3 tbsp poppy seeds

Sea salt crusted rolls
Remove the poppy seeds from the recipe. Stir 2 tsp sea salt into 2 tbsp water to dissolve, then brush over the rolls before baking.

- In a large mixing bowl, mix together the flours, yeast, sugar and salt.
- Stir in the oil and add 280 ml of warm water.
- Knead the mixture on a lightly oiled surface for 10 minutes or until smooth and elastic.
- Transfer the dough to a lightly oiled bowl, cover with oiled cling film and leave to rest for 1–2 hours.
- Knead it for 2 minutes, then divide the dough into 12 even pieces and shape into rolls.
- Transfer the rolls to a greased baking tray and cover with oiled cling film. Leave to prove for 1 hour.
- Meanwhile, preheat the oven to 220°C (200°C fan) / 425F / gas 7.
- Sprinkle the poppy seeds over the rolls, then use a knife to slash a star shape in the top of the rolls. Bake for 15–20 minutes.
- Transfer to a wire rack and leave to cool.

Cheesy olive loaf

PREPARATION TIME: 25 minutes
COOKING TIME: 20-25 minutes
SERVES: 8

2 large eggs
120 ml / 4 fl. oz / ½ cup sunflower oil
110 g / 4 oz / ¾ cup Cheddar cheese, grated
50 g / 1 ¾ oz / ⅓ cup Parmesan cheese, grate
110 g / 4 oz / ⅔ cup black olives, pitted and sliced
225 g / 8 oz / 1 ½ cups self-raising flour
2 tsp baking powder
½ tsp bicarbonate of (baking) soda
½ tsp salt

- Preheat the oven to 180°C (160° fan) / 350F / gas 4, then grease a large loaf tin.
- Beat the eggs in a jug with the oil, cheeses and olives until well mixed.
- In a large mixing bowl, mix together the flour, baking powder, bicarbonate of soda and salt, then pour in the egg mixture and stir just enough to combine.
- Scrape the mixture into the loaf tin, then bake in the oven for 20–25 minutes.
- Test with a wooden toothpick, if it comes out clean, the loaf is done. Serve warm.

Black olive and parsnip loaf
Replace the cheeses with 180 ml / 6 fl. oz / ⅔ cup Greek yogurt and 110 g / 4 oz / ¾ cup grated parsnip, then beat with the eggs and oil in a jug. Bake as normal and serve warm.

Crusty bread fingers

PREPARATION TIME: **1-2 hours**
COOKING TIME: **15-20 minutes**
MAKES: **12**

400 g / 14 oz / 2 ⅔ cups strong white bread flour, plus extra for dusting
½ tsp easy-blend dried yeast
1 tbsp caster (superfine) sugar
1 tsp fine sea salt
1 tbsp olive oil

- In a large mixing bowl, mix together the flour, yeast, sugar and salt. Stir in the oil and add 280 ml of warm water.
- Knead the mixture on a lightly oiled surface for 10 minutes or until smooth and elastic.
- Transfer the dough to a lightly oiled bowl and cover with oiled cling film. Leave to rest for 1–2 hours or until doubled in size.
- Knead for 2 minutes, then portion the dough into 12 pieces and shape into finger rolls.
- Transfer the rolls to a greased baking tray and cover with oiled cling film. Leave to prove for 1 hour or until doubled in size.
- Preheat the oven to 220°C (200° fan) / 425F / gas 7.
- Remove the cling film and dust the rolls with flour, then slash the tops with a knife.
- Transfer the tray to the top shelf of the oven, then pour a small cupful of water into the base of the oven.
- Bake for 15–20 minutes or until the rolls sound hollow underneath. Transfer to a wire rack and leave to cool.

Seeded crusty bread fingers
Before baking, sprinkle the tops of the bread rolls with white sesame seeds to add extra texture to these crusty rolls.

Oat and seed artisan loaf

PREPARATION TIME: 2 hours, 30 minutes
COOKING TIME: 35-40 minutes
MAKES: 1 loaf

200 g / 7 oz / 1 ⅓ cup stoneground wholemeal flour
200 g / 7 oz / 1 ⅓ cup malted granary flour
½ tsp easy-blend dried yeast
1 tbsp caster (superfine) sugar
1 tsp fine sea salt
100 g / 3 ½ oz / 1 cup rolled porridge oats
55 g / 2 oz / ½ cup flax seeds
1 tbsp sunflower oil

- In a large mixing bowl, mix together the flours, yeast, sugar and salt.
- Add the oats and seeds, then stir in the oil and 280 ml of warm water to bring the mixture together.
- Knead the dough on a lightly oiled surface for 10 minutes or until the dough is smooth and elastic.
- Cover the dough with cling film, then leave to rest for 1–2 hours or until doubled in size. Knead again, then shape into a loaf.
- Transfer the loaf to a greased baking tray and cover again with oiled cling film. Leave to prove for 1 hour.
- Preheat the oven to 220°C (200°C fan) / 425F / gas 7.
- When the dough has risen, slash the top with a knife, then bake for 35–40 minutes or until the loaf sounds hollow underneath. Transfer the bread to a wire rack and leave to cool.

Two-flour bread loaf

PREPARATION TIME: 2 hours, 30 minutes
COOKING TIME: 25-30 minutes
MAKES: 1 loaf

200 g / 7 oz / 1 ⅓ cup strong white bread flour, plus
extra for dusting
200 g / 7 oz / 1 ⅓ cup stone-ground wholemeal flour
½ tsp easy-blend dried yeast
1 tbsp caster (superfine) sugar
1 tsp fine sea salt
1 tbsp olive oil

- Mix together the flours, yeast, sugar and salt,
  then stir in the oil and 280 ml of warm water.
- Knead the mixture on a lightly-oiled surface
  for 10 minutes or until smooth and elastic.
- Cover with cling film and leave the dough to
  rest for 1–2 hours, or until doubled in size.
- Once the dough has finished resting, knead
  for 2 minutes and roll into a baton shape.
- Transfer the loaf to a greased baking tray and
  cover with oiled cling film. Leave to prove for
  1 hour or until doubled in size.
- Preheat the oven to 220°C (200°C fan) / 430F /
  gas 7. Dust the loaf with the remaining flour
  and slash the top with a knife.
- Bake for 25–30 minutes, or until the loaf
  sounds hollow when you tap it underneath.
- Transfer to a wire rack and leave to cool.

Parmesan and flax seed rolls

PREPARATION TIME: **2 hours, 30 minutes**
COOKING TIME: **15-20 minutes**
MAKES: **12**

400 g / 14 oz / 2 ⅔ cups strong white bread flour
½ tsp easy-blend dried yeast
1 tbsp caster (superfine) sugar
1 tsp fine sea salt
1 tbsp olive oil
100 g / 3 ½ oz / 1 cup Parmesan, finely grated
1 tbsp flax seeds

- In a large mixing bowl, mix together the flour, yeast, sugar and salt. Stir in the oil, Parmesan and 280 ml of warm water.
- Knead the mixture on a lightly oiled surface for 10 minutes or until smooth and elastic.
- Transfer the dough to a lightly oiled bowl, cover with cling film and leave to rest for 1–2 hours.
- Knead the dough for 2 minutes, then divide it into 12 even pieces and shape into rolls.
- Transfer the rolls to a greased baking tray and cover with oiled cling film. Prove for 1 hour.
- Preheat the oven to 220°C (200°C fan) / 425F / gas 7.
- Use a knife to slash the top of each roll, then sprinkle with the flax seeds. Transfer the tray to the top shelf of the oven.
- Bake for 15–20 minutes or until the rolls sound hollow underneath.
- Transfer to a wire rack and leave to cool.

Parmesan and garlic rolls
Add 1 tsp ground garlic to the mixture along with the Parmesan to give these bread rolls extra depth of flavour.

Granary bread

PREPARATION TIME: 2 hours, 30 minutes
COOKING TIME: 35-40 minutes
MAKES: 2 loaves

300 g / 10 ½ oz / 2 cups malted granary flour
100 g / 3 ½ oz / ⅔ cup strong white bread flour, plus extra for dusting
½ tsp easy-blend dried yeast
2 tbsp caster (superfine) sugar
1 tsp fine sea salt
1 tbsp olive oil

- In a large mixing bowl, mix together the flours, yeast, sugar and salt.
- Stir in the oil and add 280 ml of warm water.
- Knead the mixture on a lightly oiled surface for 10 minutes or until smooth and elastic.
- Transfer the dough to a lightly oiled bowl, cover with cling film and leave to rest for 1–2 hours.
- Knead for 2 minutes, then split into two even pieces and shape each piece into a loaf.
- Transfer the loaves to a greased baking tray and cover with oiled cling film. Leave to prove for 1 hour.
- Preheat the oven to 220°C (200°C fan) /425F / gas 7.
- When the dough is ready, dust with flour and slash the tops with a knife.
- Transfer the tray to the top shelf of the oven, then pour a small cupful of water into the base of the oven.
- Bake for 35–40 minutes. Transfer to a wire rack and leave to cool.

Seeded granary bread
Add 3 tbsp mixed seeds (such as sunflower, sesame, linseed and pumpkin seeds) to the mixture and stir until evenly combined. Sprinkle the tops with more seeds before baking.

Chorizo bread ring

PREPARATION TIME: **2 hours, 30 minutes**
COOKING TIME: **25-30 minutes**
MAKES: **1 loaf**

200 g / 7 oz / ⅓ cup strong white bread flour, plus
extra for dusting
200 g / 7 oz / 1 ⅓ cup stoneground wholemeal flour
½ tsp easy-blend dried yeast
1 tbsp caster (superfine) sugar
1 tsp fine sea salt
1 tbsp olive oil

FOR THE STUFFING
100 g / 3 ½ oz / 1 cup chorizo, chopped
75 g / 2 ½ oz / ⅓ cup sun-dried tomatoes in oil,
drained and chopped
100 g / 3 ½ oz / ⅔ cup mozzarella, cubed
1 tbsp basil leaves, chopped

- In a large mixing bowl, mix together the
  flours, yeast, sugar and salt. Stir in the oil and
  280 ml of warm water.
- Knead the mixture on a lightly oiled surface
  for 10 minutes or until smooth and elastic.
- Cover the dough with cling film, then leave to
  rest for 1-2 hours or until doubled in size.
- Combine the stuffing ingredients in a
  separate bowl.
- Roll the dough out into a rectangle, then
  spoon the stuffing in a line down the middle
  and fold in the sides. Pinch to seal.
- Curl the dough round into a ring with the
  seam on top and transfer to a greased baking
  tray. Cover with oiled cling film and leave to
  prove for 1 hour.
- Preheat the oven to 220°C (200°C fan) / 425F
  / gas 7.
- Bake for 25-30 minutes or until the loaf
  sounds hollow underneath, then dust with
  flour to finish.

Cheese and pesto bread ring
Remove the chorizo from the filling and increase
the quantities to 100 g / 3 ½ oz / ⅔ cup sun-dried
tomatoes, and 150 g / 5 ½ oz / 1 cup mozzarella,
then stir in 1 tbsp pesto and bake as normal.

Crusty baton

PREPARATION TIME: **2 hours, 30 minutes**
COOKING TIME: **25-30 minutes**
MAKES: **1 loaf**

400 g / 14 oz / 2 ⅔ cups strong white bread flour,
plus extra for dusting
½ tsp easy-blend dried yeast
1 tbsp caster (superfine) sugar
1 tsp fine sea salt
1 tbsp olive oil

- Mix together the flour, yeast, sugar and salt in
  a large mixing bowl.
- Stir in the oil and add 280 ml of warm water.
- Knead the mixture on a lightly oiled surface
  for 10 minutes or until smooth and elastic.
- Transfer the dough to a bowl and cover with
  cling film, then leave to rest for 1–2 hours or
  until doubled in size.
- Knead the dough for 2 minutes, then roll into
  a tight baton.
- Transfer the dough to a greased baking tray,
  cover with oiled cling film, then leave to prove
  for 1 hour.
- Preheat the oven to 220°C (200°C fan) / 425F
  / gas 7.
- Remove the cling film and dust the dough
  with flour, then slash the top with a knife.
- Transfer the tray to the top shelf of the oven,
  then pour a small cupful of water into the
  base of the oven.
- Bake for 25–30 minutes, then transfer to a
  wire rack and leave to cool.

Seeded wholemeal rolls

PREPARATION TIME: 2 hours, 30 minutes
COOKING TIME: 10-12 minutes
MAKES: 8 rolls

400 g / 14 oz / 2 ⅔ cups stoneground wholemeal flour
½ tsp easy-blend dried yeast
1 tbsp caster (superfine) sugar
1 tsp fine sea salt
1 tbsp olive oil
2 tbsp sunflower seeds
2 tbsp hemp seeds
3 tbsp sesame seeds
3 tbsp poppy seeds

- In a large mixing bowl, mix together the flour, yeast, sugar and salt.
- Stir the oil into 280 ml of warm water, then stir into the dry ingredients.
- Knead the mixture with most of the seed mix on a lightly oiled surface for 10 minutes or until smooth and elastic.
- Cover the dough with oiled cling film and leave to rest for 1–2 hours or until doubled in size.
- Divide the dough into 8 pieces and shape into rolls, then transfer to a greased baking tray. Cover the rolls with oiled cling film and leave to prove for 1 hour or until doubled in size.
- Preheat the oven to 220°C (200°C fan) / 425F / gas 7.
- When the rolls have risen, sprinkle with the rest of the seeds. Transfer the tray to the top shelf of the oven, then pour a small cupful of water into the base of the oven.
- Bake for 10–12 minutes or until the rolls sound hollow underneath. Transfer to a wire rack to cool.

Chocolate and cranberry bread

PREPARATION TIME: 2 hours, 30 minutes
COOKING TIME: 25-30 minutes
MAKES: 1 loaf

400 g / 14 oz / 2 ⅔ cups strong white bread flour,
plus extra for dusting
½ tsp easy-blend dried yeast
1 tbsp caster (superfine) sugar
1 tsp fine sea salt
1 tbsp sunflower oil
200 g / 7 oz / 1 ⅓ cups chocolate chips
100 g / 3 ½ oz / ⅔ cup dried cranberries

- In a large mixing bowl, combine the flour, yeast, sugar and salt.
- Stir in the oil and 280 ml of warm water, until the mixture is fully combined.
- Knead the mixture on a lightly oiled surface for 10 minutes or until smooth and elastic.
- Transfer the dough to a bowl and cover with cling film, then leave to rest for 1–2 hours or until it has roughly doubled in size.
- Sprinkle over the chocolate chips and dried cranberries, then knead for 2 more minutes until both ingredients are evenly distributed.
- Fold the edges of the dough inward to create a rough diamond shape.
- Transfer the loaf to a greased baking tray and cover with oiled cling film. Prove for 1 hour.
- Preheat the oven to 220°C (200°C fan) / 430F / gas 7.
- When fully proved, slash the top of the loaf with a knife and transfer the tray to the top shelf of the oven. Pour a small cupful of water onto the oven floor and close the door.
- Bake for 25–30 minutes or until the loaf sounds hollow underneath, then sprinkle with the remaining flour.

Chocolate chip baton
Remove the dried cranberries and add 100 g / 3 ½ oz / ⅔ cup white chocolate chips to the mixture, to give this loaf a double choc hit.

Chorizo and tomato bread

PREPARATION TIME: **2 hours, 30 minutes**
COOKING TIME: **35-40 minutes**
MAKES: **1 loaf**

400 g / 14 oz / 2 ⅔ cups strong white bread flour,
plus extra for dusting

½ tsp easy-blend dried yeast

1 tbsp caster (superfine) sugar

1 tsp fine sea salt

200 g / 7 oz cooking chorizo, cubed

100 g / 3 ½ oz / ½ cup sun-dried tomatoes

- In a large bowl, mix together the flour, yeast, sugar and salt.
- Add the chorizo and sun-dried tomatoes, then stir in 280 ml of warm water.
- Knead the mixture on the lightly oiled surface for 10 minutes, or until the dough is smooth and elastic.
- Transfer the dough to a lightly oiled bowl, cover with oiled cling film and allow to rest for 1–2 hours.
- Knock the air out of the dough with your fists, then knead for 2 minutes.
- Place the dough on a greased baking tray and cover with more oiled cling film. Leave to prove for 1 hour – the dough should double in size.
- Meanwhile, preheat the oven to 220°C (200°C fan) / 425F / gas 7.
- Bake for 35–40 minutes or until the loaf sounds hollow underneath. Leave to cool on a wire rack.

Chestnut and chorizo bread
Replace half of the strong white bread flour with 200 g / 7 oz / 1 ⅓ cup chestnut flour.

Black olive bread loaf

PREPARATION TIME: 2 hours, 30 minutes
COOKING TIME: 35-40 minutes
MAKES: 1 loaf

300 g / 10 ½ oz / 2 cups strong white bread flour, plus extra for dusting
100 g / 3 ½ oz / ⅔ cup stone-ground wholemeal flour
½ tsp easy-blend dried yeast
1 tbsp caster (superfine) sugar
1 tsp fine sea salt
100 g / 3 ½ oz / ⅔ cup black olives, pitted and sliced

- Mix together the flours, yeast, sugar and salt until combined, then stir in the olives and 280 ml of warm water.
- Knead the mixture on a lightly-oiled surface for 10 minutes or until the dough is smooth and elastic.
- Transfer the dough into a lightly-oiled bowl and cover with cling film. Leave to rest for 1–2 hours.
- When the dough is ready, knead for 2 minutes, then roll into a large sausage shape. Turn it around and roll the other way, then tuck the ends under and transfer the dough to a loaf tin, making sure the seam is underneath.
- Cover the tin loosely with oiled cling film and leave to prove for 45 minutes.
- Preheat the oven to 220°C (200°C fan) / 425F / gas 7.
- Transfer the tin to top shelf of the oven, then pour a small cup of water onto the oven floor and close the door.
- Bake for 35–40 minutes or until the loaf sounds hollow when you tap it underneath. Transfer the bread to a wire rack and leave to cool completely before slicing.

Black olive and feta loaf
Add 100 g / 3 ½ oz / ⅔ cup cubed feta cheese at the same time as the olives to make this loaf more indulgent.

Rye rolls

PREPARATION TIME: 2 hours, 30 minutes
COOKING TIME: 35-40 minutes
MAKES: 4 rolls

400 g / 14 oz / 2 ⅔ cup rye flour, plus extra for dusting
½ tsp easy-blend dried yeast
2 tbsp caster (superfine) sugar
1 tsp fine sea salt
1 tbsp olive oil
1 tbsp poppy seeds

- Mix together the flour, yeast, sugar and salt, then stir in the oil and 280 ml of warm water.

- Knead the mixture on a lightly oiled surface for 10 minutes, then transfer to a lightly oiled bowl, cover with cling film and leave to rest for 1–2 hours.

- Knead the dough for 2 minutes, then split into 4 equal pieces and shape into round rolls.

- Transfer the rolls to a greased baking tray and cover with oiled cling film. Leave to prove for 1 hour.

- Meanwhile, preheat the oven to 220°C (200°C fan) / 425F / gas 7.

- Dust the rolls with flour, sprinkle over the poppy seeds and transfer the tray to the top shelf of the oven. Pour a small cupful of water into the base of the oven and close the door.

- Bake for 35–40 minutes or until the rolls sound hollow when tapped underneath.

Rye and treacle loaf

PREPARATION TIME: 2 hours, 30 minutes
COOKING TIME: 35-40 minutes
MAKES: 1 loaf

400 g / 14 oz / 2 ⅔ cup rye flour, plus extra for dusting
1 tsp easy blend dried yeast
1 tbsp treacle
1 tbsp malt extract
1 tsp fine sea salt
1 tbsp olive oil

- In a large mixing bowl, mix together the flour, yeast, treacle, malt extract and salt.
- Stir the oil into 280 ml of warm water, then stir into the dry ingredients.
- Knead the dough on a lightly oiled surface for 10 minutes.
- Cover the dough with oiled cling film, then leave to rest for 1-2 hours or until doubled in size.
- Knead the dough for 2 more minutes, then shape it into a round loaf.
- Transfer the loaf to a greased baking tray and cover again with oiled cling film. Leave to prove for 1 hour or until doubled in size.
- Preheat the oven to 220°C (200°C fan) / 425F / gas 7.
- When the dough has risen, score the top with a knife and dust with flour.
- Bake for 35-40 minutes or until the loaf sounds hollow when tapped. Transfer the bread to a wire rack and leave to cool.

Tomato and pumpkin seed loaf

PREPARATION TIME: 15 minutes
COOKING TIME: 30-35 minutes
MAKES: 1 loaf

2 large eggs
120 ml / 4 fl. oz / ½ cup sunflower oil
180 ml / 6 fl. oz / ⅔ cup Greek yogurt
225 g / 8 oz / 1 ½ cup plain (all-purpose) flour
110 g / 4 oz / 1 cup feta, cubed
75 g / 2 ½ oz / ½ pumpkin seeds, plus extra for sprinkling
2 tsp baking powder
½ tsp bicarbonate of (baking) soda
½ tsp salt
150 g / 5 ½ oz / 1 cup cherry tomatoes, quartered

- Preheat the oven to 180°C (160°C fan) / 350F / gas 4, then line a loaf tin with greaseproof paper.
- Beat the eggs in a jug with the oil and yogurt until they are well mixed.
- In a large mixing bowl, mix together the flour, Feta, tomatoes, pumpkin seeds, baking powder, bicarbonate of soda and salt in a bowl, then pour in the egg mixture.
- Cut the tomatoes into quarters, reserving a few for the top of the loaf. Add the quartered tomatoes to the bowl and stir everything just enough to combine.
- Scrape the mixture into the tin, then stud with the reserved tomatoes and sprinkle with pumpkin seeds.
- Bake in the oven for 30–35 minutes. Test with a wooden toothpick; if it comes out clean, the cake is done.
- Transfer the loaf to a wire rack and leave to cool.

Tomato and mozzarella loaf
Replace the feta with the same quantity of mozzarella for a softer cheese filling.

Seafood loaf

PREPARATION TIME: 15 minutes
COOKING TIME: 30-35 minutes
MAKES: 1 loaf

2 large eggs
120 ml / 4 fl. oz / ½ cup sunflower oil
180 ml / 6 fl. oz / ⅔ cup Greek yoghurt
110 g / 4 oz smoked salmon, chopped
100 g / 3 ½ oz / ⅔ cup green olives, chopped
2 tbsp dill, chopped
225 g / 8 oz / 1 ½ cup plain (all-purpose) flour
2 tsp baking powder
½ tsp bicarbonate of (baking) soda
½ tsp salt

- Preheat the oven to 180 C (160 C fan) / 350F / gas 4, then line a loaf tin with greaseproof paper.
- Beat the eggs in a jug with the oil and yoghurt until well mixed.
- Mix the salmon, olives, dill, flour, baking powder, bicarbonate of soda and salt in a bowl, then pour in the egg mixture and stir just enough to combine.
- Scrape the mixture into the tin, then bake in the oven for 30–35 minutes.
- Test with a wooden toothpick; if it comes out clean, the cake is done.
- Transfer the loaf to a wire rack and leave to cool completely.

Seafood and sun-dried tomato loaf
Replace the green olives with the same quantity of sun-dried tomatoes, drained of their oil and finely chopped, to give this loaf a slightly sweeter flavour.

Date and pine nut loaf

PREPARATION TIME: 10 minutes
COOKING TIME: 45-50 minutes
MAKES: 1 loaf

100 g / 3 ½ oz / ⅔ cup self-raising flour
1 tsp baking powder
50 g / 1 ¾ oz / ½ cup ground almonds
150 g / 5 ½ oz / ⅔ cup caster (superfine) sugar
150 g / 5 ½ oz / ⅔ cup butter
3 large eggs
100 g / 3 ½ oz / ¾ cup pine nuts
100 g / 3 ½ oz / ⅔ cup dates, pitted and chopped

- Preheat the oven to 180°C (160°C fan) / 350F / gas 4, then line a loaf tin with greaseproof paper.
- Sieve the flour and baking powder into a large mixing bowl, then add the ground almonds, sugar, butter and eggs and whisk until pale and well-whipped.
- Fold in the pine nuts and dates, then spoon the mixture into the prepared loaf tin and bake for 45–50 minutes.
- Test the loaf with a toothpick; if it comes out clean, the cake is done.
- Transfer the loaf to a wire rack and leave to cool completely.

Date and walnut loaf
Replace the pine nuts with the same quantity of chopped walnuts, then sprinkle some extra nuts over the top of the cake before baking.

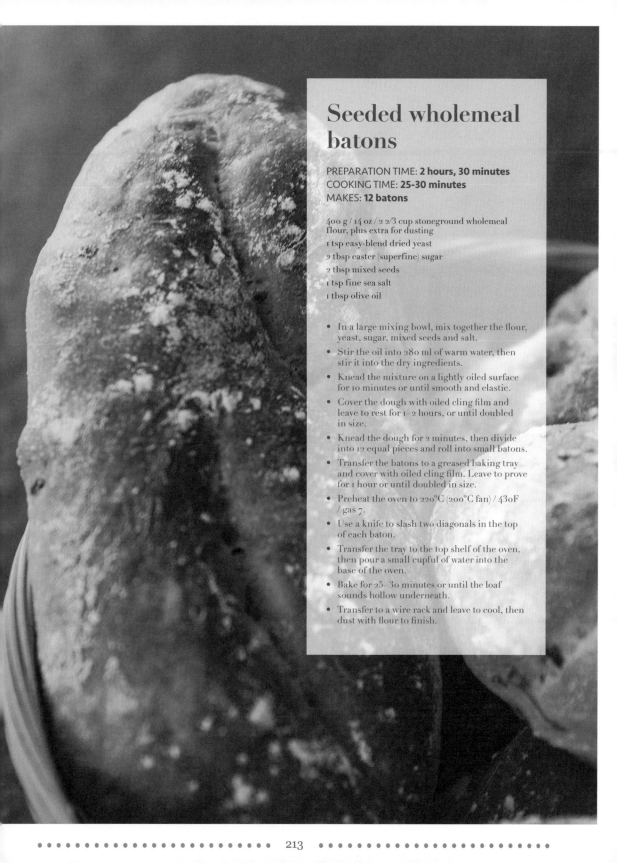

Seeded wholemeal batons

PREPARATION TIME: 2 hours, 30 minutes
COOKING TIME: 25-30 minutes
MAKES: 12 batons

400 g / 14 oz / 2 2/3 cup stoneground wholemeal
flour, plus extra for dusting
1 tsp easy-blend dried yeast
2 tbsp caster (superfine) sugar
2 tbsp mixed seeds
1 tsp fine sea salt
1 tbsp olive oil

- In a large mixing bowl, mix together the flour,
  yeast, sugar, mixed seeds and salt.
- Stir the oil into 280 ml of warm water, then
  stir it into the dry ingredients.
- Knead the mixture on a lightly oiled surface
  for 10 minutes or until smooth and elastic.
- Cover the dough with oiled cling film and
  leave to rest for 1–2 hours, or until doubled
  in size.
- Knead the dough for 2 minutes, then divide
  into 12 equal pieces and roll into small batons.
- Transfer the batons to a greased baking tray
  and cover with oiled cling film. Leave to prove
  for 1 hour or until doubled in size.
- Preheat the oven to 220°C (200°C fan) / 430F
  / gas 7.
- Use a knife to slash two diagonals in the top
  of each baton.
- Transfer the tray to the top shelf of the oven,
  then pour a small cupful of water into the
  base of the oven.
- Bake for 25–30 minutes or until the loaf
  sounds hollow underneath.
- Transfer to a wire rack and leave to cool, then
  dust with flour to finish.

Homemade wholegrain bagels

PREPARATION TIME: **2 hours, 30 minutes**
COOKING TIME: **20-25 minutes**
MAKES: **10 bagels**

400 g / 14 oz / 2 ⅔ cups stoneground
wholemeal flour
100 g / 3 ½ oz / ⅔ cup strong white bread flour
½ tsp easy-blend dried yeast
1 tbsp caster (superfine) sugar
1 tsp fine sea salt
1 tbsp sunflower oil
1 egg, beaten
50 g / 1 ¾ oz / ½ cup rolled porridge oats
50 g / 1 ¾ oz / ½ cup black and white sesame seeds

- In a large mixing bowl, mix together the
  flours, yeast, sugar and salt.
- Stir the oil into 280 ml of warm water, then
  add to the dry ingredients.
- Knead on a lightly oiled surface for 10 minutes
  or until the dough is smooth and elastic.
  Cover the dough with cling film, then leave to
  rest for 1–2 hours or until doubled in size.
- Divide the dough into 10 equal portions,
  shape into balls, then cover with cling film
  and leave to prove for 30 minutes.
- Preheat the oven to 180°C (160°C fan) / 350F /
  gas 4, then grease two baking trays.
- When the dough has risen, use your finger
  to make a hole in the centre of each ball,
  swirling to stretch the dough a little. Be
  careful not to knock all the air out of the
  dough.
- Fill a large saucepan with water until boiling.
  Place 1–2 bagels in the water at a time and
  boil for 1 minute, turning over halfway. Drain
  well and arrange the bagels on the prepared
  baking tray.
- Brush the bagels with beaten egg, top with
  the oats and seeds, then bake for 20–25
  minutes or until cooked. Transfer to a wire
  rack to cool.

Olive bread rolls

PREPARATION TIME: **2 hours, 30 minutes**
COOKING TIME: **15-20 minutes**
MAKES: **12 rolls**

400 g / 14 oz / 2 ⅔ cups bread flour, plus extra for dusting
½ tsp easy-blend dried yeast
1 tbsp caster (superfine) sugar
1 tsp fine sea salt
75 g / 2 ½ oz / ½ cup black olives, pitted and chopped
1 tbsp olive oil

- In a large mixing bowl, mix together the flour, yeast, sugar, salt and olives.
- Stir in the oil and add 280 ml of warm water.
- Knead the mixture on a lightly oiled surface for 10 minutes or until smooth and elastic.
- Cover the dough with oiled cling film and leave to rest for 1–2 hours, or until doubled in size.

- Shape the dough into 12 oval rolls, transfer to a greased baking tray and cover with cling film. Leave to prove for 1 hour.
- Preheat the oven to 220°C (200°C fan) / 425F / gas 7.
- When the dough has finished proving, slash the top of the rolls with a knife.
- Bake for 15–20 minutes or until the rolls sound hollow underneath.
- Transfer to a wire rack and leave to cool and dust with flour to finish.

Olive and Parmesan rolls
Add 75 g / 2 ½ oz / ¾ cup of finely grated Parmesan to the mixture along with the olives, stirring until combined, then bake as normal.

Cheesy chorizo and thyme loaf

PREPARATION TIME: **2 hours, 30 minutes**
COOKING TIME: **35-40 minutes**
MAKES: **1 loaf**

300 g / 10 ½ oz / 2 cups strong white bread flour,
plus extra for dusting
100 g / 3 ½ oz / ⅔ cup stoneground wholemeal flour
½ tsp easy-blend dried yeast
1 tbsp caster (superfine) sugar
1 tsp fine sea salt
100 g / 3 ½ oz / ⅔ cup chorizo, cubed
100 g / 3 ½ oz / ⅔ cup Manchego, grated
4 tbsp fresh thyme leaves

- In a large mixing bowl, mix together the flours, yeast,
  sugar and salt. Stir in the chorizo, Manchego and the
  thyme, then add 280 ml of warm water.

- Knead the mixture on a lightly oiled surface for 10
  minutes or until the dough is smooth and elastic.

- Transfer the dough to a lightly oiled bowl, cover with
  cling film and leave to rest for 1–2 hours. Line a loaf tin
  with greaseproof paper.

- Knead the dough for 2 more minutes, then roll it into a
  fat sausage. Turn it around and roll the dough tightly the
  other way, then tuck the ends under and transfer to the
  prepared tin with the seam underneath.

- Cover the tin with oiled cling film and leave for
  45 minutes.

- Preheat the oven to 220°C (200°C fan) / 425F / gas 7.

- When the dough is ready, bake for 35–40 minutes or until
  the underneath sounds hollow when tapped.

- Transfer the loaf to a wire rack to cool before serving.

Cheesy chorizo and tomato loaf
Add 100 g / 3 ½ oz / ⅔ cup sun-dried tomatoes (oil drained) to the mixture along with the chorizo to add a sweetness to this
savoury loaf.

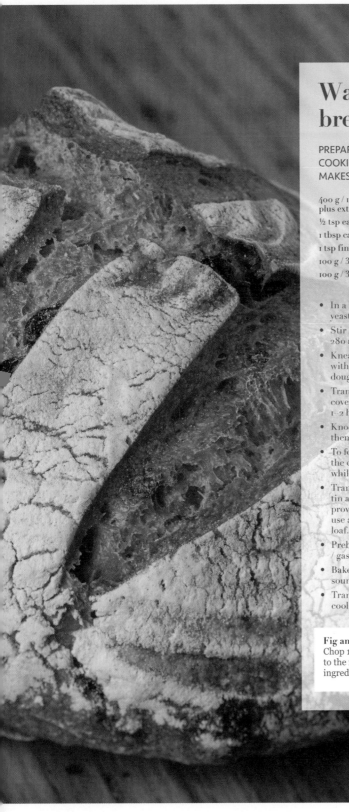

Walnut raisin bread

PREPARATION TIME: 2 hours, 30 minutes
COOKING TIME: 35-40 minutes
MAKES: 1 loaf

400 g / 14 oz / 2 ⅔ cups strong white bread flour, plus extra for dusting
½ tsp easy-blend dried yeast
1 tbsp caster (superfine) sugar
1 tsp fine sea salt
100 g / 3 ½ oz / ½ cup raisins
100 g / 3 ½ oz / ⅔ cup walnut halves

- In a large mixing bowl, mix together the flour, yeast, sugar and salt.
- Stir in the raisins and walnuts, then add 280 ml of warm water.
- Knead the mixture on a lightly oiled surface with your hands for 10 minutes or until the dough is elastic.
- Transfer the dough to a lightly oiled bowl, cover with cling film and leave to rest for 1-2 hours.
- Knock the air out of the dough with your fist, then knead for 2 minutes.
- To form a round loaf, cup your hands around the dough and move in a circular motion while pressing down.
- Transfer the dough to a greased round cake tin and cover with oiled cling film. Leave to prove for 1 hour or until doubled in size, then use a knife to slash a cross in the top of the loaf.
- Preheat the oven to 220°C (200°C fan) / 430F / gas 7.
- Bake for 35-40 minutes or until the loaf sounds hollow underneath.
- Transfer the bread to a wire rack and leave to cool completely before slicing.

Fig and walnut loaf
Chop 100 g / 3 ½ oz / ½ cup dried figs and add to the mix instead of the raisins. Ensure the ingredients are evenly distributed before baking.

Savoury bakes

Parmesan and thyme cookies

PREPARATION TIME: 10 minutes
COOKING TIME: 12-15 minutes
MAKES: 16

150 g / 5 ½ oz / 1 cup plain (all-purpose) flour
75 g / 2 ½ oz / ⅓ cup caster (superfine) sugar
110 g / 4 oz / 1 cup Parmesan, plus extra for sprinkling
2 tbsp fresh thyme leaves
½ tsp salt
150 g / 5 oz / ⅔ cup butter, cubed

- Preheat the oven to 180°C (160°C fan) / 350F / gas 4, then line a baking tray with greaseproof paper.

- In a large mixing bowl, mix together the flour, sugar, Parmesan, thyme and salt, then rub in the butter with your fingertips.

- Knead gently until the mixture forms a smooth dough, then roll out on a lightly floured surface to 5 mm thick.

- Use a cookie cutter to cut out 16 biscuits and spread them out on the baking tray, leaving room for the cookies to spread. Sprinkle a little grated Parmesan cheese over the tops.

- Bake the biscuits for 12–15 minutes, turning the tray round halfway through.

- Transfer the biscuits to a wire rack and leave to cool.

Rosemary and thyme cookies
Double up on fragrant herb flavours and add
1 tbsp dried rosemary leaves to the mixture along
with the thyme.

Ham and cheese pastry rolls

PREPARATION TIME: **10 minutes**
COOKING TIME: **10-15 minutes**
MAKES: **24**

250 g / 9 oz all-butter puff pastry
50 g / 1 ¾ oz / ⅓ cup tomato sauce
200 g / 7 oz smoked ham slices
150 g / 5 ½ oz / ⅔ cup Cheddar, grated
1 egg, beaten
spring onions (scallions), trimmed and sliced

- Preheat the oven to 220°C (200°C fan) / 425F / gas 7, then line a baking tray with greaseproof paper.
- Roll out the pastry on a lightly floured surface to about 5 mm thickness.
- Spread the pastry with a thin layer of tomato sauce. Add the slices of ham, then sprinkle over the Cheddar.
- Roll the pastry up into a tight sausage shape. Cut the roll into 2 cm (1 in) slices and arrange them on the prepared baking tray.
- Brush the rolls with the beaten egg, then bake for 10–15 minutes or until the pastry is golden.
- Transfer to a wire rack to cool slightly, then sprinkle with spring onions to finish.

Ham and mozzarella pastry rolls
Substitute the Cheddar for the same quantity of mozzarella, chopped into small pieces. Served warm, the mozzarella should be stringy.

Black sesame tuile biscuits

PREPARATION TIME: 45 minutes
COOKING TIME: 8-10 minutes
MAKES: 18

110 g / 4 oz / ⅔ cup plain (all-purpose) flour
110 g / 4 oz caster / ½ cup (superfine) sugar
2 large egg whites
110 g / 4 oz / ½ cup butter, melted
2 tbsp black sesame seeds

- Beat together the flour, sugar and egg whites until smooth.
- Beat the melted butter and sesame seeds into the mixture, then refrigerate for 30 minutes.
- Preheat the oven to 180°C (160°C fan) / 350F / gas 4, then oil two large baking trays.
- Using a teaspoon, spoon blobs of the mixture onto the baking trays. Use the back of the spoon to spread the mixture into 10 cm (4 in) circles.
- Bake the biscuits for 8–10 minutes, then use a palette knife to lift them off the trays and wrap them around a small rolling pin, or the handle of a wooden spoon.
- Leave to cool and harden.

Crispy cheese crackers

PREPARATION TIME: **10 minutes**
COOKING TIME: **8-10 minutes**
MAKES: **36**

225 g / 8 oz / 1 cup butter
½ tsp Cayenne pepper
175 g / 6 oz / 1 ¾ cups red Leicester cheese, grated
300 g / 10 ½ oz / 2 cups plain (all-purpose) flour

- Preheat the oven to 180°C (160°C fan) / 350F / gas 4, then line two baking trays with greaseproof paper.
- Melt the butter with the Cayenne pepper in a saucepan.
- Stir in most of the cheese and the flour, beating rapidly to form a paste.
- Dollop teaspoons of the mixture onto the prepared baking trays and spread the biscuits out thinly with the back of the spoon. Sprinkle over the remaining cheese.
- Bake in batches for 8–10 minutes.
- Leave the biscuits to harden on the tray for a few minutes, then transfer them to a wire rack to cool completely.

Cheese and chive crackers
Add 2 tbsp finely chopped chives to the mixture along with the cheese, stirring to combine, then bake as normal.

Olive and rosemary cookies

PREPARATION TIME: **20 minutes**
COOKING TIME: **12-15 minutes**
MAKES: **25**

150 g / 5 oz / ⅔ cup butter, cubed
225 g / 8 oz / 1 ½ cup plain (all-purpose) flour
75 g / 2 ¾ oz / ½ cup black olives, pitted and finely chopped
50 g / 1 ¾ oz / ½ cup red Leicester, grated
2 tsp dried rosemary

- Preheat the oven to 180°C (160°C fan) / 350F / gas 4, then line a baking tray with greaseproof paper.
- Use your fingertips to rub the butter into the flour, then gently stir in the olives, cheese and rosemary.
- Knead gently until the mixture forms a smooth dough, then roll out on a lightly floured surface to 1 cm (½ in) thick.
- Use a cookie cutter to cut out 25 biscuits, then spread them out onto the prepared baking tray.
- Bake the biscuits for 12–15 minutes, turning the tray round halfway through.
- Transfer the biscuits to a wire rack and leave to cool completely.

Onion and rosemary cookies
Replace the olive with 1 red onion, finely diced and fried until soft. Leave to cool before stirring into the dough with the cheese and rosemary.

THE COOKERY COLLECTION

Pretzels

PREPARATION TIME: **2 hours, 30 minutes**
COOKING TIME: **10 minutes**
MAKES: **8 small pretzels**

3oo g / 10 ½ oz / 2 cups strong white bread flour
½ tsp easy-blend dried yeast
1 tbsp butter, melted
1 tsp salt
1 egg, beaten
1 tbsp black and white sesame seeds

- In a mixing bowl, mix together the flour, yeast, butter and salt, then stir in 200 ml of warm water.
- Bring the mixture into a dough with your hands and knead for 10 minutes. Leave to rest in a warm place for 1 hour or until doubled in size.
- Divide the dough into 8 even pieces and roll each one into a long sausage.
- Twist into a classic pretzel shape and transfer to an oiled baking tray. Leave in a warm place to prove for 45 minutes.
- Meanwhile, preheat the oven to 220°C (200°C fan) / 425F / gas 7. When the pretzels are well risen, brush them with the beaten egg and sprinkle with sesame seeds, then bake for 10 minutes or until golden brown and cooked through.

Orange-glazed pretzels
Mix the juice of 2 oranges with 75 g / 2 ½ oz / ⅓ cup caster (superfine) sugar, then heat in a saucepan with the zest of 1 orange. Brush over the baked pretzels while they are cooling.

Mushroom and leek quiche

PREPARATION TIME: 1 hour
COOKING TIME: 35-40 minutes
SERVES: 6-8

1 tbsp butter
4 leeks, sliced
200 g / 7 oz chestnut mushrooms, sliced
3 large eggs, beaten
225 ml / 8 fl. oz / ¾ cup double (heavy) cream
150 g / 5 ½ oz Gruyère, grated

FOR THE PASTRY
200 g / 7 oz / 1 ⅓ cups plain (all-purpose) flour
100 g / 3 ½ oz / ½ cup butter, cubed and chilled

- Preheat the oven to 190°C (170°C fan) / 375F / gas 5.
- Make the pastry first. Sieve the flour into a large mixing bowl, then rub in the butter using your fingertips until the mixture resembles fine breaderumbs.
- Stir in just enough cold water to bring the pastry together into a pliable dough, then chill for 30 minutes.
- Roll out the pastry on a lightly floured surface and use it to line a 23 cm (9 in) round tart tin. Prick the base with a fork, line with greaseproof paper and fill with baking beans or rice.
- Bake the case for 10 minutes, then remove the greaseproof paper and baking beans. Brush the inside with beaten egg and return to the oven for 8 minutes to crisp.
- Lower the oven to 150°C (130°C fan) / 300F / gas 2.
- Heat the butter in a frying pan set over a medium-high heat, then fry the leeks for 10 minutes or until soft. Add the mushrooms and cook for a further 5 minutes, then set to one side.
- In a large mixing bowl, whisk the eggs with the double cream until combined, then stir in the leeks, mushrooms and half of the Gruyère. Pour the filling into the pastry case and scatter the rest of the cheese on top.
- Bake for 35–40 minutes or until just set.

Mushroom and pepper quiche
Finely chop 2 peppers and fry them with the mushrooms and onions until soft, then bake the quiche as normal.

Chanterelle, cheese and thyme quiche

PREPARATION TIME: **1 hour**
COOKING TIME: **35-40 minutes**
SERVES: **6-8**

50 g / 1 ¾ oz / ¼ cup butter
3 onions, thinly sliced
150 g / 5 ½ / 1 cup chanterelle mushrooms, halved
2 cloves garlic, crushed
3 large eggs
225 ml / 8 fl. oz / ¾ cup double (heavy) cream
2 tbsp thyme leaves
150 g / 5 ½ oz / 1 ½ cups Gruyère, grated
thyme sprigs to garnish

FOR THE PASTRY
100 g / 3 ½ oz / ½ cup butter, cubed
200 g / 7 oz / 1 ⅓ cups plain (all-purpose) flour

- Make the pastry first. Using your fingertips, rub the butter into the flour until the mixture resembles fine breadcrumbs, then stir in enough cold water to bind. Chill in the fridge for 30 minutes.
- Preheat the oven to 190°C (170°C fan) / 375F / gas 5.
- Roll out the pastry and use it to line a rectangular tart tin.
- Prick the base, line with greaseproof paper and fill with baking beans or rice. Bake for 10 minutes, then remove the greaseproof paper and baking beans. Brush with beaten egg and bake for another 8 minutes.
- Lower the oven to 150°C (130°C fan) / 300F / gas 2.
- Heat the butter in a frying pan set over a medium-high heat, then fry the onion and mushrooms for 10 minutes until soft. Add the garlic and fry for 2 more minutes.
- In a large mixing bowl, whisk the eggs with the double cream, then stir in the onion mixture, thyme and half of the Gruyère. Season with salt and pepper.
- Pour the filling into the pastry case and scatter the rest of the cheese on top. Bake for 35–40 minutes, then garnish with thyme.

Chanterelle and red pepper quiche
Finely chop 1 red pepper and add to the frying pan with the onion and fry until soft, then bake as normal.

Chorizo and cheese empanadas

PREPARATION TIME: 35 minutes
COOKING TIME: 50-60 minutes
MAKES: 10

1 tsp butter
100 g / 3 ½ oz / ⅔ cup chorizo, finely chopped
1 onion, finely diced
1 red pepper, finely diced
pinch of salt
1 tsp dried oregano
250 g / 9 oz potatoes, cut into small cubes
200 g / 7 oz / 2 cups Cheddar, grated
500 g / 17 ½ oz shortcrust pastry
1 egg, beaten

- Heat the butter in a small frying pan set over a medium heat, then add the chorizo and fry for 2 minutes. Transfer to a bowl and set aside.
- Add the onions, pepper, salt and oregano to the pan and cook for 10 minutes or until the vegetables are soft, stirring frequently.
- Add the potato to the pan, then cook for a further 10 minutes. Scrape into the bowl with the chorizo, add the cheese and stir everything together.
- Roll the pastry out on a lightly floured surface to a 5 mm thickness, then cut out 10 circles of pastry.
- Spoon the filling into the centre of each pastry circle, then fold the pastry in half to enclose the filling. Pinch together and crimp to seal, then transfer to a greased baking tray.
- Preheat the oven to 160°C (140°C fan) / 325F / gas 3.
- Brush the pastries with a little more beaten egg, then bake for 50–60 minutes until golden brown and cooked through.

Chorizo and pea empanadas
Add 100 g / 3 ½ oz / ⅔ cup frozen peas to the pan along with the potatoes, then bake as per the method above.

Buckwheat and mixed seed crackers

PREPARATION TIME: 15 minutes
COOKING TIME: 8-10 minutes
MAKES: 36

110 g / 4 oz / ½ cup butter
225 g / 8 oz / 1 ½ cups stone-ground wholemeal flour
225 g / 8 oz / 1 ½ cups buckwheat flour
1 tsp salt
1 tsp baking powder
110 g / 4 oz / ⅔ cup whole raw buckwheat
3 tbsp mixed seeds

- Preheat the oven to 190°C (170°C fan) / 375F / gas 5, then line two baking trays with greaseproof paper.
- Rub the butter into the wholemeal flour, then stir in the buckwheat flour, salt, baking powder and raw buckwheat.
- Add enough water to bind the mixture into a pastry-like dough, then roll out on a lightly-floured surface.
- Cut the dough into squares and sprinkle with the mixed seeds.
- Transfer the biscuits to the prepared trays in batches and bake for 8–10 minutes or until cooked through and golden brown on top.
- Transfer the biscuits to a wire rack and leave to cool.

Onion and thyme focaccia

PREPARATION TIME: **2 hours, 30 minutes**
COOKING TIME: **25-35 minutes**
SERVES: **6**

300 g / 10 ½ oz / 2 cups strong white bread flour
½ tsp easy-blend dried yeast
2 tsp fine sea salt
2 tbsp olive oil
1 red onion, finely sliced
1 tsp dried thyme leaves

- In a mixing bowl, stir together the flour, yeast and salt.
- Stir in the oil and add 280 ml of warm water.

- Knead the mixture on a lightly oiled surface for 10 minutes or until smooth and elastic.
- Cover the dough with oiled cling film and leave to rest for 1–2 hours or until doubled in size.
- Oil a rectangular cake tin, then stretch out the dough to fill the base of the tin.
- Cover the focaccia with oiled cling film and leave to prove for 1 hour or until doubled in size.
- Preheat the oven to 220°C (200°C fan) / 425F / gas 7.
- Top the focaccia with sliced onion and thyme.
- Bake for 25–35 minutes or until the top is starting to turn golden and the base is cooked through.
- Transfer to a wire rack to cool.

Onion, tomato and thyme focaccia
Add a handful of sun-dried tomatoes to the top of the focaccia along with the sliced onion and thyme, to give this savoury loaf a more substantial flavour.

Sesame seed shortbread

PREPARATION TIME: 20 minutes
COOKING TIME: 12-15 minutes
MAKES: 24

150 g / 5 oz / ⅔ cup butter, cubed
230 g / 8 oz / 1 ½ cup plain (all-purpose) flour
1 egg, beaten
1 tbsp white sesame seeds
1 tbsp black sesame seeds

Pumpkin seed shortbread
Replace the sesame seeds with the same quantity of pumpkin seeds, to give these shortbread biscuits an extra crunch.

- Preheat the oven to 180°C (160°C fan) / 350F / gas 4, then line a baking tray with greaseproof paper.
- Using your fingertips, rub the butter into the flour in a large mixing bowl.
- Knead gently on a lightly floured surface until the mixture forms a smooth dough, then roll out to 1 cm (½ in) thick.
- Use a cookie cutter to cut out 24 round biscuits, then transfer them to the prepared baking tray.
- Brush the biscuits with beaten egg, sprinkle with the sesame seeds and bake for 12–15 minutes, turning the tray round halfway through.
- Transfer the biscuits to a wire rack and leave to cool.

Mini muesli oat cake

PREPARATION TIME: 10 minutes
COOKING TIME: 15-20 minutes
MAKES: 12

110 g / 4 oz / ⅔ cup self-raising flour, sifted
110 g / 4 oz caster / ½ cup (superfine) sugar
110 g / 4 oz / ½ cup butter, softened
1 dessert apple, peeled and diced
1 tsp ground cinnamon
2 large eggs
100 g / 3 ½ oz / 1 cup muesli

- Preheat the oven to 190°C (170°C fan) / 375F / gas 5 and oil a 12-hole cupcake tin with paper cupcake cases.
- Combine the flour, sugar, butter, apple, cinnamon, eggs and half of the muesli in a bowl and whisk together until smooth.
- Divide the mixture between the paper cases and sprinkle over the rest of the muesli.
- Transfer the tin to the oven and bake for 15–20 minutes.
- Test with a wooden toothpick; if it comes out clean, the cakes are done.
- Transfer the cakes to a wire rack and leave to cool completely.

Homemade sausage rolls

PREPARATION TIME: 15 minutes
COOKING TIME: 25-30 minutes
MAKES: 20

½ small garlic clove, crushed
pinch of salt
a handful of parsley, chopped
400 g / 14 oz / 2 cups sausage meat
375 g / 13 ¼ oz all-butter puff pastry
1 egg, beaten
1 tsp dried rosemary leaves

- Preheat the oven to 200°C (180°C fan) / 400F / gas 6, then grease a baking tray.
- In a large mixing bowl, mix together the garlic, salt, parsley and sausage meat until they are combined.
- Roll the pastry out on a lightly floured surface into a large oblong shape, then cut in half, lengthways.
- Divide the sausage mixture in half, then spread along the length of each pastry strip, leaving a 1 cm (½ in) gap around the edge.
- Brush a little beaten egg along one edge, then roll the pastry tightly around the sausage mixture. Brush the ends with more egg.
- Cut each roll into 10 pieces, each about 2 ½ cm (1 in) long, then arrange on the prepared baking tray.
- Brush the tops of the pastry with more beaten egg, sprinkle with dried rosemary leaves and bake for 25–30 minutes until the pastry is crisp and the meat cooked through.
- Remove from the oven to serve warm or cold.

Chilli sausage rolls
Add 1 tsp finely chopped chilli (chili) to the sausage mixture along with the garlic to give these sausage rolls an extra kick.

Spinach and feta muffins

PREPARATION TIME: 15 minutes
COOKING TIME: 20-25 minutes
MAKES: 12

2 large eggs
120 ml / 4 fl. oz / ½ cup sunflower oil
180 ml / 6 fl. oz / ¾ cup Greek yoghurt
2 tbsp Parmesan, finely grated
250 g / 9 oz / 2 cups spinach leaves, chopped
150 g / 5 ½ oz / ¾ cup feta cheese, cubed
225 g / 8 oz / 1 ½ cup plain (all-purpose) flour
2 tsp baking powder
½ tsp bicarbonate of (baking) soda
½ tsp salt

- Preheat the oven to 180°C (160°C fan) / 35oF / gas 4, then line a 12-hole muffin tray with paper cases.
- Beat the egg in a jug with the oil, yoghurt, Parmesan, spinach and feta until well mixed.
- In a large mixing bowl, mix together the flour, baking powder, bicarbonate of soda and salt in a bowl, then pour in the egg mixture and stir just enough to combine.
- Divide the mixture between the moulds, then bake in the oven for 20–25 minutes.
- Test with a wooden toothpick; if it comes out clean, the cakes are done.

Spinach and red pepper muffins
Finely chop 1 red pepper, then add to the muffin mixture along with the spinach. Reduce the quantity of feta cheese to 100 g / 3 ½ oz / ⅔ cup, then back as normal.

Spinach and tomato quiche

PREPARATION TIME: **1 hour**
COOKING TIME: **35-40 minutes**
SERVES: **6-8**

1 tbsp butter
200 g / 7 oz / 1 ½ cups chestnut mushrooms, sliced
1 bag fresh spinach
3 large eggs, beaten
225 ml / 8 fl. oz / ¾ cup double (heavy) cream
150 g / 5 ½ oz Gruyère, grated
2 tomatoes, sliced

FOR THE PASTRY
200 g / 7 oz / 1 ⅓ cups plain (all-purpose) flour
100 g / 3 ½ oz / ½ cup butter, cubed and chilled

- Preheat the oven to 190°C (170°C fan) / 375F / gas 5.
- Make the pastry first. Sieve the flour into a large mixing bowl, then rub in the butter using your fingertips until the mixture resembles fine breadcrumbs.
- Stir in just enough cold water to bring the pastry together into a pliable dough, then chill for 30 minutes.
- Roll out the pastry on a lightly floured surface and use it to line a fluted rectangular tart tin. Prick the base with a fork, line with greaseproof paper and fill with baking beans or rice.
- Bake the case for 10 minutes, then remove the greaseproof paper and baking beans. Brush the inside with beaten egg and return to the oven for 8 minutes to crisp.
- Lower the oven to 150°C (130°C fan) / 300F / gas 2.
- Heat the butter in a frying pan set over a medium-high heat. Fry the mushrooms until soft. Add the spinach and cook until wilted.
- In a large mixing bowl, whisk the eggs with the double cream until combined, then stir in the mushrooms, spinach and half of the Gruyère. Pour the filling into the pastry case and scatter the rest of the cheese on top.
- Arrange the tomato slices on top.
- Bake for 35-40 minutes or until just set in the centre and starting to brown on top.

Spinach and ricotta pastries

PREPARATION TIME: **10 minutes**
COOKING TIME: **25-35 minutes**
MAKES: **8**

1 tsp olive oil
1 onion, finely diced
1 bag fresh spinach
150 g / 5 ½ oz / 1 cup ricotta
2 egg yolks
450 g / 1 lb all-butter puff pastry
1 egg, beaten
1 tbsp black and white sesame seeds

- Preheat the oven to 220°C (200°C fan) / 425F / gas 7.
- In a saucepan, heat the olive oil over a medium-high heat, then add the onions and cook for 10 minutes until soft, stirring occasionally. Remove from the pan and set aside in a bowl.
- Add the spinach leaves to the saucepan and cook until the leaves start to wilt. Chop the spinach and add to the bowl with the onions.
- Add the ricotta and egg yolks, then season and stir together.
- Roll out the pastry and cut into 8 squares, then transfer the squares to a baking tray.
- Dollop a spoonful of the spinach and ricotta mixture into the centre of each pastry square, leaving plenty of room around the outside.
- Brush the edges of the pastry with beaten egg, the fold the corners into the centre, so that the tips overlap. Brush the tops with beaten egg and sprinkle with sesame seeds.
- Bake in the oven for 25–35 minutes or until the pastry is golden brown.

Spinach and goat's cheese pastries
Replace the ricotta with the same quantity of goat's cheese to give these pastries a stronger cheese flavour.

Cheese and potato pasties

PREPARATION TIME: **35 minutes**
COOKING TIME: **50-60 minutes**
MAKES: **6**

1 tsp butter
1 onion, finely diced
500 g / 17 ½ oz potatoes, peeled and grated
200 g / 7 oz / 2 cups Cheddar, grated
100 g / 3 ½ oz / ⅔ cup breadcrumbs
2 eggs
pinch of salt
500 g / 17 ½ oz shortcrust pastry

- Heat the butter in a small frying pan set over a medium heat, then add the onion and fry until soft.
- In a mixing bowl, mix together the potato, Cheddar, breadcrumbs, onions and 1 egg, then season with a pinch of salt.
- Roll the pastry out on a lightly floured surface to a 5 mm thickness, then cut out 6 circles of pastry, around 16 cm (6 in) in diameter.
- Spoon the filling into the centre of each pastry circle, then beat the egg and brush a little around the edges.
- Fold up two sides of the pastry over the filling, pinch together and crimp to seal. Transfer to a greased baking tray and chill for 10 minutes.
- Preheat the oven to 160°C (140°C fan) / 325F / gas 3.
- Brush the pastries with a little more beaten egg, then bake for 50-60 minutes until golden brown and cooked through.

Cheese, pepper and potato pasties
Fry 1 finely diced red pepper with the onion until soft, then stir into the filling and bake the pasties as normal.

Parmesan and prosciutto pastries

PREPARATION TIME: 10 minutes
COOKING TIME: 10-15 minutes
MAKES: 24

250 g / 9 oz all-butter puff pastry
50 g / 1 ¾ oz / ⅓ cup butter, melted
200 g / 7 oz prosciutto slices
150 g / 5 ½ oz / ⅔ cup Parmesan, grated
a handful of basil leaves, finely chopped
1 egg, beaten

- Preheat the oven to 220°C (200°C fan) / 425F / gas 7, then line a baking tray with greaseproof paper.
- Roll out the pastry on a lightly floured surface to about 5 mm thickness.
- Spread the pastry with a thin layer of melted butter, then add the slices of prosciutto.
- Mix together the Parmesan and basil, then sprinkle over the ham.
- Roll the pastry up into a tight sausage shape. Cut the roll into 2 cm (1 in) slices and arrange them on the prepared baking tray.
- Brush the rolls with the beaten egg, then bake for 10–15 minutes or until the pastry is golden.
- Transfer to a wire rack to cool slightly before serving.

Mushroom and prosciutto muffins

PREPARATION TIME: 10 minutes
COOKING TIME: 10-15 minutes
MAKES: 12

2 large eggs
120 ml / 4 fl. oz / ½ cup sunflower oil
180 ml / 6 fl. oz / ⅔ cup Greek yogurt
75 g / 1 ¾ oz / ⅓ cup feta, crumbled
225 g / 8 oz / 1 ½ cups plain (all-purpose) flour
2 tsp baking powder
½ tsp bicarbonate of (baking) soda
½ tsp salt
200 g / 7 oz button mushrooms, sliced
6 slices prosciutto, chopped

- Preheat the oven to 180°C (160°C fan) / 350F / gas 4, then line a 12-hole muffin tray with mini paper cases.
- Beat the egg in a jug with the oil, yoghurt and feta until well mixed.
- In a large mixing bowl, mix together the flour, baking powder, bicarbonate of soda, salt, mushrooms and prosciutto in a bowl, then pour in the egg mixture and stir just enough to combine.
- Divide the mixture between the paper cases, then bake in the oven for 10–15 minutes.
- Test with a wooden toothpick; if it comes out clean, the muffins are done.

Mushroom and Stilton muffins
Remove the feta cheese and prosciutto, and instead add 100 g / 3 ½ oz / ⅔ cup Stilton to the mixture along with the mushrooms, to give these savoury muffins a stronger flavour.

Cheese and bacon quiche

PREPARATION TIME: 1 hour
COOKING TIME: 35-40 minutes
SERVES: 6-8

200 g / 7 oz smoked bacon lardons
2 tbsp olive oil
3 large eggs, beaten
225 ml / 8 fl. oz / ¾ cup double (heavy) cream
150 g / 5 ½ oz Gruyère, grated

FOR THE PASTRY
200 g / 7 oz / 1 ⅓ cups plain (all-purpose) flour
100 g / 3 ½ oz / ½ cup butter, cubed and chilled

- Preheat the oven to 190°C (170°C fan) / 375F / gas 5.
- Make the pastry first. Sieve the flour into a large mixing bowl, then rub in the butter using your fingertips until the mixture resembles fine breadcrumbs.
- Stir in just enough cold water to bring the pastry together into a pliable dough, then chill for 30 minutes.
- Roll out the pastry on a lightly floured surface and use it to line a 23 cm (9 in) round tart tin. Prick the base with a fork, line with greaseproof paper and fill with baking beans or rice.
- Bake the case for 10 minutes, then remove the greaseproof paper and baking beans. Brush the inside with beaten egg and return to the oven for 8 minutes to crisp.
- Lower the oven to 150°C (130°C fan) / 300F / gas 2.
- Fry the lardons in the oil for 5 minutes.
- In a large mixing bowl, whisk the eggs with the double cream until combined, then stir in the lardons and half of the Gruyère. Pour the filling into the pastry case and scatter the rest of the cheese on top.
- Bake for 35-40 minutes or until just set in the centre and is golden on top.

Cheese and tomato quiche
Stir 10 halved cherry tomatoes into the filling along with the bacon lardons and Gruyère, then bake as normal.

Parmesan shortbread biscuits

PREPARATION TIME: 20 minutes
COOKING TIME: 12-15 minutes
MAKES: 24

150g / 5 oz / ⅔ cup butter, cubed
230 g / 8 oz / 1 ½ cup plain (all-purpose) flour
50 g / 1 ¾ oz / ½ cup Parmesan, grated
pinch black pepper
2 tsp flax seeds

- Preheat the oven to 180°C (160°C fan) / 35oF / gas 4, then line a baking tray with greaseproof paper.
- Using your fingertips, rub the butter into the flour, then stir in the Parmesan and black pepper.
- Knead gently until the mixture forms a smooth dough, then roll out on a lightly floured surface to 5 mm thick.
- Use a flower-shaped cookie cutter to cut out 24 biscuits and transfer them to the prepared baking tray.
- Sprinkle the flax seeds over the biscuits.
- Bake the biscuits for 12–15 minutes, turning the tray round halfway through.
- Transfer the biscuits to a wire rack and leave to cool.

Courgette and herb loaf

PREPARATION TIME: **10 minutes**
COOKING TIME: **55 minutes**
MAKES: **1 loaf**

300 g / 10 ½ oz / 2 cups self-raising flour
2 tsp baking powder
250 g / 9 oz / 1 ¼ cup butter, softened
5 large eggs
100 g / 3 ½ oz / 1 cup Cheddar cheese, grated
1 courgette (zucchini), grated
1 tbsp flat leaf parsley, chopped
2 tbsp basil, chopped

- Preheat the oven to 170°C (150°C fan) / 340F / gas 3, then line a large loaf tin with greaseproof paper.
- Sieve the flour and baking powder into a large mixing bowl, then add the butter and eggs. Beat the mixture until smooth and well-whipped.
- Fold in the cheese, courgette and herbs, then scrape the mixture into the prepared loaf tin.
- Bake for 55 minutes. Test the cake with a toothpick; if it comes out clean, the cake is done.
- Transfer the cake to a wire rack and leave to cool completely before serving.

Pepper and herb loaf
Replace the Cheddar with the same quantity of Parmesan cheese, then substitute the courgette with a finely chopped red pepper.

Cheese and chive scones

PREPARATION TIME: **20 minutes**
COOKING TIME: **15-20 minutes**
MAKES: **12**

300 g / 10 ½ oz / 2 cup self-raising flour, plus extra for dusting
1 tbsp caster (superfine) sugar
1 tsp salt
50 g / 1 ¾ oz / ⅓ cup butter, softened
300 ml / 10 fl. oz / 1 ¼ cups milk
100 g / 3 ½ oz / ⅔ cup Parmesan, grated
2 tbsp chives, chopped
1 egg, beaten

- Preheat the oven to 220° (200°C fan) / 425F / gas 7, then grease a baking tray. Sieve the flour, sugar and salt into a large mixing bowl, then use your fingertips to rub in the butter until the mixture resembles fine breadcrumbs.
- Make a well in the centre of the dry ingredients, then add the milk, Parmesan and chives. Stir until the dough starts to come together.
- Knead the dough on a lightly floured surface, then roll out to about 3 cm (1 ¼ in) thickness and use a circular cutter to cut out 12 scones. Transfer to the prepared baking tray, then brush with beaten egg. Bake for 15–20 minutes. Test with a wooden toothpick. Transfer to a wire rack to cool, then sprinkle with flour to finish.

Parmesan and herb scones
Replace the chopped chives with 1 tbsp chopped basil and 1 tbsp dried oregano to give these scones an extra herby flavour.

Bacon and herb muffins

PREPARATION TIME: **15 minutes**
COOKING TIME: **10-15 minutes**
MAKES: **24**

1 tsp olive oil
150 g / 5 oz / 1 cup streaky bacon, cubed
2 large eggs
120 ml / 4 fl. oz / ½ cup sunflower oil
50 g / 1 ¾ oz / ½ cup Cheddar, grated
225 g / 8 oz / 1 ½ cups plain (all-purpose) flour
½ tsp dried rosemary leaves, chopped
½ tsp dried thyme leaves
2 tsp baking powder
½ tsp bicarbonate of soda
½ tsp salt

- Heat the olive oil in a frying pan set over a medium-high heat, then add the bacon and fry for 10 minutes or until cooked.
- Preheat the oven to 180°C (160°C fan) / 350F / gas 4, then line a 24-hole mini muffin tin with paper cases (or line two 12-hole muffin trays with mini paper cases).
- Beat the egg in a jug with the sunflower oil and Cheddar until well mixed.
- In a large mixing bowl, mix together the flour, rosemary, thyme, baking powder, bicarbonate of soda and salt, then pour in the egg mixture and stir just enough to combine.
- Stir the cooked bacon until evenly distributed through the mixture.
- Divide the mixture between the paper cases, then bake in the oven for 10–15 minutes.
- Test with a wooden toothpick; if it comes out clean, the muffins are done.

Bacon and red Leicester muffins
Replace the Cheddar with the same quantity of red Leicester cheese, to give these muffins a lightly different flavour.

Onion and thyme mini muffins

PREPARATION TIME: 15 minutes
COOKING TIME: 10-15 minutes
MAKES: 12

1 tbsp butter
1 onion, finely diced
2 large eggs
120 ml / 4 fl. oz / ½ cup sunflower oil
180 ml / 6 fl. oz / ¾ cup Greek yoghurt
2 tbsp Parmesan, finely grated
2 tbsp fresh thyme leaves
225 g / 8 oz / 1 ½ cups plain (all-purpose) flour
2 tsp baking powder
½ tsp bicarbonate of (baking) soda
½ tsp salt

- Heat the butter in a small frying pan set over a medium-high heat, then add the onion. Cook for 10 minutes until soft, stirring occasionally.
- Preheat the oven to 180°C (160°C fan) / 350F / gas 4, then line a 12-hole muffin tray with paper cases.
- Beat the eggs in a jug with the oil, yoghurt, Parmesan and thyme until well mixed.
- In a large mixing bowl, mix together the flour, baking powder and bicarbonate of soda, then pour in the egg mixture and stir just enough to combine.
- Stir in the onion and mix until evenly distributed.
- Divide the mixture between the cases, then bake in the oven for 10–15 minutes.
- Test with a wooden toothpick; if it comes out clean, the cakes are done.

Spinach and feta tart

PREPARATION TIME: **1 hour**
COOKING TIME: **35–40 minutes**
SERVES: **6–8**

1 tbsp olive oil
1 onion, finely diced
2 bags fresh spinach
3 large eggs, beaten
225 ml / 8 fl. oz / ¾ cup double (heavy) cream
150 g / 5 ½ oz / 1 cup feta, cubed

FOR THE PASTRY
200 g / 7 oz / 1 ⅓ cups plain (all-purpose) flour
100 g / 3 ½ oz / ½ cup butter, cubed and chilled

- Preheat the oven to 190°C (170°C fan) / 375F / gas 5.
- Make the pastry first. Sieve the flour into a large mixing bowl, then rub in the butter using your fingertips until the mixture resembles fine breadcrumbs.
- Stir in just enough cold water to bring the pastry together into a pliable dough, then chill for 30 minutes.
- Roll out the pastry on a lightly floured surface and use it to line a 23 cm (9 in) round tart tin. Prick the base with a fork, line with greaseproof paper and fill with baking beans or rice.
- Bake the case for 10 minutes, then remove the greaseproof paper and baking beans. Brush the inside with beaten egg and return to the oven for 8 minutes to crisp.
- Lower the oven to 150°C (130°C fan) / 300F / gas 2.
- Heat the oil in a frying pan set over a medium-high heat, then add the onion and cook for 10 minutes or until soft. Add the spinach to the pan and cook until wilted.
- In a large mixing bowl, whisk the eggs with the double cream until combined, then stir in the spinach, onion and half of the feta. Pour the filling into the pastry case and scatter the rest of the cheese on top.
- Bake for 35–40 minutes or until just set in the centre and starting to brown.

Spinach and ricotta tart
Substitute the feta for the same quantity of ricotta for a milder, creamier flavour.

Salmon and dill muffins

PREPARATION TIME: **15 minutes**
COOKING TIME: **20-25 minutes**
MAKES: **12**

2 large eggs
120 ml / 4 fl. oz / ½ cup sunflower oil
180 ml / 6 fl. oz / ⅔ cup Greek yogurt
110 g / 4 oz smoked salmon, chopped
2 tbsp dill, chopped
225 g / 8 oz / 1 ½ cups plain (all-purpose) flour
2 tsp baking powder
½ tsp bicarbonate of (baking) soda
½ tsp salt

- Preheat the oven to 180°C (160°C fan) / 350F / gas 4, then line a 12-hole muffin tin with paper cases.
- Beat the eggs in a jug with the oil and yogurt until well mixed.
- In a large mixing bowl, mix together the salmon, dill, flour, baking powder, bicarbonate of soda and salt in a bowl, then pour in the egg mixture and stir just enough to combine.
- Spoon the mixture into the prepared paper cases, then bake in the oven for 20–25 minutes. Test with a wooden toothpick; if it comes out clean, the muffins is done.
- Transfer the muffins to a wire rack and leave to cool completely.

Salmon and goat's cheese muffins
Add 110 g / 4 oz goat's cheese to the mixture along with the eggs, oil and yogurt, then bake as normal.

Parmesan and olive shortbread

PREPARATION TIME: 20 minutes
COOKING TIME: 15-20 minutes
MAKES: 16

150 g / 5 oz / ⅔ cup butter, cubed
230 g / 8 oz / 1 ½ cup plain (all-purpose) flour
50 g / 1 ¾ oz / ½ cup Parmesan, grated
50 g / 1 ¾ oz / ⅓ cup green olives, pitted and finely chopped
1 tsp olive oil

- Preheat the oven to 180°C (160°C fan) / 350F / gas 4, then line a baking tray with greaseproof paper.
- Use your fingertips to rub the butter into the flour, then stir in the Parmesan, olives and olive oil.
- Knead gently until the mixture forms a smooth dough, then form into a cylinder 6 cm (2 ½ in) in diameter.
- Slice the roll into 1 cm (½ in) thick slices and spread them out on the prepared baking tray.
- Bake the biscuits for 15–20 minutes, turning the tray round halfway through.
- Transfer to a wire rack and leave to cool.

Salty bacon and onion muffins

PREPARATION TIME: 20 minutes
COOKING TIME: 10-15 minutes
MAKES: 12

1 tsp olive oil
150 g / 5 ½ oz / ⅔ cup bacon lardons
2 large eggs
120 ml / 4 fl. oz / ½ cup sunflower oil
180 ml / 6 fl. oz / ¾ cup Greek yoghurt
2 tbsp Parmesan, finely grated
2 spring onions (scallions), trimmed and finely chopped
225 g / 8 oz / 1 ½ cup plain (all-purpose) flour
2 tsp baking powder
½ tsp bicarbonate of (baking) soda
½ tsp salt

- Heat the olive oil in a frying pan set over a medium-high heat, then add the bacon and fry for 10 minutes or until cooked to your preference.
- Preheat the oven to 180°C (160°C fan) / 350F / gas 4, then line a 12-hole muffin tray with paper cases.
- Beat the eggs in a jug with the sunflower oil, yoghurt, Parmesan and most of the spring onions until well mixed.
- In a large mixing bowl, mix together the flour, baking powder, bicarbonate of soda and seasoning in a bowl, then pour in the egg mixture and stir enough to combine.
- Stir through the bacon lardons until evenly distributed.
- Divide the mixture between the cases, then bake in the oven for 10–15 minutes. Test with a wooden toothpick; if it comes out clean, the muffins are done.
- Transfer to a wire rack to cool slightly, then sprinkle with the remaining spring onions to finish.

Chorizo and spring onion muffins
Replace the bacon with the same quantity of finely chopped chorizo. Fry for a few minutes over a low heat, then stir into the cake mixture before baking,

Parmesan and bacon mini muffins

PREPARATION TIME: 15 minutes
COOKING TIME: 10-15 minutes
MAKES: 24

1 tsp olive oil

150 g / 5 oz / 1 cup streaky bacon, cubed

2 large eggs

120 ml / 4 fl. oz / ½ cup sunflower oil

100 g / 3 ½ oz / 1 cup Parmesan, grated

225 g / 8 oz / 1 ½ cup plain (all-purpose) flour

2 tsp baking powder

½ tsp bicarbonate of (baking) soda

½ tsp salt

- Heat the olive oil in a frying pan set over a medium-high heat, then add the bacon and fry for 10 minutes or until cooked to your preference.
- Preheat the oven to 180°C (160°C fan) / 350F / gas 4, then line a 24-hole mini muffin tin with paper cases (or line two 12-hole muffin trays with mini paper cases).
- Beat the egg in a jug with the sunflower oil and Parmesan until they are well mixed.
- In a large mixing bowl, mix together the flour, baking powder, bicarbonate of soda and salt, then pour in the egg mixture and stir just enough to combine.
- Stir in the cooked bacon until evenly distributed.
- Divide the mixture between the paper cases, then bake in the oven for 10–15 minutes.
- Test with a wooden toothpick; if it comes out clean, the muffins are done.

Brie and bacon mini muffins
Replace the Parmesan with small cubes of brie, then add 50 g / 1 ¾ oz / ⅓ cup dried cranberries to the muffin mixture along with the bacon.

Olive and tomato mini muffins

PREPARATION TIME: **15 minutes**
COOKING TIME: **10-15 minutes**
MAKES: **24**

2 large eggs

120 ml / 4 fl. oz / ½ cup sunflower oil

180 ml / 6 fl. oz / ⅔ cup Greek yoghurt

2 tbsp Parmesan, finely grated, plus extra
for sprinkling

225 g / 8 oz / 1 ½ cups plain (all-purpose) flour

2 tsp baking powder

½ tsp bicarbonate of (baking) soda

½ tsp salt

75 g / 2 ½ oz / ½ cup black olives,
stoned and chopped

100 g / 3 ½ oz / ⅔ cup sun-dried tomatoes, chopped

- Preheat the oven to 180°C (160°C fan) / 350F
  / gas 4, then line a 24-hole mini muffin tin
  with paper cases (or line two 12-hole muffin
  tins with mini paper cases).
- Beat the eggs in a jug with the oil, yoghurt
  and cheese until well mixed.
- In a large mixing bowl, mix together the flour,
  baking powder, bicarbonate of soda, salt,
  olives and sun-dried tomatoes in a bowl, then
  pour in the egg mixture and stir just enough
  to combine.
- Divide the mixture between the paper cases,
  then bake in the oven for 10 15 minutes.
- Test with a wooden toothpick; if it comes out
  clean, the muffins are done.
- Serve warm, sprinkled with more grated
  Parmesan cheese.

Olive and rosemary muffins
Replaces the sun-dried tomatoes with 2 tbsp
chopped, fresh rosemary to give these muffins
a herby flavour. Stir into the mixture along with
the olives, then bake as normal.

Parmesan and rosemary biscuits

PREPARATION TIME: **20 minutes**
COOKING TIME: **12-15 minutes**
MAKES: **25**

150 g / 5 oz / 2/3 cup butter, cubed
225 g / 8 oz / 1 ½ cup plain (all-purpose) flour
50 g / 1 ¾ oz / ½ cup Parmesan, grated
2 tsp dried rosemary

- Preheat the oven to 180°C (160°C fan) / 350F / gas 4. Line a baking tray with greaseproof paper.
- Use your fingertips to rub the butter into the flour, then stir in the Parmesan and rosemary.
- Knead gently until the mixture forms a smooth dough, then roll out on a lightly floured surface to 1 cm (½ in) thick.
- Use a fluted cookie cutter to cut out 25 biscuits, then spread out onto the prepared baking tray.
- Bake the biscuits for 12–15 minutes, turning the tray round halfway through.
- Transfer the biscuits to a wire rack and leave to cool completely.

Parmesan and herb shortbread
For a different herby flavour, substitute the rosemary for 2 tsp herbs de Provence, stirring into the mixture with the Parmesan, then bake as normal.

Feta and pepper muffins

PREPARATION TIME: **15 minutes**
COOKING TIME: **10-15 minutes**
MAKES: **12**

2 large eggs
120 ml / 4 fl. oz / ½ cup sunflower oil
180 ml / 6 fl. oz / ¾ cup Greek yoghurt
150 g / 5 ½ oz / 1 cup feta, cubed
1 red pepper, deseeded and finely diced
225 g / 8 oz / 1 ½ cup plain (all-purpose) flour
1 tsp dried rosemary leaves
2 tsp baking powder
½ tsp bicarbonate of (baking) soda
½ tsp salt

- Preheat the oven to 180°C (160°C fan) / 350F / gas. Line a 12-hole muffin tray with paper cases.
- Beat the eggs in a jug with the oil, yoghurt, feta and red pepper until well mixed.
- In a large mixing bowl, mix together the flour, dried rosemary, baking powder, bicarbonate of soda and salt in a bowl, then pour in the egg mixture and stir to combine. Divide the mixture between the cases, then bake in the oven for 10–15 minutes. Test with a wooden toothpick.

Feta and sun-dried tomato muffins
Replace the red pepper with the same quantity of sun-dried tomatoes, drained of their oil and chopped into small pieces. Bake as normal.

Asparagus and red onion quiche

PREPARATION TIME: 1 hour
COOKING TIME: 35-40 minutes
SERVES: 6

1 tbsp butter
3 red onions, peeled and sliced
8 asparagus stalks
3 large eggs, beaten
225 ml / 8 fl. oz / ¾ cup double (heavy) cream
150 g / 5 ½ oz Gruyère, grated

FOR THE PASTRY
200 g / 7 oz / 1 ⅓ cups plain (all-purpose) flour
100 g / 3 ½ oz / ½ cup butter, cubed and chilled

* Preheat the oven to 190°C (170°C fan) / 375F / gas 5.
* Make the pastry first. Sieve the flour into a large mixing bowl, then rub in the butter using your fingertips until the mixture resembles fine breadcrumbs.
* Stir in just enough cold water to bring the pastry together into a pliable dough, then chill for 30 minutes.
* Roll out the pastry on a lightly floured surface and use it to line a fluted tart tin. Prick the base with a fork, line with greaseproof paper and fill with baking beans or rice.
* Bake the case for 10 minutes, then remove the greaseproof paper and baking beans. Brush the inside with beaten egg and return to the oven for 8 minutes to crisp.
* Lower the oven to 150°C (130°C fan) / 300F / gas 2.
* Heat the butter in a frying pan, then fry the onion over a low heat until soft and caramelised. Add the asparagus and cook for 2 more minutes.
* In a large mixing bowl, whisk the eggs with the double cream until combined, then stir in the red onions and half of the Gruyère. Pour the filling into the pastry case and scatter the rest of the cheese on top.
* Arrange the asparagus on top of the quiche, then bake for 35–40 minutes or until just set in the centre.

Index

Almond and coconut
  sponge cookies, 131

Almond and lemon curd cake, 86

Almond and lemon pie, 146

Almond and lemon torte, 161

Almond and oat flour cake, 140

Almond and orange flower
  shortbread, 128

Almond and pistachio biscotti, 80

Almond and raspberry loaf cake, 29

Almond and rose water pie, 146

Almond and star anise
  shortbread stars, 83

Almond biscotti, 80

Almond cakes, 38

Almond cookies, 111

Almond crescent biscuits, 21

Almond, lemon and treacle tart, 152

Almond, raspberry and white
  chocolate loaf, 29

Almond sponge cookies, 131

Almond torte, 161

Apple, almond and honey tarts, 61

Apple, almond and vanilla tart, 108

Apple and blackberry crumble, 128

Apple and cinnamon cake, 11

Apple and cinnamon pie, 91

Apple and oat crumble, 152

Apple and raisin cake, 11

Apple cider loaf cake, 66

Apple crumble tart, 152

Apple crumble, 128

Apple, pecan and cinnamon loaf, 107

Apple upside-down cake, 6

Apple, walnut and honey tarts, 61

Apricot and almond tartes, 77

Apricot and honey tarte Tatin, 78

Apricot and nut fruit cake, 87

Apricot cupcakes, 104

Apricot galette, 67

Apricot jam biscuits, 83

Apricot jam cupcakes, 104

Asparagus and red onion quiche, 250

Bacon and herb muffins, 242

Bacon and red Leicester muffins, 242

Baked pecan mini muffins, 71

Banana and apricot loaf, 17

Banana and chocolate spring rolls, 90

Banana and double chocolate
  loaf cake, 127

Banana and nut loaf cake, 142

Banana and walnut spiced loaf, 97

Banana, carrot and ginger loaf, 99

Banana, chocolate and cashew loaf, 127

Banoffee tart, 70

Basil and Parmesan biscuits, 155

Basil and sun-dried tomato biscuits, 155

Beer and mustard seed loaf, 170

Beer bread, 170

Blackberry and cream
  cheese muffins, 138

Blackberry and pistachio
  mini muffins, 41

Blackberry cake, 72

Blackberry, chocolate and pistachio
  muffins, 41

Blackberry custard tarts, 163

Black cherry cheesecake brownies, 18

Black Forest gateau, 144

Black olive and feta loaf, 207

Black olive and parsnip loaf, 196

Black olive bread loaf, 207

Black sesame tuile biscuits, 222

Blood orange upside-down cake, 98

Blueberry and lemon curd tartlets, 65

Blueberry and orange muffins, 19

Blueberry cake, 72

Blueberry carrot muffins, 124

Blueberry ricotta tartlets, 48

Brie and bacon mini muffins, 248

Buckwheat and mixed seed
  crackers, 228

Bundt cake, 134

Bundt cake with lemon, 134

Buttercream cupcakes, 50

Caramel and chocolate chip cookies, 14

Caramel fudge cookies, 14

Carrot and Roquefort loaf, 177

Carrot and rye cake, 141

Carrot and walnut loaf, 177

Carrot, orange and walnut cake, 76

Chanterelle and red pepper quiche, 226

Chanterelle, cheese and
  thyme quiche, 226

Cheese and bacon quiche, 239

Cheese and chive crackers, 223

Cheese and chive scones, 241

Cheese and onion bread, 186

Cheese and onion loaf, 178

Cheese and pesto bread ring, 202

Cheese and potato pasties, 236

Cheese and tomato quiche, 239

Cheese, pepper and potato pasties, 236

Cheese-stuffed bread rolls, 171

Cheesy chorizo and thyme loaf, 216

Cheesy chorizo and tomato loaf, 216

Cheesy olive loaf, 196

Cherry and almond cookies, 8

Cherry and cranberry tart, 112

Cherry and hazlenut cookies, 8

Cherry clafoutis, 51

Cherry scones, 77

Chestnut and chorizo bread, 206

Chilli chocolate and walnut cookies, 155

Chilli sausage rolls, 232

Chocolate almond cakes, 38

Chocolate and almond biscotti, 44

Chocolate and almond brownies, 113

Chocolate and blackberry sandwich, 158

Chocolate and buttercream biscuits, 58

Chocolate and cranberry bread, 205

Chocolate and ginger ganache cupcakes, 92

Chocolate and hazelnut loaf cake, 14

Chocolate and hazelnut shortbread, 36

Chocolate and hazelnut torte, 88

Chocolate and ice cream cookie, 56

Chocolate and peanut butter brownies, 32

Chocolate and peanut squares, 8

Chocolate and pecan bundt cake, 145

Chocolate and pink peppercorn cookies, 140

Chocolate and pistachio cookies, 47

Chocolate and pistachio shortbread, 53

Chocolate and strawberry gateau, 148

Chocolate and walnut loaf, 31

Chocolate and walnut spring rolls, 90

Chocolate biscuit brownies, 89

Chocolate cake squares, 49

Chocolate chip and pistachio cookie, 56

Chocolate chip baton, 205

Chocolate chip blondies, 92

Chocolate chip muffins, 133

Chocolate chip quinoa cookies, 54

Chocolate chip raspberry blondies, 92

Chocolate chunk cookies, 164

Chocolate cream and raspberry cupcakes, 20

Chocolate cream cherry cupcakes, 20

Chocolate cream muffins, 137

Chocolate-dipped biscotti, 44

Chocolate-dipped hazelnut shortbread, 26

Chocolate-dipped pistachio biscotti, 126

Chocolate fudge loaf cake, 80

Chocolate ganache cupcakes, 92

Chocolate gateau with cherries, 64

Chocolate gingerbread stars, 56

Chocolate loaf cake, 80

Chocolate, orange and almond brownies, 113

Chocolate orange cinnamon shortbread, 119

Chocolate pecan mini muffins, 71

Chocolate, pistachio and cherry tart, 96

Chocolate, raisin and hazelnut loaf cake, 14

Chocolate shortbread, 53

Chocolate spice cookies, 140

Chocolate sponge fingers, 25

Chocolate tart with cherries, 96

Chocolate torte, 123

Chocolate truffle loaf, 79

Chorizo and cheese empanadas, 227

Chorizo and olive loaf cake, 180

Chorizo and pea empanadas, 227

Chorizo and spring onion muffins, 247

Chorizo and tomato bread, 206

Chorizo bread ring, 202

Cinnamon and raisin bagels, 182

Cinnamon and raisin cookies, 44

Cinnamon and raisin oatmeal cookies, 98

Cinnamon cookies, 44

Cinnamon oatmeal cookies, 98

Cinnamon shortbread, 101

Cinnamon snaps, 35

Cinnamon spice loaf cake, 132

Classic carrot cake, 154

Classic coffee cake, 100

Clementine upside-down cake, 6

Coconut and lemon cake, 86

Coconut and pine nut cookies, 125

Coconut cookies, 125

Coconut shortbread, 101

Coffee and chocolate cake, 15

Coffee and chocolate chip cookies, 23

Coffee caramel nut muffins, 35

Coffee nut muffins, 35

Coffee sponge fingers, 25

Colourful buttercream cupcakes, 50

Corn bread, 185

Cottage cheese and walnut loaf, 147

Courgette and herb loaf, 241

Cranberry and almond muffins, 164

Cranberry and apple loaf cake, 104

Cranberry and pistachio biscotti, 126

Cranberry brownies, 89

Cranberry loaf cake, 104

Cranberry muffins, 164

Cream puffs, 131

Crispy cheese crackers, 223

Crusty baton, 203

Crusty bread fingers, 197

Crusty bread rolls, 189

Daisy cupcakes, 149

Date and fig bread, 191

Date and oatmeal cookies, 71

Date and pine nut loaf, 212

Date and walnut loaf, 212

Date, cherry and oatmeal cookies, 71

Double choc cookies, 120

Double chocolate and hazelnut cookies, 47

Double chocolate and pecan cookies, 41

Double chocolate button cookies, 116

Double chocolate cherry cookies, 116

Double chocolate cinnamon cookies, 120

Double chocolate coffee cookies, 23

Double chocolate raspberry and banana loaf, 156

Dried fig bread loaf, 191

Dutch caramel waffles, 24

Egg custard tarts, 12

Feta and pepper muffins, 250

Feta and sun-dried tomato muffins, 250

Fig and almond tarts, 77

Fig and honey muffins, 63

Fig and honey tarte Tatin, 78

Fig and lemon loaf, 89

Fig and orange muffins, 19

Fig and walnut loaf, 217

Fig and white chocolate loaf, 89

Focaccia with rosemary, 190

Frosted apple loaf, 26

Frosted pear loaf, 26

Fruit and nut chocolate tart, 105

Fruit cake, 114

Fruit scones, 77

Ginger and raisin snaps, 161

Gingerbread, 110

Gingerbread stars, 56

Ginger muffins, 94

Ginger shortbread, 74

Ginger snap biscuits, 160

Ginger spice loaf cake, 132

Gluten and dairy-free banana loaf cake, 118

Gluten-free chocolate sponge, 101

Gluten-free coconut loaf, 153

Gluten-free sponge, 101

Gooseberry pudding, 57

Granary bread, 201

Granary corn bread, 185

Ham and cheese pastry rolls, 221

Ham and mozzarella pastry rolls, 221

Herby cheese and tomato loaf, 187

Herby cheese loaf, 187

Homemade sausage rolls, 232

Homemade wholegrain bagels, 214

Honey cake with cherries, 68

Honey cake with raspberries, 68

Iced almond shortbread stars, 83

Iced cinnamon hearts, 30

Iced cinnamon snaps, 35

Iced lemon and blueberry loaf, 162

Iced lemon loaf cake, 162

Iced nutmeg and hazelnut biscuits, 86

Iced nutmeg biscuits, 86

Iced orange loaf cake, 122

Iced rose water hearts, 30

Indulgent chocolate and berry cake, 93

Kamut loaf, 179

Key lime pie, 50

Lavender lemon loaf cake, 59

Lavender lemon shortbread biscuits, 38

Lavender shortbread biscuits, 38

Lemon and almond cake, 140

Lemon and ginger shortbread, 47

Lemon and lime madeleines, 81

Lemon and poppy seed cakes, 113

Lemon and poppy seed loaf, 121

Lemon and poppy seed shortbread, 137

Lemon and thyme cakes, 113

Lemon bundt cake, 60

Lemon curd bundt cake, 60

Lemon curd tart, 136

Lemon drizzle muffins, 157

Lemon-ginger apple cake, 22

Lemon-ginger cake, 22

Lemon meringue cupcakes, 122

Lemon meringue pie, 37

Lemon shortbread, 74

Lemon shortbread biscuits, 47

Lemon surprise cupcakes, 115

Lemon thyme loaf cake, 59

Lemon-ginger apple cake, 22

Light orange and honey loaf, 110

Light orange loaf cake, 110

Lime and lemon pie, 50

Marmalade biscuits, 146

Melt-in-the-middle chocolate puddings, 75

Milk bread rolls, 168

Mini chocolate cupcakes, 134

Mini muesli oat cake, 231

Mini vanilla cupcakes, 134

Mini white chocolate loaf cakes, 135

Mixed berry Swiss roll, 139

Mixed fruit loaf, 39

Mushroom and leek quiche, 225

Mushroom and pepper quiche, 225

Mushroom and prosciutto muffins, 238

Mushroom and Stilton muffins, 238

Nectarine cake, 17

Nutmeg and lemon cookies, 53

Nutmeg cookies, 53

Nutmeg egg custard tarts, 12

Nutty almond biscotti, 80
Nutty berry tarts, 125
Nutty chocolate brownies, 32
Nutty cookies, 69
Nutty granary bread, 174

Oat and cranberry cookies, 95
Oat and seed artisan loaf, 198
Oat, raisin and cranberry cookies, 95
Olive and Parmesan rolls, 215
Olive and rosemary cookies, 223
Olive and rosemary muffins, 249
Olive and sun-dried tomato loaf, 180
Olive and tomato mini muffins, 249
Olive bread rolls, 215
Onion and rosemary cookies, 223
Onion and thyme focaccia, 229
Onion and thyme mini muffins, 243
Onion bread, 186
Onion, tomato and thyme focaccia, 229
Orange and chocolate shortbread, 119
Orange and cinnamon rolls, 28
Orange and poppy seed loaf, 122
Orange and sesame seed cupcakes, 11
Orange and treacle tart, 152
Orange and walnut cake, 33
Orange-glazed pretzels, 224
Orange polenta cake, 7
Orange treacle tart, 45

Parmesan and bacon mini muffins, 248
Parmesan and flax seed rolls, 200
Parmesan and garlic rolls, 200
Parmesan and herb scones, 241
Parmesan and herb shortbread, 250
Parmesan and olive shortbread, 246
Parmesan and prosciutto pastries, 237

Parmesan and rosemary biscuits, 250
Parmesan and thyme cookies, 220
Parmesan shortbread biscuits, 240
Peach cake, 17
Pear, almond and vanilla tart, 108
Pear and caramel tarte Tatin, 59
Pear and chocolate sponge, 117
Pear and chocolate tarte Tatin, 59
Pear and cinnamon pie, 91
Pear and ginger upside-down cake, 82
Pear and golden syrup cake, 62
Pear and honey cake, 62
Pear, pecan and ginger loaf, 107
Pecan and cranberry oat cookies, 16
Pecan pie, 84
Pepper and herb loaf, 241
Pineapple upside-down cake, 34
Plum and chocolate loaf cake, 74
Plum and honey loaf cake, 74
Plum and mascarpone tart, 151
Plum galette, 67
Poppy seed and hazelnut shortbread, 36
Poppy seed rolls, 195
Poppy seed shortbread biscuits, 137
Poppy seed twist bread, 172
Pound cake, 10
Pretzels, 224
Pumpkin and raisin cupcakes, 158
Pumpkin and raisin loaf cake, 65
Pumpkin and walnut pie, 103
Pumpkin loaf cake, 65
Pumpkin pie, 103
Pumpkin seed shortbread, 230
Pumpkin spice cupcakes, 158
Pumpkin spice loaf cake, 27

Quinoa and cranberry cookies, 23

Quinoa and fruit cookies, 54
Quinoa, raisin and chocolate
    cupcakes, 23

Raisin and poppy seed loaf cake, 159
Raisin and walnut ginger bread, 110
Raspberry and chocolate sandwich, 158
Raspberry and cream cheese
    muffins, 138
Raspberry and lemon curd tartlets, 65
Raspberry and lemon loaf, 116
Raspberry and rose water loaf, 116
Raspberry cheesecake brownies, 18
Raspberry meringue cupcakes, 122
Raspberry meringue roulade, 85
Raspberry muffins, 107
Raspberry Swiss roll, 139
Redcurrant and white
    chocolate muffins, 73
Redcurrant muffins, 73
Rhubarb and apple crumble, 109
Rhubarb loaf cake, 20
Rhubarb and strawberry crumble, 109
Rhubarb custard tart, 40
Rhubarb loaf cake, 20
Rich chocolate caramel tart, 106
Rose and almond shortbread
    biscuits, 128
Rose water cherry cupcakes, 32
Rose water daisy cupcakes, 149
Rose water white chocolate cupcakes, 32
Rosemary and olive focaccia, 190
Rosemary and thyme cookies, 220
Round spelt loaf, 173
Rum and raisin loaf cake, 119
Rum, chocolate and raisin loaf, 119
Rustic rye bread, 192
Rustic wholemeal olive loaf, 183

Rye and ginger bread, 192
Rye and treacle loaf, 209
Rye rolls, 208

Salmon and dill muffins, 245
Salmon and goat's cheese muffins, 245
Salted caramel shortcake, 43
Salted chocolate and walnut cookies, 41
Salty bacon and onion muffins, 247
Sea salt crusted rolls, 195
Seafood and sun-dried tomato loaf, 211
Seafood loaf, 211
Seeded crusty bread fingers, 197
Seeded granary bread, 201
Seeded wholemeal rolls, 204
Seeded wholemeal batons, 213
Sesame baguettes, 181
Sesame seed and cinnamon cookies, 149
Sesame seed shortbread, 230
Spiced blood orange upside-
    down cake, 98
Spiced carrot and ginger loaf, 95
Spiced carrot loaf cake, 95
Spiced cranberry bagels, 182
Spiced fruit cake, 114
Spinach and feta muffins, 233
Spinach and feta tart, 244
Spinach and goat's cheese pastries, 235
Spinach and red pepper muffins, 233
Spinach and ricotta pastries, 235
Spinach and ricotta tart, 244
Spinach and tomato quiche, 234
Sponge fingers, 130
Sticky chocolate brownies, 68

Sticky chocolate orange brownies, 68
Sticky oat and banana cookies, 29
Stilton-stuffed bread rolls, 171
Strawberry and mascarpone tart, 151
Strawberry and mint muffins, 107
Strawberry cream puffs, 131
Strawberry cream tartlets, 62
Strawberry custard tarts, 163
Strawberry jam biscuits, 83
Strawberry meringue roulade, 85
Strawberry mess tartlets, 62
Strawberry ricotta tartlets, 48
Summer berry buttercream
    cupcakes, 42
Summer berry pudding, 9
Summer berry tarts, 125
Summer fruit tart, 129
Sun-dried tomato and feta bread, 175
Sunflower seed chocolate cookies, 149
Sweet plum tart, 55

Toffee and chocolate drizzle cake, 150
Toffee drizzle cake, 150
Tomato and mozzarella loaf, 210
Tomato and pumpkin seed loaf, 210
Treacle and oat cookies, 29
Treacle bread, 169
Tuscan bloomer, 194
Two-flour bread loaf, 199

Vanilla cream muffins, 137

Walnut and chocolate squares, 8
Walnut bread, 176

Walnut cake, 33
Walnut choc-chip cookies, 155
Walnut raisin bread, 217
White bloomer loaves, 193
White chocolate and almond loaf, 46
White chocolate and pecan
    bundt cake, 145
White chocolate and pistachio loaf, 46
White chocolate and raspberry
    banana loaf, 156
White chocolate cake squares, 49
White chocolate caramel shortcake, 43
White chocolate chunk cookies, 164
White chocolate hazelnut
    shortbread, 26
White walnut bread, 176
Wholemeal apple and caramel cake, 143
Wholemeal banana and apricot loaf, 17
Wholemeal banana loaf cake, 165
Wholemeal chocolate and nut
    cookies, 143
Wholemeal chocolate chip cookies, 143
Wholemeal chocolate loaf, 31
Wholemeal chocolate muffins, 102
Wholemeal glazed chocolate cake, 13
Wholemeal pear and caramel cake, 143
Wholemeal poppy seed loaf, 188
Wholemeal sesame baguettes, 181
Wholemeal sun-dried tomato
    and feta bread, 175
Wholemeal sun-dried tomato bread, 184
Wholemeal twist bread, 172

Zesty ginger and carrot loaf, 52
Zesty orange cupcakes, 11